Cooking Light

THE COMPLETE
QUICK
COOK

D0126656

ISBN-13: 978-0-8487-3442-8
ISBN-10: 0-8487-3442-4
Library of Congress Control Number: 2011931616
Printed in the United States of America
First printing 2011

Be sure to check with your health-care provider before making any changes in your diet.

OXMOOR HOUSE

VP, PUBLISHING DIRECTOR:	Jim Childs
EDITORIAL DIRECTOR:	Susan Payne Dobbs
CREATIVE DIRECTOR:	Felicity Keane
BRAND MANAGER:	Michelle Turner Aycock
SENIOR EDITOR:	Heather Averett
MANAGING EDITOR:	Laurie S. Herr

COOKING LIGHT®
THE COMPLETE QUICK COOK

PROJECT EDITOR:	Holly D. Smith
ASSISTANT DESIGNER:	Allison Sperando Potter
DIRECTOR, TEST KITCHENS:	Elizabeth Tyler Austin
ASSISTANT DIRECTORS, TEST KITCHENS:	Julie Christopher, Julie Gunter
TEST KITCHENS PROFESSIONALS:	Wendy Ball, RD; Allison E. Cox; Victoria E. Cox; Margaret Monroe Dickey; Alyson Moreland Haynes; Stefanie Maloney; Callie Nash; Catherine Crowell Steele; Leah Van Deren
PHOTOGRAPHY DIRECTOR:	Jim Bathie
SENIOR PHOTO STYLIST:	Kay E. Clarke
ASSOCIATE PHOTO STYLIST:	Katherine Eckert Coyne
ASSISTANT PHOTO STYLIST:	Mary Louise Menendez
SENIOR PRODUCTION MANAGER:	Greg A. Amason

Contributors

AUTHORS:	Bruce Weinstein, Mark Scarbrough
DESIGNER:	Amy R. Bickell
COPY EDITORS:	Jasmine Hodges, Dolores Hydock
PROOFREADERS:	Norma Butterworth-McKittrick, Tara Trenary
INDEXER:	Mary Ann Laurens
INTERNS:	Erin Bishop, Maribeth Browning, Laura Hoxworth, Alison Loughman, Mamie McIntosh, Lindsay A. Rozier
TEST KITCHENS PROFESSIONAL:	Kathleen Royal Phillips
PHOTOGRAPHERS:	Beau Gustafson, Lee Harrelson, Beth Dreiling Hontzas, Mary Britton Senseney, Becky Luigart-Stayner
PHOTO STYLISTS:	Mindi Shapiro Levine, Celine Russell
NUTRITIONAL ANALYSIS:	Caroline Glagola Dunn, Kate Grigsby

Time Home Entertainment Inc.

PUBLISHER:	Richard Fraiman
VP, STRATEGY & BUSINESS DEVELOPMENT:	Steven Sandonato
EXECUTIVE DIRECTOR, MARKETING SERVICES:	Carol Pittard
EXECUTIVE DIRECTOR, RETAIL & SPECIAL SALES:	Tom Mifsud
EXECUTIVE DIRECTOR, NEW PRODUCT DEVELOPMENT:	Peter Harper
DIRECTOR, BOOKAZINE DEVELOPMENT & MARKETING:	Laura Adam
PUBLISHING DIRECTOR:	Joy Butts
FINANCE DIRECTOR:	Glenn Buonocore
ASSOCIATE GENERAL COUNSEL:	Helen Wan

Cooking Light®

EDITOR:	Scott Mowbray
CREATIVE DIRECTOR:	Carla Frank
DEPUTY EDITOR:	Phillip Rhodes
EXECUTIVE EDITOR, FOOD:	Ann Taylor Pittman
SPECIAL PUBLICATIONS EDITOR:	Mary Simpson Creel, MS, RD
SENIOR FOOD EDITOR:	Julianna Grimes
SENIOR EDITOR:	Cindy Hatcher
ASSOCIATE FOOD EDITOR:	Timothy Q. Cebula
ASSISTANT EDITOR, NUTRITION:	Sidney Fry, MS, RD
ASSISTANT EDITORS:	Kimberly Holland, Phoebe Wu
TEST KITCHEN DIRECTOR:	Vanessa T. Pruett
ASSISTANT TEST KITCHEN DIRECTOR:	Tiffany Vickers Davis
RECIPE TESTERS AND DEVELOPERS:	Robin Bashinsky, Adam Hickman, Deb Wise
ART DIRECTOR:	Fernande Bondarenko
JUNIOR DEPUTY ART DIRECTOR:	Alexander Spacher
ASSOCIATE ART DIRECTOR:	Rachel Lasserre
DESIGNER:	Chase Turberville
JUNIOR DESIGNER:	Hagen Stegall
PHOTO DIRECTOR:	Kristen Schaefer
ASSISTANT PHOTO EDITOR:	Amy Delaune
SENIOR PHOTOGRAPHER:	Randy Mayor
SENIOR PHOTO STYLIST:	Cindy Barr
PHOTO STYLIST:	Leigh Ann Ross
CHIEF FOOD STYLIST:	Charlotte Autry
SENIOR FOOD STYLIST:	Kellie Gerber Kelley
FOOD STYLING ASSISTANT:	Blakeslee Wright
COPY CHIEF:	Maria Parker Hopkins
ASSISTANT COPY CHIEF:	Susan Roberts
RESEARCH EDITOR:	Michelle Gibson Daniels
EDITORIAL PRODUCTION DIRECTOR:	Liz Rhoades
PRODUCTION EDITOR:	Hazel R. Eddins
ASSISTANT PRODUCTION EDITOR:	Josh Rutledge
ADMINISTRATIVE COORDINATOR:	Carol D. Johnson
COOKINGLIGHT.COM EDITOR:	Allison Long Lowery
NUTRITION EDITOR:	Holley Johnson Grainger, MS, RD
PRODUCTION ASSISTANT:	Mallory Daugherty

To order additional publications, call 1-800-765-6400 or 1-800-491-0551.
For more books to enrich your life, visit **oxmoorhouse.com**
To search, savor, and share thousands of recipes, visit **myrecipes.com**

COVER: Chicken with Lemon-Leek Linguine (page 283); Timer: Tony Hutchings/Photographer's Choice/Getty Images
PAGE 1: Chinese Five-Spice Steak with Rice Noodles (page 202); PAGE 3: Pork Medallions with Port Wine–Dried Cherry Pan Sauce (page 286);
PAGE 5: Prosciutto and Melon Pasta Salad (page 109); PAGE 6: Hello Dolly Bars (page 340)

Cooking Light
THE COMPLETE
QUICK
COOK

BY BRUCE WEINSTEIN & MARK SCARBROUGH

Oxmoor
House

39

73

92

291

181

151

201

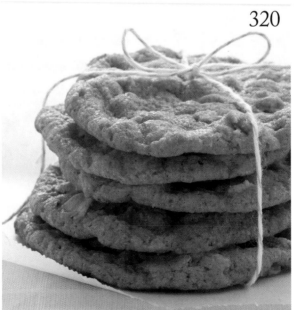

320

CONTENTS

LET'S FACE IT:

It takes time to cook. And time is precisely the one thing we don't seem to have! But there's good news. Becoming a quick cook is a skill that can be learned—much like chopping an onion or deglazing a pan.

In *Cooking Light The Complete Quick Cook,* we'll show you how investing a little time up front—planning, shopping, stocking, and organizing—means you can spend far less time in the kitchen. Now that's a deal no one can turn down!

Throughout this 352-page, practical guide to smart, fast cooking, we'll show you how to plan your meals, speed up your shopping, and organize your kitchen—even how to clean up more effectively. In fact, we're ready to teach you every skill you'll need to get in and out of the kitchen in no time, put a nutritious meal on the table, and still have time left over for yourself.

After writing more than 20 cookbooks, teaching countless cooking classes, and developing hundreds of recipes for *Cooking Light,* we've learned a thing or two about quick, healthy cooking—most importantly, how to combine great taste with efficiency and grace. So with our knowledge and experience, coupled with the expertise of the *Cooking Light* staff, we bring you *Cooking Light The Complete Quick Cook.*

Here are hundreds of recipes that won't chain you to the stove. But far more than that, here's a manual that will help you learn the skills you need to be a quick cook. That's an investment that will pay off for years to come. Let's get cooking!

Bruce Weinstein and Mark Scarbrough

TOP 10 SECRETS OF A QUICK COOK

Nailing Down the Basics

A QUICK COOK IS SOMEONE WHO UNDERSTANDS WHY WE COOK IN THE FIRST PLACE. She's found the right balance between process and product; she goes into the kitchen to get to the table! Given that, cooking quickly can be pure pleasure, ability, and task perfectly matched.

Just to be clear, let's say that again: Ability balanced to task. In other words, it's a combination of your confidence and a recipe designed to get you out of the kitchen with little folderol. It's not all on your shoulders. Some of it falls on ours, too.

Let's face it: There are a lot of recipes for fast-track meals that simply cannot be done without a battalion of sous chefs, personal assistants, and assistant producers. It takes a village to make short rib hash in 20 minutes.

Too bad most of us face the stove alone. Even if there are 10 people in the kitchen, chances are one person is doing the heavy lifting.

And nobody wants a bad strain. That's why even professional athletes rely on their coaches and why we're here now—because cooking quickly is a skill. And like any other, from gymnastics to ice-dancing, it can be coached. There's always something new to learn or some new path to accomplishment. And something that can be forgotten, too.

It's easy to lapse into wandering in the wilderness, adrift between counter and stove, multitasking without really doing much. It's even easier to stumble headlong into a mad dash hither and yon for ingredients and tools at 5:30 p.m.

Remember this: Cooking quickly is not innate or genetic, something you either have or you don't, like blue eyes. It's honed over time. It's not only about how you work in the kitchen but also about how you think about doing that work.

Now more than ever, we need to learn these skills. Our days are packed, schedules full to bursting— a blur of two-thumbed texting and rush-rush commitments. By the dinner hour, we often find ourselves at loose ends, exhausted. The last thing we want to do is spend another hour at the stove—not to mention the time spent cleaning up afterward. We want good nutrition and good taste in minutes. We want it all. And why not?

And even if we're already proficient in the kitchen, we need to hone those skills time and again. They go rusty and are in need of a refresher course. When ability slacks off and slides away, you're left able to accomplish only the simplest tasks. You're boiling dinner in bags or buying fast-food burgers that hardly give you the big, balanced flavors you want—not to mention the nutrition you need.

So let's get to our quick-cook coaching. Our first step, even before we jump into the game with our recipes, is to nail down the basics. Let's do it in the form of the Top 10 Secrets of a Quick Cook. Each is a general

principle, followed by some specifics on how to put it into practice. Consider these the basic outline of what we all need to learn—the skill sets we have to master. Because that's the heart of the matter: competence. That is, learning it, refining it. Well, that and recipes designed to meet that competence head-on.

After you've read through these Top 10 Secrets, you'll be ready to go straight to the recipes. Nothing teaches like experience. There, you'll learn how to put these principles into practice. Be sure to return to this introductory chapter occasionally for little reviews along the way. Make it your goal to refine what you're doing in the kitchen—all so you can get out and enjoy your life.

But first, enjoy what you're doing in the kitchen, too. Our principle is pleasure: big tastes, fresh ingredients, family favorites, and new ways to put what we want on the table. To that end, the real secret to cooking quickly is to have fun. Nothing is a bigger time-waster than a bad mood. Have a blast learning as you go. You'll be a quick cook before you know it, competent and confident. Best of all, you can carry that confidence into the rest of your life, the better to relish every precious moment it affords.

SECRET #1

Invest Time to Save Time

Cooking takes time. You can either put in the time at the stove when you're dusted with flour and up to your ears in olive oil, or you can bank a few minutes in advance so things go quickly—and smoothly—once you get going in the kitchen.

The truth of the matter is that you've got to spend time to save it. Yes, planning takes time. But any time you invest up front will pay off as you find yourself seated at the dinner table without having broken a sweat—and without the kitchen looking like a demolition crew has passed through.

☑ Make menu planners.

Sit down once or twice a week, and figure out what you'll fix over the course of the next few days. Sunday afternoons are a natural time, but any day will do. Why?
• You'll be able to plan out what you need at the grocery store.
• You can look up unfamiliar terms or ingredients.
• There'll be no dithering over what to make on any given night.
• You'll be mentally prepared for the meals to come.

☑ Be open to change.

In other words, don't plan too far in advance. It might sound good to set your dinner menus a month in advance, but it can be pretty stifling, too. What if you hear someone mention a great idea for asparagus or read an article about newfangled burgers? You'll want to scratch that itch, satisfy that craving—and stop by the store on your way home from work to pick up the necessary ingredients. Or to be more mundane, what if next Thursday comes and you don't want salmon? Or the salmon you bought two weeks ago is freezer-burned? Give yourself the freedom to make changes, to fly by the seat of your pants. A little grace in the kitchen—and in life, too—goes a long way.

☑ Practice recipe grazing.

Flip through this book to figure out where you want to go. It's a road atlas for meals ahead. Make cookbooks and cooking magazines part of your night-table reading. Browse and select, looking for dishes you want to prepare.

☑ Read the recipe before you go shopping.

In fact, make shopping lists from written recipes. These are your best guides to what you'll need—and what you'll need to do.

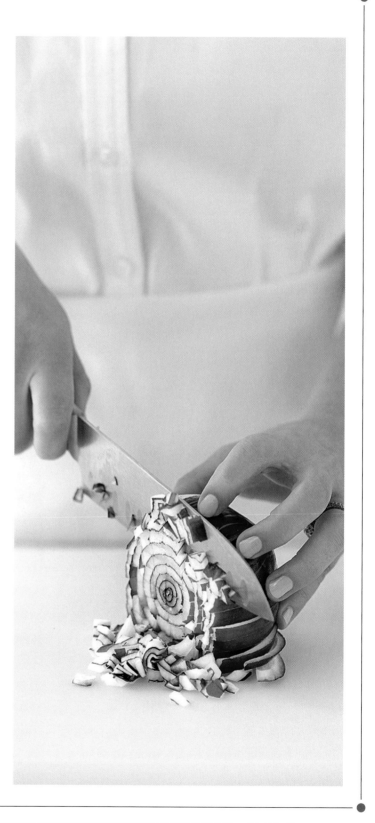

☑ **Check recipes not only for ingredients but also for any tools you will need.**

Nothing slows you down like having to MacGyver-ize some tool a recipe requires. Do you need a fine-mesh sieve or a balloon whisk? You can buy either at the supermarket while you're picking up ingredients.

☑ **When you chop one onion, chop two.**

You can chop two onions more quickly than you can chop one on two separate occasions. Scoop the second chopped onion into a zip-top plastic bag, and squirrel it away in the freezer for a future meal. The same goes for celery, carrots, and bell peppers.

☑ **Know your ingredients.**

There's nothing worse than that moment when a lonely artichoke sits on your cutting board, and you have no clue what to do with it. Check out cookbooks, reference books, and cooking magazines. Or download apps or quick reference guides for your smartphone.

☑ **Start with a fairly clean kitchen.**

No, you don't have to get out the abrasive cleanser, but do empty the sink. And the trash, if it needs it. A sink full of pots and pans when you're trying to drain pasta or wheat berries is not a good thing.

☑ **Use downtime to keep the kitchen in working order.**

Chances are, the kitchen is the most heavily used room in your home—even if you don't cook that much. The spices get moved; the knives get put in the wrong drawer. Use downtime to rearrange one drawer, one cabinet. Don't do the whole kitchen. Don't get carried away. Smaller, discrete tasks offer you a sense of accomplishment, as well as some deserved downtime later. For example, today you might want to clean out the refrigerator drawers and get rid of those science experiments masquerading as onions.

☑ **Make a fresh start.**

Put away any thoughts of past failures, and turn to the dish at hand. Remember: It's just dinner, not a personal referendum.

SECRET #2

"Mise" Your Kitchen

When quick cooks set to work, they always do their *mise en place (meez-on-PLAHS)*, French for "set in place," often abbreviated to "mise," as in "Have you done your *mise* yet?" In other words, you have the recipe ingredients chopped or diced ready to use; completing the dish is then tossing them into the pan and making sure not to burn them.

The value of this whole *mise* technique holds true for your kitchen as well. If you want to be a quick cook, you need to set things in place to make your work environment work for you. If you're running hither and yon to find your spices or dig out a saucepan from a pile of plastic containers, you're wasting energy—and time.

1
Declutter your counters.

You need room to work, so open up that precious real estate. Maybe you can mount the microwave under the cabinets. Maybe you can move the telephone and phone books to another room. Or maybe you can put away that big fruit bowl until it's actually filled with fruit.

3
Consider hanging your pots and pans.

A rack is a great way to organize your cookware, always right within reach. As a bonus, you won't stack nonstick skillets or pans on top of each other, a good way to nick them and render them ineffective.

2
Declutter your drawers, too.

Don't dig for measuring spoons; organize those drawers—especially your knife drawer! You can get a nasty cut digging through it when you're looking for a vegetable peeler or a can opener. Besides, knives should never be stored free-floating in a drawer. Buy a knife holder made for drawers. Or keep the knives in a block on the counter.

4

Move food and dishware farther from the stove, tools closer.

Arrange your kitchen so that the things you use at the stove are near it. Move your pots, pans, whisks, and wooden spoons to the island or cabinets and drawers nearby so you have them ready to access. You don't need the stemware near the burners!

6

Stack sealable containers and baking dishes in the cabinets.

If these things fall out of the cabinet when you open the doors, you'll waste time shoving them back in before you can get back to the stove. A little investment in neatness really pays off.

7

Don't forget to *mise* the refrigerator.

Put the things you use often in the front of the shelves. The milk should be in front of the fish sauce—unless you're making tons of Thai dishes!

5

Use a spice drawer or spinning rack.

If you can afford the space, lay the bottles of dried herbs and spices in a drawer or on a spinning rack near the stove. It's easier to see them all serried up, rather than having to dig through bottles on a shelf to find that dried tarragon.

Keep a Well-Stocked Pantry

Too many of us end up at the supermarket at 6 p.m., desperately looking for that bottle of dried thyme or box of pasta. In truth, a well-stocked pantry makes dinner not only faster, but also easier.

To that end, we've got a list of what a quick-cook pantry should contain. These are the essentials—what you should have on hand to make dinners in a snap. Yes, the whole list can be a bit of a budget-buster right up front. But just as Rome wasn't built in a day, there's no reason you have to stock your pantry from day one either. Rather, this is an aspirational list, something to work toward. It's where you want to end up, rather than start out.

TIPS FOR STOCKING UP Before we get to the list itself, here are a few ideas to make the process of building a quick-cook pantry go more smoothly.

• *Mise* **your pantry,** just like your kitchen. Keep ingredients in order—and in groups: all the vinegars together, all the flours together.

• **Keep a dry-erase board** near the pantry so you can jot down the things you need to buy to restock next time you're at the store. Or keep a running list on your smartphone, always at the ready.

• **Consider your refrigerator and its freezer** part of your pantry. These, too, should be stocked with ingredients to make dinners in a snap: frozen shrimp and frozen ground beef, for example. Or unsalted butter and deli mustard. Later, when we get to the No-Shopping Suppers chapter, we'll make meals strictly out of this pantry, without having to go to the store at all.

THE COMPLETE *QUICK* COOK PANTRY ESSENTIALS

Flours
- ❏ All-purpose flour, preferably unbleached
- ❏ Whole-wheat flour

Baking Necessities
- ❏ Baking powder, preferably double-acting
- ❏ Baking soda
- ❏ Chocolate: bittersweet or dark squares or chips, semisweet chips, unsweetened squares or chips
- ❏ Cocoa powder
- ❏ Cornmeal
- ❏ Cornstarch
- ❏ Unseasoned whole-wheat breadcrumbs

Sugars and Sweeteners
- ❏ Honey, preferably an aromatic wildflower variety
- ❏ Maple syrup
- ❏ Molasses
- ❏ Sugar: brown, granulated, and powdered

Fats and Oils
- ❏ Canola oil
- ❏ Cooking spray
- ❏ Olive oil
- ❏ Peanut oil
- ❏ Sesame oil

Vinegars and Condiments
- ❏ Balsamic vinegar
- ❏ Barbecue sauce
- ❏ Broth: beef, chicken, and vegetable, preferably fat-free, lower-sodium
- ❏ Capers
- ❏ Chili sauce
- ❏ Cider vinegar
- ❏ Dry vermouth (use in place of wine for sauces)
- ❏ Hoisin sauce
- ❏ Hot red pepper sauce
- ❏ Jarred olives, preferably pitted
- ❏ Ketchup
- ❏ Mayonnaise, preferably light or reduced-fat mayonnaise
- ❏ Mustard, preferably smooth Dijon mustard

- ❏ Peanut butter, preferably natural-style peanut butter
- ❏ Red wine vinegar
- ❏ Soy sauce, preferably lower-sodium soy sauce
- ❏ Vanilla extract
- ❏ White wine vinegar
- ❏ Worcestershire sauce

Grains and Pasta

- ❏ Buckwheat
- ❏ Bulgur wheat
- ❏ Cornmeal, preferably yellow cornmeal
- ❏ Couscous
- ❏ Egg noodles
- ❏ Farfalle (bow tie pasta), penne, or rigatoni
- ❏ Orzo
- ❏ Quick-cooking barley
- ❏ Quinoa
- ❏ Rice
- ❏ Rice noodles
- ❏ Rolled oats
- ❏ Thin spaghetti

Herbs, Spices, and Seasonings

- ❏ Bay leaves
- ❏ Black peppercorns (grind fresh)
- ❏ Celery seed
- ❏ Cinnamon sticks
- ❏ Crushed red pepper
- ❏ Curry powder
- ❏ Dried basil
- ❏ Dried cilantro
- ❏ Dried dill
- ❏ Dried oregano
- ❏ Dried rosemary
- ❏ Dried sage

- ❏ Dried thyme
- ❏ Dry mustard
- ❏ Garlic powder
- ❏ Grated nutmeg
- ❏ Ground allspice
- ❏ Ground cinnamon
- ❏ Ground cloves
- ❏ Ground cumin
- ❏ Ground ginger
- ❏ Lemon-pepper seasoning, preferably salt-free
- ❏ Mild paprika
- ❏ Salt
- ❏ Smoked paprika, preferably mild

Nuts

- ❏ Pecans
- ❏ Pine nuts
- ❏ Sliced almonds
- ❏ Walnuts

Protein

- ❏ Canned tuna, packed in water
- ❏ Canned clams
- ❏ Tofu, preferably a silken firm tofu that does not require refrigeration

Fruits and Vegetables

(both in the fridge and/or in the pantry)

- ❏ Bagged salad greens
- ❏ Bagged slaw mix
- ❏ Canned artichoke hearts, preferably packed in water
- ❏ Canned beans: white, black, chickpeas, and pinto
- ❏ Canned diced green chiles
- ❏ Canned diced tomatoes, preferably unseasoned and no-salt-added

- ❏ Celery
- ❏ Dried fruits: raisins, apricots, and prunes
- ❏ Dried mushrooms, preferably porcini
- ❏ Garlic, bottled or fresh
- ❏ Ginger, bottled
- ❏ Onions
- ❏ Potatoes
- ❏ Sliced mushrooms, preferably cremini
- ❏ Tomato paste, preferably no-salt-added

The Freezer Pantry

- ❏ Boneless center-cut pork chops
- ❏ Frozen bell pepper strips
- ❏ Frozen broccoli florets
- ❏ Frozen mixed vegetables
- ❏ Frozen pearl onions
- ❏ Frozen tilapia fillets

- ❏ Ground beef, preferably 96% lean
- ❏ Ground turkey
- ❏ Shrimp, preferably medium-sized, peeled, and deveined
- ❏ Skinless, boneless chicken breasts
- ❏ Strip steaks

The Refrigerator Pantry

- ❏ Eggs, large
- ❏ Hard grating cheese like Parmigiano-Reggiano, preferably in a block
- ❏ Jarred pesto, preferably low-fat
- ❏ Milk, preferably low-fat
- ❏ Pasteurized egg substitute
- ❏ Soft melting cheese like Jarlsberg or Gruyère
- ❏ Sour cream, preferably low-fat
- ❏ Unsalted butter
- ❏ Yogurt, preferably low-fat

SECRET #4

Cook Fewer Times Than You Eat

When you're planning your menus, think about ways to repurpose whatever you cook.

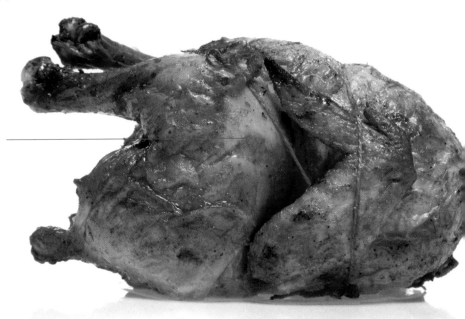

Sometimes bigger is better.

If you're in the mood for chicken, sometimes you might want to roast a whole bird rather than just breasts. No, not every time. It will certainly take more time. But you'll have meat for sandwiches, pasta salads, and stir-fries later in the week. A big bowl of cooked quinoa will also mean grain salads and vegetarian wraps in the days ahead. In the end, you're not just saving time while you cook; you're cooking to save time. It's a trade-off. We usually want to work with smaller things so they cook more quickly. But a big bird in the oven can also mean many quick meals down the road.

Always be on the lookout for good freezer leftovers.

Making a meat loaf may be a bit of a chore, but those slices in the freezer mean quick microwave dinners later.

Double the rice.

Make a large pot on the first night for a side dish, and then save the extra in the fridge for fried rice (using frozen shrimp and frozen mixed vegetables), a rice salad for lunch, or even rice pudding for dessert.

Double the dressing.

If you're making pasta salad or a shrimp Caesar, don't just make enough dressing for one meal. Double or triple the batch, and keep the remaining dressing in the fridge for another meal in the coming days—you could serve it with steamed broccoli on a baked potato.

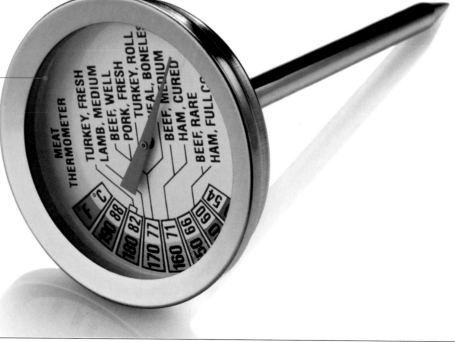

Double the pasta.

Make twice as much as you need, and then save the leftovers in the fridge for pasta salads in the week ahead.

Roast for meals ahead.

Roasts yield enough meat that is suitable for several menus. Consider roasting that turkey breast tonight while you're making a different meal altogether. Set it in the oven, let it go through dinner, even into your TV hours, and then take it out when it's perfect, sometime later in the evening. You've just banked meals for days. Again, it's not a normal, everyday strategy, but as quick cooks, we're less about the rules and more about getting it done efficiently.

SECRET #5

Get In and Out of the Supermarket Fast

While a trip to the grocery store can be a learning experience for new foods and flavors, most of us want to get in and out as quickly as possible. Sure, it'd be great to spend 30 minutes on a Sunday afternoon checking out quinoa flour or the stock of fruit chutneys, but mostly we're in the place late on a weekday afternoon and trying to get home.

A trip to the supermarket requires advance planning—that is, investing time up front to save it later on. You need to know what you want so you can get it as quickly as possible. We know one friend whose goal is for the wheels of her cart to never stop turning. She grabs ingredients on the fly! Such efficiency may be beyond most of us, but here are a few ways to come close without running over other shoppers on your way in and out.

1

Make a list based on the recipes you want to cook—and check the list twice.

If you have a list on a dry-erase board or your smartphone of the pantry items you need to restock, make sure you add those items to your shopping list. And take a quick look at what's still in the pantry. Maybe there's only a cup of flour left in the bin. Better to buy it now, rather than to have to run to the store when you're in the middle of a recipe.

3

Don't shop hungry.

If it's 1:30 p.m. and you still haven't had lunch, or if you've just come from the gym, it's probably not the best time to go to the supermarket. You're hungry and more likely to lose your concentration. You're also more likely to pick up convenience fare or snacks—not the things on your list that will make nutritious meals in the days ahead.

2

Organize your list.

You know how your local supermarket is laid out. In fact, it's probably laid out like almost every other supermarket. So order your list with the usual categories: dairy, meat, fresh vegetables, frozen foods, dry goods, condiments, oils, juice, baking necessities, and cleaning products. If you really want to go all out, write out these categories on a sheet of paper—or on your computer—with lots of space between them, and then copy or print off a stack to keep in a drawer, a list at the ready.

Call ahead.

If you're in a rush, give the supermarket a ring. The butcher or fish counter can have your order ready for you when you arrive. They'll have the pork loin trimmed and tied for you. They'll grind bottom round for you, if you'd rather have it than what's in the case. Call for large deli orders—or bakery orders. Also phone ahead for unusual items. No need to waste time searching for an Indonesian sweet soy sauce if the store doesn't have it in the first place.

If possible, avoid the grocery store rush hour.

The market's the most crowded after work on weekdays and on Saturday afternoons. Consider shopping after dinner one evening—or right after breakfast. Even a lunch break as a shopping run is better than the traffic jam that awaits you at 6 p.m.

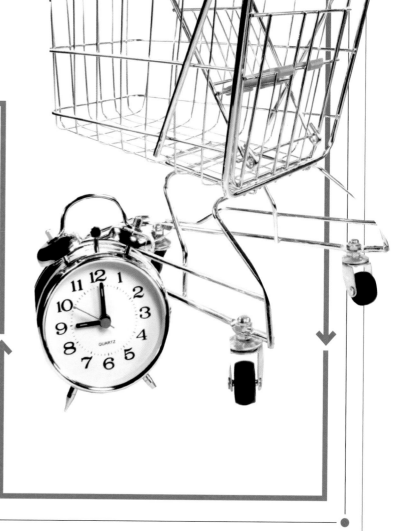

Shop alone.

No doubt about it, kids speed you up during most of your day but slow you down at the supermarket! If at all possible, shop while your kids are at school—or leave them with the babysitter or your mother. And never make grocery shopping a social event. Plan on coffee with your friends at another time.

SECRET #6

Embrace Convenience—But Examine It

Convenience products are a boon to us quick cooks: canned tomatoes, frozen corn, preminced ginger. We've had some around our kitchens for so long, we might not even remember they were invented to be shortcuts in the first place. Canned broth, anyone?

However, convenience has to be examined, especially because we're also serious about a healthy lifestyle. There's no reason to embrace convenience at the cost of good nutrition.

So take your reading glasses to the supermarket. Check those labels. Know what you're buying. A good convenience product has in it only what you would put in it. The ingredients on a jar of marinara sauce should read like a recipe, not a chemical lab report.

Don't fall in love at first sight. Instead, shop with your eyes open (and your glasses on).

And remember that many convenience products are doped with too much sodium. Search out lower-sodium—or even no-sodium—alternatives among the offerings. You should control the salt in your own meal, not let someone else give you way more than you need.

1 Be wary of label call-outs. "Low-sugar" is often just an excuse for higher fat; "low-fat" is sometimes an excuse for higher sugar. Skip the ad copy, and look at the ingredients.

2 There's often no need to thaw.
Many frozen vegetables and fruits don't need to be thawed before they can be used in recipes: berries, corn, bell pepper strips, broccoli florets, cauliflower florets. These can be thrown right into hot woks, skillets, and pots. Our recipes will let you know when you can shave off the thawing time.

3 Stock up on quick-cooking grains.
Consider these options for the quick cook:
- Boil-in-bag brown rice
- Buckwheat
- Instant polenta
- Quick-cooking barley
- Quick-cooking bulgur (sometimes called "instant bulgur")
- Quinoa

4 Buy some shelf-stable milk for the pantry.

It's easy to run out of milk in a busy household. Consider buying a few cartons of shelf-stable, no-refrigeration milk in aseptic packaging, often available in the beverage aisle; store in the pantry, a far easier alternative to running to the store when you run out. (Just make sure you keep those expiration dates in mind.)

5 If you buy in bulk, don't store in bulk.

Separate that 5-pound box of mushrooms into 2-cup bags for the fridge so the mushrooms are easier to use. And don't shove that 20-pound bag of flour in a zip-top plastic bag and seal it up. It'll take more time fighting with the bag to get the flour out. Instead, store the flour in a sealable container with a 1-cup measuring cup inside.

6 Take a quick spin through the produce section.

Many supermarkets stock chopped bell peppers, shredded carrots, and even cubed butternut squash in the refrigerator case of the produce section near the bagged salad greens. Once you know what's there, you'll have a convenient resource for shaving minutes off recipes.

Think Small

SECRET #7

In general terms, the bigger something is, the longer it takes to cook. For example, baby vegetables cook more quickly than their full-grown counterparts. Don't go for the football-sized baking potatoes; dig for the smallest potatoes in the bin.

As a general rule, don't be seduced by the giant roasts in the meat section; head for the turkey scaloppine or the pork tenderloin, which can be sliced into medallions.

Yes, we've said that roasting a whole chicken makes for quick meals later in the week. And sometimes the payoff is worth it. But no doubt about it, a whole chicken takes longer to roast than three or four bone-in skinless chicken breasts. Nine times out of ten, think rack of lamb, not leg of lamb. Or think meatballs instead of meat loaf. It's the same mixture; it's just how it's been shaped! The same goes for veggies: small broccoli florets cook more quickly than big knobs.

Given all that, here are our basic meat choices.

QUICK-COOKING CUTS

BEEF
- ❏ flank steak
- ❏ sirloin steaks
- ❏ strip steaks
- ❏ rib-eye steaks
- ❏ T-bone steaks
- ❏ porterhouse steaks
- ❏ tenderloin steaks (aka filet mignon)
- ❏ London broil

CHICKEN
- ❏ skinless, boneless chicken breasts and thighs

DUCK
- ❏ breasts

LAMB
- ❏ loin chops
- ❏ rib chops
- ❏ loin
- ❏ sirloin
- ❏ rack of lamb

PORK
- ❏ loin chops
- ❏ rib chops
- ❏ tenderloin
- ❏ bacon
- ❏ boneless center-cut chops

TURKEY
- ❏ scaloppine
- ❏ turkey London broil

VEAL
- ❏ scaloppine
- ❏ rib chops
- ❏ loin chops (also known as veal porterhouse steaks or veal T-bone steaks)

LONG-COOKING CUTS

BEEF
- ❏ brisket
- ❏ chuck roast
- ❏ blade steaks
- ❏ bottom round
- ❏ oxtail, eye-of-round roast
- ❏ stew meat
- ❏ shanks
- ❏ whole tenderloin roast
- ❏ standing rib roast

CHICKEN
- ❏ bone-in cuts
- ❏ whole birds

DUCK
- ❏ legs, whole birds

LAMB
- ❏ shoulder chops
- ❏ leg
- ❏ stew meat
- ❏ breast
- ❏ shanks

PORK
- ❏ whole pork loin
- ❏ ham
- ❏ shanks
- ❏ shoulder
- ❏ Boston butt
- ❏ belly
- ❏ rib roasts

TURKEY
- ❏ whole breast
- ❏ leg quarters
- ❏ wings
- ❏ whole birds

VEAL
- ❏ brisket
- ❏ leg
- ❏ breast
- ❏ rib roast
- ❏ stew meat

And here are our vegetable choices in two generalized categories.

QUICK-COOKING VEGGIES

- ❏ Onions
- ❏ Green beans
- ❏ Broccoli florets
- ❏ Zucchini
- ❏ Summer (or yellow) squash
- ❏ Eggplant
- ❏ Asparagus
- ❏ Sugar snap peas
- ❏ Cauliflower florets
- ❏ Corn
- ❏ Radishes
- ❏ Shelled peas
- ❏ Fennel
- ❏ Bell peppers
- ❏ Mushrooms
- ❏ Bean sprouts
- ❏ Tomatoes
- ❏ Brussels sprouts

LONG-COOKING VEGGIES

- ❏ Broccoli stems
- ❏ Potatoes
- ❏ Winter squash (such as butternut or acorn squash)
- ❏ Celeriac (celery root)
- ❏ Turnips
- ❏ Parsnips
- ❏ Rutabaga
- ❏ Beets
- ❏ Sweet potatoes
- ❏ Cassava (Yuca)
- ❏ Carrots

Raw is an option

Most quick-cooking vegetables can be eaten raw—and so cooking is actually a matter of choice.

Versatile veggies

Many quick-cooking vegetables can also be long-cookers, like mushrooms, tomatoes, and fennel. These can go a long time over the heat, breaking down and becoming much sweeter over time.

Small is fast

Almost all long-cooking vegetables can be quick-cookers if they are cut into very small bits. The prime example is carrots, added to many a quick sauté once they are sliced into paper-thin coins or shredded through the large holes of a box grater.

Crank Up the Heat

There's a reason your oven goes up to 500° and your burners go up to high.
You need a lot of heat, especially when you're cooking quickly.
Things get browned more quickly. Crisper, too. And tastier. Plus, they cook
more quickly. Talk about a win-win!

☑ Don't leave the stove.

If you're turning up the heat, you can't answer the telephone or get locked in a chain of texts.

☑ Follow the recipe.

While we want to encourage you to turn up the heat when you sauté meat or sweat vegetables, we don't want you to neglect a stated recipe temperature, especially when it comes to baking and roasting. Tested recipes were designed to work in specific ways.

☑ Follow the cues.

Most recipes include both a time and a visual cue: 10 minutes or until lightly browned. While the timing is a nice guide, go with the cue first and foremost. Your diced onion or sliced chicken breasts might be done sooner because your stove puts out more heat or your dice is smaller than ours. Don't wait for the stated time to elapse—move on. You're ahead of us!

☑ Practice with a wok.

There's no better way to practice high-heat searing than with stir-fries. Give one a go early on to get yourself used to working in a higher-heat environment.

Use Gadgets to Save Time

Everybody knows sharp knives make kitchen work a breeze. But there are a host of gadgets that can shave off time spent in the kitchen. Most gadgets are not gimmicks. But how do you know which are useful and which are unnecessary?

As you stand in the cookware store or browse through online sites, think about the tasks you actually do in the kitchen. Make a lot of apple pies or cherry crisps? If not, an apple corer or cherry pitter may not be the best value for your money. Make a lot of pan gravies? If so, a fat separator is right for you.

Follow this rule of thumb: Start with good knives, cutting boards, measuring tools, and cookware. After that, do a little cooking before you decide what other gadgets you need. You'll be well versed in the tools that would make your life easier.

Here are some gadgets we use way more often than we use our microwave oven.

Knife sharpener
A dull knife is actually more dangerous than a sharp one—it can slip off an onion and cut your finger. Invest in a good knife sharpener so your main cooking tools will be at their best.

Kitchen scissors
Sharp, dishwasher-safe shears can open food packages, cut the fat off chicken breasts, snip fresh herbs, cut a roast turkey into its parts, and even dice dried fruit. What's more, you can chop whole tomatoes right in the can by snipping them into small bits.

Extra measuring cups and spoons
Buy a spare set or two of measuring spoons and cups so you can toss the dirty ones in the sink without cleaning them. Also, consider the same advice for wooden spoons and heat-safe rubber spatulas—three of each is optimal.

Large mixing bowls

You can't make tuna salad for four in a small mixing bowl without getting everything all over the counter. Bigger mixing bowls mean less mess—and less time cleaning up.

Instant-read meat thermometer

Take the guesswork out of knowing when any piece of meat is done. Plus, it's your best guarantee for food safety.

Immersion blender

Stick it in a pot of soup and you'll have a puree in seconds. And you don't have to worry about spilling hot soup all over the kitchen as you try to get it from the stove to the blender. Make sure you get an immersion blender with a detachable blade for easy cleanup.

Food processor

Chop, dice, and grind huge quantities of vegetables, meat, or breadcrumbs in a fraction of the time it takes to do it by hand. Make sure you get the shredding blade for slaws.

High-quality pots and pans

Heavy-duty pots hold their heat to cook evenly and efficiently. High-quality nonstick coatings will shave minutes off any meal—not only in the cleanup but right at the stove. Nothing pays off like good cookware over the years.

Keep It Clean

SECRET #10

One reason many of us shy away from the kitchen is fear of the mess afterward. Don't give in to that fear! Discover ways to limit the damage. Faster doesn't mean messier. Instead, cleaning up should be integrated into the process of cooking, not left to the end when everyone's full, content, and maybe even a little tired. So multitask: Clean as you go. It's the best way to shave lots of time off the end of the process—and make it far less daunting all around.

1

Have a garbage bowl.

Limit your trips to the trash can. Set an extra bowl out on the counter as you cook. It can collect all the potato skins, onion bits, and trimmed fat from the ingredients of your meal, not to mention any packaging or containers.

3

Clean your oven.

Be sure to clean your oven at least every six months, if not every four. You're much more likely to turn up the heat if the oven doesn't threaten to smoke up the kitchen.

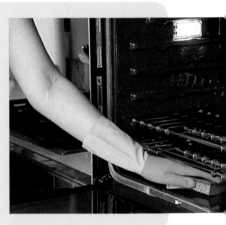

2

Line your roasting pans with aluminum foil.

You'll get the benefit of a heavy, metal pan with the ease and convenience of a quick cleanup. Line the pan thoroughly, and you might not even need to wash it afterward.

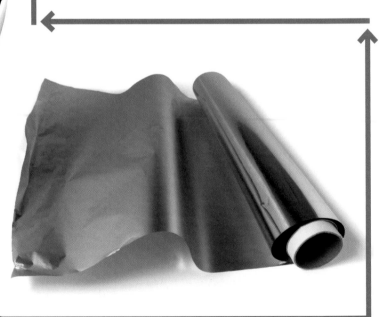

4

Water is the best cleanup tool.

Set pots and pans in the sink, and fill them with hot water to soak while you're at dinner. For really burned-on bits and even caramelized sugar, deglaze the mess: Fill the skillet or pan halfway with water, cover it, bring it to a boil over high heat, and boil for 1 minute. There'll be much less scrubbing afterward. Just be sure not to follow this procedure with a nonstick skillet. It will damage the pan. It's not recommended to heat nonstick skillets above medium-high heat.

5

Have fun!

Don't worry about the mess. Sure, it needs cleaning up. But worries slow you down. Concentrate on the meal ahead, and the pleasure of your family and friends. There's no inducement to efficiency quite like contentment!

DRESS IT UP!

Our Essential Dressings and Sauces

THESE MAKE-AHEADS ARE AN EXTREMELY IMPORTANT PART OF A QUICK COOK'S REPERTOIRE, like the corners of a jigsaw puzzle. They lay the foundation for a well-stocked pantry.

Time spent up front means less time spent later. Most of these recipes will keep for a week; some for up to two weeks. Dry rubs, a staple for flavorful summertime dinners, will last even longer.

But beyond their make-ahead value, these recipes also remind us that our task is twofold. Yes, we want to be quick cooks, in and out of the kitchen in a flash and back to our lives. However, we also want to be healthy cooks, offering family and friends the best options, even in a limited amount of time. Put simply, we want to honor both nutrition and speed.

So in many ways, these recipes for salad dressings, sauces, and marinades are the perfect place to start. They remind us of our twin goals, helping us put the healthiest, most nutritious and flavorful meals on the table even when we're counting the minutes on the clock.

That's the very heart of our quick-cook plan.

Enlightened Greek Dressing

The anchovy gives this dressing—which pairs perfectly with Enlightened Greek Salad on page 84—a little zip and balances the other flavors nicely. Make a double batch, and save extra in the fridge, covered, for up to 1 week. This easy dressing also makes a great marinade for cuts of beef like bottom round, flank steak, skirt steak, or short ribs.

1 canned anchovy fillet

3 tablespoons fresh lemon juice

2½ tablespoons olive oil

2 tablespoons red wine vinegar

2 teaspoons Worcestershire sauce

1 teaspoon dried oregano

¼ teaspoon dried dill

¼ teaspoon freshly ground black pepper

1 garlic clove, pressed

1. Mash anchovy fillet in a small bowl with a fork. Add lemon juice and remaining ingredients, stirring with a whisk until blended. Store, covered, in refrigerator for up to 1 week. **YIELD:** ½ cup (serving size: 2 tablespoons).

CALORIES 107; **FAT** 9.5g (sat 1.2g, mono 6.3g, poly 0.9g); **PROTEIN** 3.8g; **CARB** 2.1g; **FIBER** 0.2g; **CHOL** 21mg; **IRON** 0.4mg; **SODIUM** 133mg; **CALC** 10mg

MORE CHOICES: Consider substituting fresh herbs for the dried by doubling the stated amounts. However, keep in mind that a dressing with fresh herbs must be used within a day or two; otherwise, the herbs turn black and look unappealing.

Creamy Raspberry Dressing

You can have a bright spark of summer any time of year with this easy dressing. You can even make and refrigerate it for up to a week in advance. Try it on a spinach salad with some chopped hard-cooked egg and shredded carrot—or a fruit salad with plenty of hulled strawberries and sliced peaches.

⅓ cup honey

¼ cup raspberry vinegar

¼ cup plain fat-free yogurt

1 tablespoon Dijon mustard

2 teaspoons olive oil

¼ teaspoon salt

¼ teaspoon freshly ground black pepper

1. Combine all ingredients; stir with a whisk until creamy. Store, covered, in refrigerator for up to 1 week. **YIELD:** ¾ cup (serving size: 3 tablespoons).

CALORIES 120; **FAT** 2.6g (sat 0.3g, mono 1.8g, poly 0.3g); **PROTEIN** 1.2g; **CARB** 25.1g; **FIBER** 0.1g; **CHOL** 0mg; **IRON** 0.4mg; **SODIUM** 257mg; **CALC** 39mg

savvy IN A SNAP

Salad dressings like this one are also great marinades for chicken, pork, or fish. Just remember that food can be kept in a vinegary environment for only a couple of hours.

Shallot and Grapefruit Dressing

Drizzle this zesty dressing over mixed salad greens topped with goat cheese. Squeeze the juice from juicy grapefruit, or look for fresh grapefruit juice in the produce section of the grocery store.

1 teaspoon olive oil

½ cup chopped shallots

2 cups fresh grapefruit juice (about 3 grapefruit)

2 tablespoons chopped fresh cilantro

2 teaspoons sugar

¼ teaspoon freshly ground black pepper

2 tablespoons olive oil

1. Heat 1 teaspoon oil in a large nonstick skillet over medium heat. Add shallots; cook 5 minutes or until golden brown. Stir in juice. Bring to a boil over medium-high heat; cook until reduced to 1 cup, about 6 minutes. Remove from heat; cool to room temperature.

2. Place grapefruit juice mixture, cilantro, sugar, and pepper in a food processor; process until smooth. With processor on, slowly pour 2 tablespoons oil through food chute; process until smooth. Store, covered, in refrigerator for up to 1 week. **YIELD:** 1 cup (serving size: 1 tablespoon).

CALORIES 35; **FAT** 2g (sat 0.3g, mono 1.5g, poly 0.2g); **PROTEIN** 0.3g; **CARB** 4.2g; **FIBER** 0.1g; **CHOL** 0mg; **IRON** 0.1mg; **SODIUM** 1mg; **CALC** 4mg

MORE CHOICES: This dressing is flavorful enough to stand up to assertive salad greens such as arugula, frisée, and endive.

Maple-Mustard Dressing

This dressing is best suited to subtle, delicate greens like Boston, Bibb, or almost any other butterhead lettuce.

⅓ cup maple syrup

2 tablespoons finely chopped shallots

3 tablespoons whole-grain Dijon mustard

2 tablespoons red wine vinegar

1 tablespoon canola oil

¼ teaspoon freshly ground black pepper

⅛ teaspoon salt

1. Combine all ingredients in a medium bowl, stirring with a whisk. Store, covered, in refrigerator for up to 1 week. **YIELD:** about ¾ cup (serving size: 1 tablespoon).

CALORIES 40; **FAT** 1.5g (sat 0.1g, mono 0.8g, poly 0.5g); **PROTEIN** 0.3g; **CARB** 6.7g; **FIBER** 0.1g; **CHOL** 0mg; **IRON** 0.3mg; **SODIUM** 120mg; **CALC** 12mg

MORE CHOICES: Use this dressing as a barbecue mop for swordfish steaks—or ears of corn placed right on the grill rack.

Orange-Sesame Dressing

This bold dressing is best on salads stocked with big flavors such as those found in sliced fruit, chopped nuts, diced bell peppers, and broccoli florets.

½ cup fresh orange juice (about 2 large oranges)

⅓ cup rice vinegar

2 tablespoons sesame seeds

1 tablespoon Chinese hot mustard

1 teaspoon sugar

¼ teaspoon salt

1 garlic clove, minced

2 tablespoons canola oil

1 teaspoon dark sesame oil

1. Combine first 7 ingredients in a medium bowl. Slowly drizzle oils into juice mixture, stirring constantly with a whisk. Store, covered, in refrigerator for up to 10 days. **YIELD:** 1½ cups (serving size: 4 teaspoons).

CALORIES 27; FAT 2.3g (sat 0.2g, mono 1.2g, poly 0.8g); PROTEIN 0.2g; CARB 1.2g; FIBER 0.1g; CHOL 0mg; IRON 0.2mg; SODIUM 45mg; CALC 11mg

MORE CHOICES: Try this dressing over pasta salads, particularly those filled with Asian vegetables. Try a combination of shredded baby bok choy, sliced water chestnuts, and chopped green onions with cooked whole-wheat ziti.

Asian Ginger-Carrot Dressing

Here's a healthier take on the flavorful dressing found on salads in Japanese restaurants across North America.

3 tablespoons finely shredded carrot

3 tablespoons mirin (sweet rice wine)

¼ cup minced peeled fresh ginger

¼ cup lower-sodium soy sauce

2 tablespoons rice vinegar

1. Combine all ingredients in a medium bowl, stirring with a whisk. Store, covered, in refrigerator for up to 3 days. **YIELD:** about 1 cup (serving size: 2 tablespoons).

CALORIES 21; **FAT** 0g (sat 0g, mono 0g, poly 0g); **PROTEIN** 0.6g; **CARB** 3g; **FIBER** 0.1g; **CHOL** 0mg; **IRON** 0.1mg; **SODIUM** 197mg; **CALC** 3mg

Blue Cheese Dressing

A dressing as bold as this one needs salad greens that can stand up to its assertiveness. Try it on a mix of chopped arugula, radicchio, and endive, the classic tricolor salad. Halve the recipe for a smaller batch, suitable for 6 servings.

½ cup (2 ounces) crumbled blue cheese

½ cup plain fat-free yogurt

2 tablespoons light mayonnaise

1. Combine all ingredients in a small bowl. Store, covered, in refrigerator for up to 4 days. **YIELD:** ¾ cup (serving size: 1 tablespoon).

CALORIES 29; **FAT** 2g (sat 1g, mono 0.6g, poly 0.4g); **PROTEIN** 1.6g; **CARB** 1g; **FIBER** 0g; **CHOL** 5mg; **IRON** 0mg; **SODIUM** 92mg; **CALC** 44mg

savvy IN A SNAP

Moldy **blue cheese** should be tossed out. Yes, those blue veins are a form of penicillin mold in the cheese—but any green, brown, or black molds blooming outside those veins can spell trouble.

Easy Herb Vinaigrette

This recipe makes plenty of dressing to keep on hand, so having a salad with dinner is effortless any night of the week. Because of the fresh herbs, the dressing lasts for only a couple of days.

9 tablespoons white wine vinegar

1½ tablespoons honey

½ teaspoon salt

1 cup canola oil

3 tablespoons chopped fresh basil

3 tablespoons minced fresh chives

1. Combine first 3 ingredients in a medium bowl; slowly add oil, stirring with a whisk until combined. Stir in basil and chives. Store, covered, in refrigerator for up to 2 days. **YIELD:** 1 cup (serving size: 1 tablespoon).

CALORIES 160; **FAT** 17.2g (sat 1.2g, mono 10.2g, poly 5.1g); **PROTEIN** 0.1g; **CARB** 2.1g; **FIBER** 0.1g; **CHOL** 0mg; **IRON** 0mg; **SODIUM** 89mg; **CALC** 2mg

savvy IN A SNAP

QUICK & EASY VINAIGRETTES

A good vinaigrette is all about simplicity. Grab a bowl, whisk together the oil and vinegar, add a pinch of salt, and you've done most of the work. Dull lettuce springs to life, veggies go from bland to bold, and meat finds a tangy marinade.

There's actually a secret to this magic: good ingredients. Because so few are necessary, it pays to reach for the top-shelf stuff.

It also pays to give your forearm a little workout. Thoroughly blend the oil with the watery vinegar. When properly emulsified, ingredients are suspended throughout the mix. A broken vinaigrette will have clear separation between the oil and the vinegar.

From there, all you need to do is flavor as you see fit. Additions can be as simple as a pinch of salt and pepper or as complex as a bit of honey, fresh herbs, or minced shallots. Store fresh-made vinaigrette in a covered container in the fridge for 3 to 4 days. Stir well with a whisk before serving.

Chile-Garlic Vinaigrette

The heat of a chile isn't in its seeds; it's in the white membranes (the fruit's placenta) that hold the seeds to the chile. When cut, those membranes spray the chemical defense onto their seeds. For less heat, cut the top and bottom off the chile, then stand it upright on your cutting board. Slice down between the chile and the membranes, removing the green flesh without cutting into the membranes.

1 tablespoon chopped serrano chile

¼ teaspoon salt

6 garlic cloves, crushed

1 canned anchovy fillet

3 tablespoons red wine vinegar

2 tablespoons water

2 tablespoons fresh lemon juice

1½ tablespoons extra-virgin olive oil

1. Combine first 4 ingredients in a mortar; mash to a paste with a pestle. Combine chile paste mixture, vinegar, and remaining ingredients in a small bowl, stirring with a whisk. Store, covered, in refrigerator for up to 1 week.

YIELD: ¾ cup (serving size: 1 tablespoon).

CALORIES 21; **FAT** 1.7g (sat 0.2g, mono 1.2g, poly 0.2g); **PROTEIN** 0.3g; **CARB** 1.1g; **FIBER** 0.1g; **CHOL** 1mg; **IRON** 0.7mg; **SODIUM** 219mg; **CALC** 8mg

MORE CHOICES: Use this piquant dressing on green salads loaded with shredded raw vegetables like zucchini, yellow squash, daikon radish, and cucumber.

Versatile Vinaigrette

Cornstarch, commonly used as a thickening agent, gives this red wine vinaigrette body so it can better coat a salad. Store any remaining vinaigrette in a sealed container in the refrigerator for up to a week.

1 cup vegetable broth

2 teaspoons cornstarch

2 tablespoons red wine vinegar

1 tablespoon extra-virgin olive oil

1 teaspoon sugar

¼ teaspoon salt

⅛ teaspoon freshly ground black pepper

1. Combine broth and cornstarch in a small saucepan, stirring with a whisk. Bring broth mixture to a boil over medium heat; cook 1 minute, stirring constantly. Remove from heat, and stir in remaining ingredients. Store, covered, in refrigerator for up to 1 week. Whisk before serving. **YIELD:** 1 cup (serving size: 2 tablespoons).

CALORIES 21; **FAT** 1.8g (sat 0.2g, mono 1.2g, poly 0.1g); **PROTEIN** 0.3g; **CARB** 1.3g; **FIBER** 0g; **CHOL** 0mg; **IRON** 0.1mg; **SODIUM** 199mg; **CALC** 0.mg

MORE CHOICES: To make a Dijon vinaigrette, add 2 teaspoons Dijon mustard to the broth mixture with the red wine vinegar and remaining ingredients. To make a cumin-lime "vinaigrette," omit the vinegar; add 3 tablespoons fresh lime juice and ¼ teaspoon ground cumin to the broth mixture with the oil and remaining ingredients.

Essential Lemon Dressing

There's just something about that mix of lemon juice and olive oil—so Mediterranean, so irresistible.

1 tablespoon grated lemon rind

1 tablespoon minced fresh dill or 1 teaspoon dried dill

3 tablespoons lemon juice

¼ teaspoon salt

¼ teaspoon freshly ground black pepper

2 tablespoons olive oil

1. Combine lemon rind and next 4 ingredients (through pepper) in a medium bowl, stirring with a whisk. Slowly add olive oil in a thin stream, stirring constantly with a whisk until combined. **YIELD:** 4 servings (serving size: 1¾ tablespoons).

CALORIES 64; **FAT** 6.8g (sat 0.9g, mono 4.9g, poly 0.7g); **PROTEIN** 0.1g; **CARB** 1.3g; **FIBER** 0.2g; **CHOL** 0mg; **IRON** 0.1mg; **SODIUM** 148mg; **CALC** 4mg

QUICK TIP: Always keep fresh lemons on hand. A squeeze added to soups and stews at the end of their cooking time brightens the flavors considerably.

Korean Barbecue Wet Rub ▶

Here is a traditional-tasting Korean rub that goes on just before the food is grilled. It's great on salmon, steaks, pork tenderloin, dark-meat chicken, or any game bird, such as duck or quail.

¼ cup packed dark brown sugar

½ teaspoon salt

4 teaspoons bottled minced garlic

2 teaspoons lower-sodium soy sauce

2 teaspoons dark sesame oil

1. Combine all ingredients. Store in an airtight container in refrigerator for up to 1 week. **YIELD:** about 3 tablespoons (serving size: 1½ teaspoons).

CALORIES 53; FAT 1.6g (sat 0.2g, mono 0.6g, poly 0.6g); **PROTEIN** 0.2g; **CARB** 9.8g; **FIBER** 0.1g; **CHOL** 0mg; **IRON** 0.3mg; **SODIUM** 271mg; **CALC** 12mg

Cajun Blackening Dry Rub ▶

Try this fiery rub on chicken breasts or white-fleshed fish fillets such as catfish or snapper. Or try it on shell-on shrimp for a real Cajun feast. You can also sprinkle it on burgers of any variety, from turkey to beef—or over corn on the cob.

2½ tablespoons paprika

2 teaspoons salt

1½ teaspoons ground cumin

1½ teaspoons dried thyme

1 teaspoon freshly ground black pepper

½ teaspoon garlic powder

½ teaspoon ground red pepper

1. Combine all ingredients. Store in an airtight container at room temperature for up to 2 months. **YIELD:** about ⅓ cup (serving size: 1 teaspoon).

CALORIES 5; FAT 0.2g (sat 0g, mono 0g, poly 0.1g); **PROTEIN** 0.2g; **CARB** 0.9g; **FIBER** 0.6g; **CHOL** 0mg; **IRON** 0.4mg; **SODIUM** 201mg; **CALC** 6mg

Texas Barbecue Dry Rub

Try this rub on lamb chops, skinless chicken thighs, or strip steaks—or any meat that could be seared and cooked quickly on the grill.

2 tablespoons chili powder

2 tablespoons brown sugar

1½ teaspoons salt

2 teaspoons freshly ground black pepper

1 teaspoon dry mustard

1 teaspoon ground cumin

¼ teaspoon ground red pepper

1. Combine all ingredients. Store in an airtight container at room temperature for up to 2 months. **YIELD:** about ⅓ cup (serving size: 1 teaspoon).

CALORIES 9; FAT 0.1g (sat 0g, mono 0g, poly 0g); **PROTEIN** 0.1g; **CARB** 2g; **FIBER** 0.3g; **CHOL** 0mg; **IRON** 0.2mg; **SODIUM** 219mg; **CALC** 4mg

MORE CHOICES: A coarse-grained sea salt will offer more crunch in a dry rub, often a nice touch on the grill, particularly in fast-cooked items like fish fillets.

MORE CHOICES: Add a dribble of Asian red chile sauce, sambal oelek, or even hot pepper sauce for some kick against the sweetness.

MORE CHOICES: You can also use this rub on meats braised in a slow cooker. Or use it as a spice mixture to flavor chilis and stews.

Jalapeño-Lime Marinade

Although great on chicken or pork, this marinade also works well on fish or shellfish, smeared on just as they hit the hot grill rack or pan.

½ cup thawed orange juice concentrate, undiluted

1 teaspoon grated lime rind

¼ cup fresh lime juice (about 2 limes)

¼ cup honey

2 teaspoons ground cumin

3 teaspoons bottled minced garlic

¼ teaspoon salt

2 jalapeño peppers, seeded and finely chopped

1. Combine all ingredients; stir well. Store in an airtight container in refrigerator for up to 1 week. **YIELD:** 1⅓ cups (serving size: 1 tablespoon).

CALORIES 26; **FAT** 0.1g (sat 0g, mono 0.1g, poly 0g); **PROTEIN** 0.3g; **CARB** 6.5g; **FIBER** 0.1g; **CHOL** 0mg; **IRON** 0.2mg; **SODIUM** 29mg; **CALC** 6mg

savvy IN A SNAP

Bottled minced garlic can go bad, even tightly sealed in the fridge. Replace any that is brown or has a funky, musty smell.

◄ Ginger-Molasses Marinade

This is a sweet but savory marinade, best on beef or burgers. For more flavor, use 1 teaspoon bottled minced peeled ginger instead of the ground ginger.

½ cup lower-sodium soy sauce

¼ cup molasses

1 tablespoon olive oil

1 teaspoon ground ginger

1. Combine all ingredients; stir well. Store, covered, in refrigerator for up to 2 weeks. **YIELD:** ¾ cup (serving size: 1 tablespoon).

CALORIES 48; **FAT** 1.7g (sat 0.2g, mono 1.3g, poly 0.1g); **PROTEIN** 0g; **CARB** 7g; **FIBER** 0g; **CHOL** 0mg; **IRON** 0.5mg; **SODIUM** 393mg; **CALC** 21mg

Zesty Dijon Marinade ►

Rather than using an expensive aged balsamic vinegar, look for a flavorful, slightly sweet bottling, one that will offer an elegant but economical pop to this pantry staple. Marinate chicken or pork for a couple of hours—or use this marinade as a barbecue mop when chicken or pork is on the grill.

1 cup balsamic vinegar

½ cup Dijon mustard

¼ cup olive oil

½ teaspoon freshly ground black pepper

¼ teaspoon salt

2 garlic cloves, minced

1. Combine all ingredients; stir well. Store in an airtight container in refrigerator for up to 2 weeks. **YIELD:** 1½ cups (serving size: 1 tablespoon).

CALORIES 28; **FAT** 2.6g (sat 0.3g, mono 1.8g, poly 0.2g); **PROTEIN** 0g; **CARB** 0.8g; **FIBER** 0g; **CHOL** 0mg; **IRON** 0mg; **SODIUM** 173mg; **CALC** 1mg

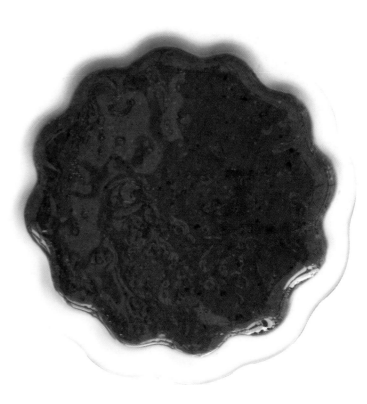

Tangy Tamarind Sauce

This sauce is great mopped onto grilled or broiled beef, chicken, pork, lamb, or veal. It's sweet and sticky with a little fire underneath—a perfect combination.

½ cup tamarind puree or concentrate

6 tablespoons water

¼ cup chopped onion

½ teaspoon salt

½ teaspoon ground cumin

1 large jalapeño pepper, halved and seeded

1 garlic clove, peeled

1. Combine all ingredients in a blender or mini food processor; process until smooth. Store, covered, in refrigerator for up to 1 week. **YIELD:** 1 cup (serving size: 1 tablespoon).

CALORIES 5; **FAT** 0g (sat 0g, mono 0g, poly 0g); **PROTEIN** 0.1g; **CARB** 1.1g; **FIBER** 0.1g; **CHOL** 0mg; **IRON** 0.1mg; **SODIUM** 74mg; **CALC** 3mg

savvy IN A SNAP

Tamarind puree or concentrate is a sour, sticky mixture made from the tropical fruit. You can find the puree or concentrate in most grocery stores, sometimes in the Asian aisle, sometimes in the Latin American section, and sometimes among the condiments.

MORE CHOICES: Add more flavor to Aioli by substituting olive oil for the canola oil. Or go nuts with walnut or almond oil for an even bolder flavor.

6 *simple* sauces for CHICKEN

Jazz up a basic chicken breast with these versatile sauces. All are made with six or fewer ingredients.

1. WHITE WINE SAUCE

This classic sauce deserves a place in your repertoire. It takes everyday dishes up a notch with a touch of elegance and lots of flavor, yet very little effort. Pair it with a sautéed chicken breast, a tilapia fillet, or a pork loin. It's also good on pasta.

Cooking spray

⅓ cup finely chopped onion

½ cup fat-free, lower-sodium chicken broth

¼ cup dry white wine

2 tablespoons white wine vinegar

2 tablespoons butter

2 teaspoons finely chopped fresh chives

1. Heat a skillet over medium-high heat. Coat pan with cooking spray. Add onion to pan; sauté 2 minutes. Stir in broth, wine, and vinegar; bring to a boil. Cook until reduced to ¼ cup (about 5 minutes). Remove from heat; stir in butter and chives. Serve warm. **YIELD:** 6 tablespoons (serving size: 1½ tablespoons).

CALORIES 59; **FAT** 5.7g (sat 3.6g, mono 1.5g, poly 0.2g); **PROTEIN** 0.6g; **CARB** 1.6g; **FIBER** 0.4g; **CHOL** 15mg; **IRON** 0.2mg; **SODIUM** 90mg; **CALC** 8mg

2. TANGY MUSTARD SAUCE

Dijon mustard and maple syrup combine in a sweet-savory pan sauce that adds a velvety richness to chicken. This pan sauce reduces in about 5 minutes, so you can make it while your chicken cooks.

2 teaspoons olive oil

2 garlic cloves, minced

¼ cup dry white wine

¼ cup fat-free, lower-sodium chicken broth

2 tablespoons maple syrup

2 tablespoons Dijon mustard

¾ teaspoon chopped fresh rosemary

½ teaspoon freshly ground black pepper

1. Heat olive oil in a skillet over medium-high heat. Add garlic to pan; cook 30 seconds, stirring constantly. Stir in wine, broth, syrup, and mustard; bring to a boil. Cook until reduced to ¼ cup (about 5 minutes), stirring occasionally. Stir in rosemary and pepper. Serve warm. **YIELD:** ¼ cup (serving size: 1 tablespoon).

CALORIES 54; **FAT** 2.3g (sat 0.3g, mono 1.7g, poly 0.3g); **PROTEIN** 0.3g; **CARB** 8.2g; **FIBER** 0.2g; **CHOL** 0mg; **IRON** 0.3mg; **SODIUM** 87mg; **CALC** 13mg

3. CREAMY WHITE SAUCE

This white sauce is an easy go-to recipe that you can whip up in minutes to use on hot or cold chicken, or as a zesty sandwich spread. It also works well with fish and chips.

¼ cup canola mayonnaise

2 teaspoons white vinegar

1 teaspoon fresh lemon juice

½ teaspoon freshly ground black pepper

¼ teaspoon salt

1 garlic clove, minced

1. Combine all ingredients, stirring well. **YIELD:** about ⅓ cup (serving size: about 4 teaspoons).

CALORIES 47; **FAT** 4.5g (sat 0g, mono 2.5g, poly 1.5g); **PROTEIN** 0.1g; **CARB** 0.5g; **FIBER** 0.1g; **CHOL** 0mg; **IRON** 0mg; **SODIUM** 238mg; **CALC** 2mg

4. CLASSIC VINAIGRETTE

This classic vinaigrette recipe is so simple you'll soon know it by heart. It's great on steamed fresh veggies and salads, or drizzled on sprouts in a sandwich. Experiment with different vinegars to change things up from time to time.

1½ tablespoons red wine vinegar

1 tablespoon chopped shallots

1 tablespoon Dijon mustard

¼ teaspoon salt

⅛ teaspoon pepper

3 tablespoons extra-virgin olive oil

1. Combine vinegar, shallots, mustard, salt, and pepper. Gradually add oil, stirring until incorporated. **YIELD:** 6 tablespoons (serving size: 1½ tablespoons).

CALORIES 94; **FAT** 10.1g (sat 1.4g, mono 7.4g, poly 1.1g); **PROTEIN** 0.1g; **CARB** 0.7g; **FIBER** 0g; **CHOL** 0mg; **IRON** 0.1mg; **SODIUM** 178mg; **CALC** 2mg

5. PARSLEY PESTO

A nice twist on traditional basil pesto, this version uses flat-leaf parsley for a fresh, herbal flavor. Great on pastas, bruschetta, pizzas, and sandwiches, this pesto is just as versatile as the classic.

2 cups fresh flat-leaf parsley leaves

2 tablespoons pine nuts, toasted

1½ tablespoons grated Parmigiano-Reggiano cheese

1 teaspoon extra-virgin olive oil

¼ teaspoon salt

1. Combine all ingredients in a food processor; process until smooth. **YIELD:** ½ cup (serving size: 2 tablespoons).

CALORIES 59; **FAT** 4.8g (sat 0.7g, mono 1.9g, poly 1.6g); **PROTEIN** 2.3g; **CARB** 2.8g; **FIBER** 1.2g; **CHOL** 2mg; **IRON** 2.1mg; **SODIUM** 211mg; **CALC** 64mg

6. SPICY ORANGE SAUCE

Save your weeknight chicken from the doldrums. Grated fresh ginger and orange marmalade add a little sweet-and-spicy Asian flair. Hesitant to buy sambal oelek (chile paste) just for this recipe? It's one of our favorite pantry staples because it adds heat and spice to many great recipes. Serve this sauce warm.

Cooking spray

1 tablespoon grated peeled fresh ginger

⅔ cup fat-free, lower-sodium chicken broth

3 tablespoons orange marmalade

1½ tablespoons lower-sodium soy sauce

1½ teaspoons fresh lemon juice

¾ teaspoon chile paste with garlic (such as sambal oelek) or other hot chile sauce

1. Heat a skillet over medium-high heat. Coat pan with cooking spray. Add ginger; cook 1 minute, stirring constantly. Stir in broth, marmalade, and soy sauce; bring to a boil. Cook until mixture is slightly thick. Stir in lemon juice and sambal oelek. **YIELD:** about ¾ cup (serving size: about 3 tablespoons).

CALORIES 45; **FAT** 0.1g (sat 0g, mono 0.1g, poly 0g); **PROTEIN** 0.8g; **CARB** 11.2g; **FIBER** 0.4g; **CHOL** 0mg; **IRON** 0.2mg; **SODIUM** 273mg; **CALC** 10mg

UP AND AT 'EM!

Starting the Day Off Right

WHAT'S FOR BREAKFAST? For a lot of us, a cup of coffee. Sorry, but that doesn't cut it. We all need breakfast. Think of the word: Break the fast. It's been a long time since your last meal. It may be good for the soul, but fasting is tough on the body. It throws your glucose and insulin levels out of whack. An empty stomach can be the wellspring of acid reflux. And having no food for hours often means you're just plain cranky.

Studies show that those of us who regularly eat breakfast perform better during the course of our day. We have more endurance for physical activity and better cognitive performance at work and school.

Still not sold on that morning meal? Get this: Those of us who eat breakfast by and large weigh less than those who skip it. One reason is that we are better able to stave off hunger until lunch—not tempted to snack or carbo-load through thousands of calories before the noon whistle blows.

Plus, people who eat breakfast are already in the mindset to make healthy choices all day.

For the best start, think grains—like a bowl of hot oat bran and a drizzle of maple syrup. Better yet, whole grains will start you out right and hold you until lunch.

So here's to healthy morning meals. Some of these ideas may be better for the weekend, but all are quick—and a delicious way to start the day by eating right.

Make-Ahead Muesli with Apples and Honey

Here's a hearty, old-world, whole-grain, make-ahead morning treat that's popular across the Alps—and ready when you are. A full-flavored honey is the key—look for orange blossom, wildflower, star thistle, or even chestnut, which are all delicate and perfumy and pair well with the dried apples.

2 cups old-fashioned rolled oats

2 cups 1% low-fat milk

¾ cup unsweetened apple juice

½ cup chopped dried apples

¼ cup toasted wheat germ

¼ cup unsalted sunflower seed kernels

2 tablespoons honey

½ teaspoon ground cinnamon

¼ teaspoon salt

Ground cinnamon (optional)

1. Combine all ingredients (except cinnamon) in a large bowl; cover and refrigerate overnight. Store in refrigerator for up to 2 days. When serving, garnish with cinnamon, if desired. **YIELD:** 4 servings (serving size: about 1 cup).

CALORIES 365; **FAT** 9.5g (sat 1.7g, mono 3g, poly 3.1g); **PROTEIN** 13.3g; **CARB** 60g; **FIBER** 7.3g; **CHOL** 6mg; **IRON** 3mg; **SODIUM** 277mg; **CALC** 160mg

savvy IN A SNAP

Wheat germ is a mineral-rich part of the wheat kernel, stocked with vitamin E, folate, phosphorus, and zinc. It's removed during processing for all-purpose and cake flour but is present in whole-wheat flour. Wheat germ is sold toasted and untoasted. Either kind can go rancid if exposed to air or sunlight. Once opened, the jar can be stored in the fridge for several months.

Pistachio Granola

This easy stovetop method makes preparing granola a breeze. Handle the cooled granola according to your preference—leave it in larger chunks, or break it up into smaller pieces. Serve it with low-fat milk, low-fat yogurt (try vanilla-flavored), or even almond milk. It's so good, you might want to put a serving in a zip-top plastic bag for a post-workout snack.

⅔ cup packed brown sugar

¼ cup apple cider

2 cups old-fashioned rolled oats

⅔ cup chopped pistachios

⅔ cup nutlike cereal nuggets

⅔ cup dried sweet cherries

½ cup sunflower seed kernels

½ teaspoon ground cinnamon

¼ teaspoon salt

1. Combine sugar and cider in a large nonstick skillet; cook over medium-high heat 3 minutes or until sugar dissolves, stirring frequently. Stir in oats and remaining ingredients; cook 5 minutes or until granola is lightly browned, stirring frequently. Cool completely. Store in an airtight container for up to 2 weeks. **YIELD:** 10 servings (serving size: ½ cup).

CALORIES 263; **FAT** 8.4g (sat 1g, mono 3.1g, poly 3.7g); **PROTEIN** 6.9g; **CARB** 42.9g; **FIBER** 4.6g; **CHOL** 0mg; **IRON** 3.9mg; **SODIUM** 149mg; **CALC** 45mg

savvy IN A SNAP

Oats come in at least three varieties, all of which are whole-grain: quick-cooking, rolled (sometimes called regular), and steel-cut, a long-cooking, extra-chewy sort, long favored in Ireland and Scotland. (You can also track down oat groats, the whole grain without any processing; it is often available at health-food stores.) A stocked pantry always has the rolled (or regular) kind on hand. (Who knows when you're going to want oatmeal cookies?) But a well-stocked pantry has at least one of the other types in stock, too, depending on your preferences.

Whole-Grain Hot Cereals— The Perfect Pick-You-Up

A boxed, whole-grain cold cereal is a wonderful way to start the day—but a hot cereal is just so much more satisfying. Sure, we all know about oatmeal; but for a filling, healthy, whole-grain cereal as part of your morning routine, you might also consider:

INSTANT OATS

OAT GROATS

FRANCE

Brown rice farina

Cream of rye

Creamy buckwheat cereal

Hard red wheat cereal, sometimes called "bear mush"

Multi- or seven-grain hot cereals

REGULAR (ROLLED) OATS

STEEL-CUT (IRISH) OATS

100-CALORIE OPTIONS

Any of the cereals at left can be made in the microwave for a superfast morning starter.
And don't forget to jazz them up with some flavorful add-ins. Swirl, sprinkle, or top your hot cereal
with any one of these 18 options for less than 100 calories each.

- 1 tablespoon peanut butter
- 1 tablespoon toasted flaked coconut
- 1 tablespoon chocolate syrup

- ½ bacon slice, crumbled
- 1½ tablespoons shredded cheese
- ¼ cup plain 2% reduced-fat Greek yogurt

- 2 tablespoons diced apple
- ¼ cup sliced strawberries
- ¼ cup blueberries

- 1 tablespoon dried cherries
- 1 tablespoon diced dried apricots
- 1 tablespoon diced dried figs

- 1 tablespoon sliced almonds
- 1 tablespoon chopped cashews
- 1 tablespoon chopped walnuts

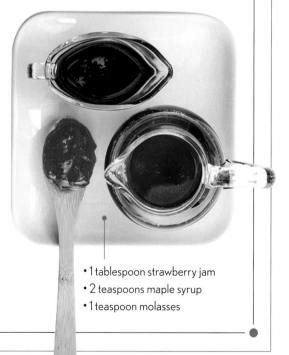

- 1 tablespoon strawberry jam
- 2 teaspoons maple syrup
- 1 teaspoon molasses

Multigrain Malt Waffle Mix

9 ounces all-purpose flour (about 2½ cups)

9.5 ounces whole-wheat flour (about 2 cups)

1.8 ounces spelt flour (about 6 tablespoons)

1 cup yellow cornmeal

½ cup sugar

½ cup malted milk powder

3 tablespoons baking powder

2 tablespoons toasted wheat germ

1 tablespoon salt

1. Weigh or lightly spoon flours into dry measuring cups; level with a knife. Combine flours and remaining ingredients in a large bowl, stirring with a whisk. Store in an airtight container in refrigerator. **YIELD:** 7¼ cups.

CALORIES 120; **FAT** 0.8g (sat 0.3g, mono 0.1g, poly 0.2g); **PROTEIN** 3.4g; **CARB** 25g; **FIBER** 1.5g; **CHOL** 1.3mg; **IRON** 1mg; **SODIUM** 242mg; **CALC** 20mg

waffling AROUND

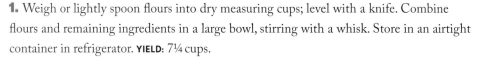

Waffles are a quick breakfast option—especially when you're thinking of eating breakfast for dinner! Here are some tips and tricks for keeping the process quick and simple.

- **Spray the waffle iron** with cooking spray before preheating to prevent sticking.

- **Pour the batter** in the middle of the waffle iron, and spread close to the edge using a rubber spatula.

- **After spreading the batter,** keep the waffle iron lid closed for a couple of minutes to prevent the top and bottom of the waffle from separating.

- **Although the general rule** is to cook until the waffle stops steaming, cooking times can vary, so follow the manufacturer's instructions.

- **Waffles freeze well.** Cool them to room temperature; freeze in a single layer on a baking sheet. Store in a freezer-safe zip-top plastic bag for up to 3 months. To reheat, place frozen waffles on a baking sheet in a 350° oven for 10 minutes, or in a toaster.

- **Let the waffle iron cool** completely before you clean it. To do so, wipe it with a damp paper towel to pick up any remaining crumbs—no soap is needed.

Multigrain Malt Waffles

Your kids will be so happy to know that waffles are always at the ready—and you'll be so happy to know that you've got a great, healthy, whole-grain mix as the base. Walnut oil is a lovely, nutty indulgence here, but you can also substitute any other nut oil.

Cooking spray

1 cup plus 2 tablespoons **Multigrain Malt Waffle Mix** (page 60)

⅔ cup 1% low-fat milk

2 tablespoons toasted walnut oil

1 teaspoon vanilla extract

1 large egg

1. Coat a waffle iron with cooking spray; preheat.

2. Place Multigrain Malt Waffle Mix in a bowl. Combine milk and remaining ingredients in another bowl, stirring well with a whisk; add to waffle mix, stirring well. Let batter stand 5 minutes.

3. Spoon about ⅓ cup batter per 4-inch waffle onto hot waffle iron, spreading batter to edges. Cook 5 minutes or until steaming stops; repeat procedure with remaining batter.

YIELD: 5 servings (serving size: 1 waffle).

CALORIES 200; **FAT** 7.8g (sat 1.2g, mono 1.8g, poly 4.3g); **PROTEIN** 5.6g; **CARB** 27g; **FIBER** 1.5g; **CHOL** 45mg; **IRON** 1.2mg; **SODIUM** 270mg; **CALC** 64mg

Peanut Butter Pancakes

Conventional chunky peanut butter works best in this recipe; the natural-style peanut butter (ground peanuts and oil) is difficult to stir into a liquid batter. For a P-B-and-J morning treat, serve these with a fruit syrup—or an all-fruit strawberry spread.

6.75 ounces all-purpose flour (about 1½ cups)

6 tablespoons sugar

2 teaspoons baking powder

¼ teaspoon salt

1¼ cups fat-free milk

¼ cup chunky peanut butter

1 tablespoon vegetable oil

½ teaspoon vanilla extract

2 large eggs, lightly beaten

1. Weigh or lightly spoon flour into dry measuring cups; level with a knife. Combine flour, sugar, baking powder, and salt in a large bowl. Combine milk and next 4 ingredients (through eggs); add to flour mixture, stirring until smooth.

2. Spoon about ¼ cup batter per pancake onto a hot nonstick griddle or large nonstick skillet. Cook 2 minutes or until tops are covered with bubbles and edges look cooked. Carefully turn pancakes over; cook 2 minutes or until bottoms are lightly browned.

YIELD: 5 servings (serving size: 2 pancakes).

CALORIES 349; **FAT** 11.7g (sat 2.5g, mono 5.1g, poly 3.2g); **PROTEIN** 12.2g; **CARB** 49.4g; **FIBER** 1.2g; **CHOL** 90mg; **IRON** 2.5mg; **SODIUM** 432mg; **CALC** 204mg

EVEN *faster*

The night before, mix the dry ingredients in one bowl and the wet in another. Store the dry ingredients, covered, on the kitchen counter; store the wet, also covered, in the fridge. Want some whole grains in these pancakes? Use 1 cup all-purpose flour and ½ cup whole-wheat flour in the batter.

Oven-Puffed Pancake

This is a lightened version of a "Dutch baby," a skillet pancake that provides a great start to a chilly weekend morning. Make sure the cast-iron skillet is well seasoned so the pancake doesn't stick as it bakes.

2.25 ounces all-purpose flour (about ½ cup)

½ cup fat-free milk

2 tablespoons granulated sugar

¼ teaspoon salt

1 large egg

1 large egg white

1 tablespoon butter

Powdered sugar (optional)

1. Preheat oven to 425°.

2. Weigh or lightly spoon flour into a dry measuring cup; level with a knife. Combine flour and next 5 ingredients (through egg white); stir until moist.

3. Melt butter in a 10-inch cast-iron skillet over medium heat. Pour batter into pan; cook 1 minute (do not stir). Bake at 425° for 18 minutes or until golden. Sprinkle with powdered sugar, if desired. Cut into quarters; serve immediately.

YIELD: 4 servings.

CALORIES 141; **FAT** 4.4g (sat 2.3g, mono 1.4g, poly 0.4g); **PROTEIN** 5.2g; **CARB** 19.9g; **FIBER** 0.4g; **CHOL** 64mg; **IRON** 0.9mg; **SODIUM** 222mg; **CALC** 48mg

ON THE SIDE: As the pancake bakes, stir together 3 cups diced, cored apples, a couple of tablespoons of apple cider, and a teaspoon of brown sugar in a saucepan over medium-low heat to make a quick, fiber-rich, applesauce-like compote for this breakfast treat.

QUICK TIP: Make sure you've got dried fruit in the pantry for quick morning breakfasts. A few dried apple rings or a handful of dried cherries alongside one of these muffins is a perfect start to the day!

Refrigerator Bran Muffins

There's just something so comforting about going to bed at night knowing that breakfast is ready to go in the morning. Here, you can make a whole-grain muffin batter and store it in the fridge for up to two weeks, baking up as many muffins in the morning as you need. Now that's a breakfast anyone can love! Make sure you bake an extra muffin for a snack later in the day.

2 cups shreds of wheat bran cereal (natural high-fiber cereal)

1⅓ cups boiling water

⅔ cup oat bran

6 ounces all-purpose flour (about 1⅓ cups)

4.5 ounces whole-wheat flour (about 1 cup)

1 tablespoon baking soda

1 teaspoon ground cinnamon

½ teaspoon salt

2 cups low-fat buttermilk

1 cup packed light brown sugar

½ cup toasted walnut oil

½ cup honey

2 large eggs

Cooking spray

1. Combine first 3 ingredients in a large bowl; let stand 15 minutes.

2. Weigh or lightly spoon flours into dry measuring cups; level with a knife. Combine flours and next 3 ingredients (through salt) in a bowl, stirring with a whisk.

3. Add buttermilk and next 4 ingredients (through eggs) to bran mixture, stirring well with a whisk. Add flour mixture; stir just until moist. Cover and refrigerate batter for up to 1 week.

4. Preheat oven to 375°.

5. Spoon batter for desired number of muffins into muffin cups coated with cooking spray, filling cups half full.

6. Bake at 375° for 20 minutes or until muffins spring back when touched lightly in center. **YIELD:** 30 servings (serving size: 1 muffin).

CALORIES 140; **FAT** 4.7g (sat 0.5g, mono 1.1g, poly 2.9g); **PROTEIN** 3.1g; **CARB** 25g; **FIBER** 2.3g; **CHOL** 15mg; **IRON** 1.4mg; **SODIUM** 200mg; **CALC** 48mg

mastering MUFFINS

Ready in a flash and delightful as can be, our muffins will disappear from your table almost as quickly as you can whip them up. They are the perfect quick breakfast idea—particularly when made ahead. Muffins are easy to master—just follow our tips, and you will be on your way.

5 QUICK TIPS FOR PERFECT MUFFINS:

1. **LEAVE A FEW LUMPS IN THE BATTER.** Overstirring can toughen a muffin. Just think—you actually save time by not having to stir as thoroughly as you thought!

2. **SPRAY THE MUFFIN CUPS WITH COOKING SPRAY BEFORE ADDING THE BATTER.** This step prevents a messy and time-consuming cleanup.

3. **CHECK FOR DONENESS EARLY** (about 5 minutes before the specified time) because ovens can vary in temperature.

4. **COOL MUFFINS IN THE PAN FOR 5 MINUTES,** and then eat them warm or remove them to a rack so they don't get soggy.

5. **STORE MUFFINS CORRECTLY SO THEY STAY FRESH.** Keep muffins in an airtight container for a day or two. Simply grab and go for breakfast on the run. Or wrap muffins individually in plastic wrap, place them in a zip-top plastic bag, and freeze them for up to 1 month. Thaw them at room temperature or in the microwave for 10 to 30 seconds. Breakfast has never been quicker!

Sour Cream Muffins with Poppy Seed Streusel

Keep these orange-scented muffins around for a quick breakfast or sweet snack.

Streusel:

3 tablespoons sugar

2 tablespoons all-purpose flour

1 tablespoon butter, melted

1 teaspoon poppy seeds

Muffins:

9 ounces all-purpose flour (about 2 cups)

¾ cup sugar

2 teaspoons baking powder

1 teaspoon baking soda

½ teaspoon salt

¾ cup nonfat buttermilk

¼ cup butter, melted

1 tablespoon grated orange rind

1 teaspoon vanilla extract

1 large egg, lightly beaten

1 (8-ounce) carton reduced-fat sour cream

Cooking spray

1. Preheat oven to 375°.

2. To prepare streusel, combine first 4 ingredients in a small bowl; set aside.

3. To prepare muffins, weigh or lightly spoon 9 ounces flour (about 2 cups) into dry measuring cups; level with a knife. Combine flour, ¾ cup sugar, baking powder, baking soda, and salt in a medium bowl, stirring with a whisk. Make a well in center of mixture. Combine buttermilk and next 5 ingredients (through sour cream) in a small bowl; add to flour mixture, stirring just until moist. Spoon batter into 15 muffin cups coated with cooking spray. Sprinkle streusel evenly over batter. Bake at 375° for 18 minutes or until golden brown. Remove muffins from pans immediately; place on a wire rack. **YIELD:** 15 servings (serving size: 1 muffin).

CALORIES 180; **FAT** 6.3g (sat 3.2g, mono 2.3g, poly 0.4g); **PROTEIN** 3.3g; **CARB** 27.8g; **FIBER** 0.5g; **CHOL** 31mg; **IRON** 1mg; **SODIUM** 277mg; **CALC** 77mg

Blueberry Oatmeal Muffins

Tossing frozen blueberries with flour before adding them to the batter keeps them from turning the batter purple while they bake. If you use fresh blueberries, skip that step.

1²⁄₃ cups quick-cooking oats

3 ounces all-purpose flour (about ²⁄₃ cup)

2.33 ounces whole-wheat flour (about ½ cup)

¾ cup packed light brown sugar

2 teaspoons ground cinnamon

1 teaspoon baking powder

1 teaspoon baking soda

¾ teaspoon salt

1½ cups low-fat buttermilk

¼ cup canola oil

2 teaspoons grated lemon rind

2 large eggs

2 cups frozen blueberries

2 tablespoons all-purpose flour

Cooking spray

2 tablespoons granulated sugar

1. Preheat oven to 400°.

2. Place oats in a food processor; pulse 5 to 6 times or until oats resemble coarse meal. Place in a large bowl.

3. Weigh or lightly spoon flours into dry measuring cups; level with a knife. Add flours and next 5 ingredients (through salt) to oats; stir well. Make a well in center of mixture.

4. Combine buttermilk and next 3 ingredients (through eggs). Add to flour mixture; stir just until moist.

5. Toss berries with 2 tablespoons all-purpose flour, and gently fold into batter. Spoon batter into 16 muffin cups coated with cooking spray; sprinkle granulated sugar evenly over batter. Bake at 400° for 20 minutes or until muffins spring back when touched lightly in center. Remove from pans immediately; place on a wire rack. **YIELD:** 16 servings (serving size: 1 muffin).

CALORIES 190; **FAT** 5g (sat 0.6g, mono 2.4g, poly 1.2g); **PROTEIN** 4.2g; **CARB** 33.3g; **FIBER** 2.4g; **CHOL** 23mg; **IRON** 1.6mg; **SODIUM** 248mg; **CALC** 74mg

EVEN *faster*

Once cooled, the muffins can be stored in a zip-top plastic bag in the freezer for up to 1 month. Thaw one in the microwave by cooking on HIGH for 25 to 35 seconds, or just take it out the night before, and leave it on the counter.

QUICK TIP: These scones can be frozen in a sealed plastic bag for up to 3 months. Thaw as many as you need for breakfast on the counter overnight.

Sour Cream Scones

Whole-wheat flour adds nutty flavor to a basic scone recipe. Split a scone in half, and spread it with your choice of jam, preserves, or lemon curd.

6.75 ounces all-purpose flour (about 1½ cups)

3 ounces whole-wheat flour (about ⅔ cup)

⅓ cup packed brown sugar

2 tablespoons granulated sugar

2 teaspoons baking powder

½ teaspoon baking soda

¼ teaspoon salt

⅔ cup reduced-fat sour cream

3 tablespoons butter, melted and cooled

1 large egg white

⅓ cup dried currants or raisins

Cooking spray

1 tablespoon granulated sugar

¼ teaspoon ground cinnamon

1. Preheat oven to 400°.

2. Weigh or lightly spoon flours into dry measuring cups; level with a knife. Combine flours and next 5 ingredients (through salt) in a large bowl; stir well with a whisk.

3. Combine sour cream, butter, and egg white in a small bowl. Add sour cream mixture to flour mixture, stirring just until moist. Stir in currants.

4. Turn dough out onto a lightly floured surface; knead lightly 6 to 12 times with floured hands. (Dough will be crumbly.) Divide dough in half. Pat each half into a 6-inch circle on a baking sheet coated with cooking spray. Cut each circle into 6 wedges; do not separate.

5. Combine 1 tablespoon granulated sugar and cinnamon. Lightly coat top of dough with cooking spray. Sprinkle evenly with cinnamon mixture. Bake at 400° for 15 minutes or until lightly browned. **YIELD:** 1 dozen (serving size: 1 scone).

CALORIES 175; **FAT** 4.8g (sat 2.9g, mono 1.3g, poly 0.3g); **PROTEIN** 3.6g; **CARB** 30.2g; **FIBER** 1.4g; **CHOL** 14mg; **IRON** 1.3mg; **SODIUM** 219mg; **CALC** 81mg

QUICK TIP: Get a coffee-maker with a program-mable feature. You can set it the night before to be ready when you are the next morning.

Simple Baked Eggs

Baked eggs are a delicious morning treat. Because heat toughens egg whites, they need the protection of a little fat. Cream to the rescue! This is the easiest way to prepare and serve several individual portions.

1 tablespoon butter

6 large eggs

1 teaspoon freshly ground black pepper

¾ teaspoon salt

2 tablespoons whipping cream

1. Preheat oven to 350°.

2. Coat each of 6 (6-ounce) ramekins or custard cups with ½ teaspoon butter. Break 1 egg into each prepared ramekin. Sprinkle eggs evenly with pepper and salt; spoon 1 teaspoon cream over each egg. Place ramekins in a 13 x 9–inch glass or ceramic baking dish; add hot water to pan to a depth of 1¼ inches. Bake at 350° for 25 minutes or until eggs are set.

YIELD: 6 servings (serving size: 1 egg).

CALORIES 109; **FAT** 8.7g (sat 3.9g, mono 2.9g, poly 0.8g); **PROTEIN** 6.5g; **CARB** 0.8g; **FIBER** 0.1g; **CHOL** 223mg; **IRON** 0.9mg; **SODIUM** 380mg; **CALC** 32mg

ON THE SIDE: You'll want whole-wheat toast, of course, to dip the points in those lovely yolks. But also consider some bacon. Bake it in the oven on its own baking sheet right alongside the eggs; bake, without turning, until crisp, about 20 minutes or maybe a little less, depending on how crunchy you like it.

Eggs Pipérade

Pipérade is a dish from the Basque region of France that always includes tomatoes and bell peppers. This version with eggs is similar to a frittata.

1 teaspoon olive oil

¾ cup chopped red bell pepper

¾ cup chopped green bell pepper

1 garlic clove, minced

½ teaspoon dried thyme

¼ teaspoon salt

¼ to ½ teaspoon ground red pepper

1 (14.5-ounce) can diced tomatoes, undrained

4 large eggs, lightly beaten

1 tablespoon chopped fresh parsley (optional)

1. Heat oil in a large nonstick skillet over medium-high heat. Add bell peppers and garlic; sauté 5 minutes. Add thyme, salt, ground red pepper, and tomatoes; cover, reduce heat to medium, and cook 7 minutes or until bell peppers are tender. Uncover and cook 1 minute or until liquid almost evaporates. Gently stir in eggs; cover and cook 3 minutes or until set. Garnish with parsley, if desired. Cut into 4 wedges. **YIELD:** 4 servings (serving size: 1 wedge).

CALORIES 134; **FAT** 6.8g (sat 1.8g, mono 2.8g, poly 1g); **PROTEIN** 8.1g; **CARB** 10.7g; **FIBER** 1.4g; **CHOL** 221mg; **IRON** 2.2mg; **SODIUM** 476mg; **CALC** 67mg

QUICK TIP: Look for chopped bell pepper at the salad bar in your supermarket.

In-a-Rush Migas

This Tex-Mex favorite can also become breakfast-on-the-go. Just roll the tortillas closed in foil, and then peel back the foil for an in-the-hand meal. (Remember to keep the foil sealed at the bottom so the salsa doesn't leak on you!) You can double or even triple this recipe—although you might consider reducing the amount of minced chile in larger batches.

2 (6-inch) corn tortillas

Cooking spray

2 teaspoons unsalted butter

¼ cup minced red onion

1 tablespoon minced pickled jalapeño peppers

4 large eggs, lightly beaten

2 tablespoons 1% low-fat milk

3 tablespoons shredded sharp cheddar cheese

½ cup salsa

¼ teaspoon ground black pepper

1. Preheat broiler.

2. Heat a medium nonstick skillet over medium-low heat. Add tortillas, 1 at a time, to pan. Cook 1 minute or until warm and soft, turning after 30 seconds. Transfer warm tortillas to a baking sheet coated with cooking spray.

3. Melt butter in skillet over medium heat; add onion and jalapeño peppers. Cook 2 minutes or until onion is tender, stirring occasionally. While the onion and peppers cook, whisk eggs and milk in a small bowl until smooth; add to onion mixture, and cook 2 minutes. Do not stir until mixture begins to set on bottom. Draw a heat-resistant spatula through egg mixture to form large curds. Do not stir constantly. Egg mixture is done when thickened but still moist.

4. Spoon egg mixture evenly over tortillas. Top evenly with cheese, salsa, and black pepper. Broil 2 minutes or until cheese melts. Serve immediately. **YIELD:** 2 servings (serving size: 1 miga).

CALORIES 325; **FAT** 18.7g (sat 7.5g, mono 4.9g, poly 1.5g); **PROTEIN** 17g; **CARB** 24g; **FIBER** 1.4g; **CHOL** 445mg; **IRON** 2mg; **SODIUM** 535mg; **CALC** 188mg

MORE CHOICES: There's a world of salsas to choose from: green, red, peach, mild, hot, insanely hot. Have several on hand, the better to customize these easy migas to everyone's tastes.

Breakfast Polenta with Warm Berry Compote

This makes a lot of compote, so if you prefer less with your polenta, reserve some to use as a topping for pancakes, waffles, or ice cream.

Compote:

1 tablespoon butter

3 tablespoons honey

1 tablespoon fresh lemon juice

Dash of ground cinnamon

1 (12-ounce) bag frozen assorted berries

Polenta:

3 cups 1% low-fat milk

½ cup quick-cooking polenta

2 tablespoons sugar

½ teaspoon salt

1. To prepare compote, melt butter in a medium saucepan over medium heat. Add honey, juice, cinnamon, and berries; bring to a boil. Reduce heat; simmer 5 minutes or until thoroughly heated. Keep warm.

2. To prepare polenta, bring milk to a boil in a medium saucepan. Slowly add polenta, stirring constantly with a whisk. Stir in sugar and salt, and cook 5 minutes or until thick, stirring constantly. Serve with compote. **YIELD:** 4 servings (serving size: ⅔ cup polenta and ⅓ cup compote).

CALORIES 285; **FAT** 4.9g (sat 3g, mono 1.4g, poly 0.2g); **PROTEIN** 8.5g; **CARB** 54.2g; **FIBER** 3.9g; **CHOL** 15mg; **IRON** 1.2mg; **SODIUM** 386mg; **CALC** 541mg

MORE CHOICES: Try this polenta on its own as a bed for a fried egg for a delicious, grain-filled breakfast. Have lots of ground black pepper at the ready!

12 Smart Ideas for Breakfast On-the-Go

Set yourself up for healthy-breakfast success by stocking your shelves with items you can grab and go.

Cheese Slices
Reduced-fat cheese slices are good to keep on hand for breakfast sandwiches.

Sausage
Soy or lean turkey sausage patties can be eaten alone or put in a breakfast wrap or sandwich. Watch the salt content, though.

Almonds
A tablespoon or two of nuts adds protein to your yogurt or oatmeal. Stir frozen berries into oatmeal or yogurt to boost the vitamin content.

Preserves
A tablespoon or two of fruit preserves or chopped dried fruit stirred into plain instant oatmeal adds a touch of sweetness to otherwise savory dishes. See pages 58-59 for other quick whole-grain cereal suggestions and stir-ins.

Waffles
Whole-wheat toaster waffles need to be simply topped with a tablespoon of peanut butter and/or fruit preserves. Fold them in half like a sandwich, and you're out the door!

Cottage Cheese

Single-serving cartons of low-fat, low-sodium cottage cheese are a good source of protein; stir in berries or other fruit for fiber.

Cereal

Preportioned servings of whole-grain cereal in sealable bowls are packed with vitamins and minerals. Watch for added sugar.

English Muffin

Whole-grain English muffins can serve as a base for a breakfast sandwich. Spread on peanut butter, a satisfying source of protein and heart-healthy fats.

String Cheese

String cheese pairs well with whole-wheat crackers.

Yogurt

Small cartons of low-fat yogurt provide a good combination of carbohydrates and protein.

Boiled Egg

Hard-cooked eggs are excellent to have on hand for busy mornings.

Breakfast Wrap

Breakfast wraps with whole-wheat tortillas make a quick healthy breakfast; roll in lean protein, such as turkey and reduced-fat cheese, scrambled eggs with diced peppers and onions, or peanut butter and bananas.

Linzer Smoothie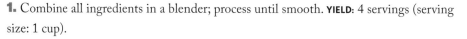

A Linzer tart is made with almonds and raspberries—so why not make a smoothie modeled on those flavors? It's a great morning pick-you-up. Frozen raspberries will make the drink icier—and ideal for a hot summer morning.

1 ripe banana

¾ cup frozen raspberries

½ cup plain low-fat yogurt

¼ cup unsweetened apple juice

1 tablespoon honey

¼ teaspoon almond extract

1. Place all ingredients in a blender; process until smooth, scraping sides. **YIELD:** 1 serving (serving size: 1⅔ cups).

CALORIES 316; **FAT** 1.6g (sat 1.3g, mono 0g, poly 0g); **PROTEIN** 7.2g; **CARB** 73g; **FIBER** 6.8g; **CHOL** 10mg; **IRON** 1mg; **SODIUM** 88mg; **CALC** 218mg

Blackberry-Mango Breakfast Shake

Use silken soft tofu to achieve a smooth consistency in this quick morning starter. This delicious, creamy drink is loaded with protein, fiber, and heart-protective vitamin C. Store leftovers in the refrigerator for up to one day, but stir before serving.

1½ cups frozen blackberries

1 cup refrigerated mango slices

1 cup (about 6½ ounces) reduced-fat silken soft tofu

1 cup orange juice

3 tablespoons honey

1. Combine all ingredients in a blender; process until smooth. **YIELD:** 4 servings (serving size: 1 cup).

CALORIES 155; **FAT** 0.8g (sat 0.1g, mono 0.2g, poly 0.4g); **PROTEIN** 4g; **CARB** 35.9g; **FIBER** 3.7g; **CHOL** 0mg; **IRON** 1mg; **SODIUM** 39mg; **CALC** 44mg

MORE CHOICES: If you don't like the seeds in blackberries, substitute frozen blueberries.

EVEN *faster*

Omit the honey, and use vanilla low-fat yogurt in this smoothie.

Spiced Winter Fruit

Serve this warm and comforting fruit compote over plain, low-fat yogurt, particularly super-thick Greek yogurt. Or, for a weekend treat, try it instead of syrup on whole-grain waffles.

1 cup packed light brown sugar

1 teaspoon ground ginger

1 teaspoon ground cinnamon

½ teaspoon ground nutmeg

2 tablespoons butter

2 quinces (about ¾ pound), each cut into 8 wedges

3 cups sliced peeled Bartlett or Anjou pear (about 1½ pounds)

2½ cups sliced peeled Granny Smith apple (about 1½ pounds)

¼ teaspoon freshly ground black pepper

Cinnamon sticks (optional)

1. Combine first 4 ingredients in a small bowl; set aside.

2. Melt butter in a large nonstick skillet over medium heat. Add quinces; cover and cook 6 minutes, stirring occasionally. Add sugar mixture, pear, and apple; cover and cook 12 minutes, stirring occasionally. Stir in pepper; garnish with cinnamon sticks, if desired. Store in an airtight container in the refrigerator for up to 3 days; reheat over low heat 3 minutes before serving. **YIELD:** 8 servings (serving size: ¾ cup).

CALORIES 219; **FAT** 3.6g (sat 1.9g, mono 0.9g, poly 0.3g); **PROTEIN** 0.7g; **CARB** 50.1g; **FIBER** 4.5g; **CHOL** 8mg; **IRON** 1.1mg; **SODIUM** 38mg; **CALC** 38mg

savvy IN A SNAP

Quince, in season in the winter months, is a yellow-skinned fruit that looks and tastes like a cross between an apple and a pear; cooking mellows the tartness. (If you can't find quince, just use two additional apples or pears cut into wedges.)

Grilled Goat Cheese Sandwiches with Fig and Honey

Great for breakfast, these sandwiches are equally good for a quick lunch with a salad on the side. Mixing honey with the goat cheese makes it easier to spread over the cinnamon-raisin bread.

2 teaspoons honey

¼ teaspoon grated lemon rind

1 (4-ounce) package goat cheese

8 (1-ounce) slices cinnamon-raisin bread

2 tablespoons fig preserves

2 teaspoons thinly sliced fresh basil

Cooking spray

1 teaspoon powdered sugar

1. Combine first 3 ingredients, stirring until well blended. Spread 1 tablespoon goat cheese mixture on each of 4 bread slices; top each slice with 1½ teaspoons preserves and ½ teaspoon basil. Top with remaining bread slices. Lightly coat outside of bread with cooking spray.

2. Heat a large nonstick skillet over medium heat. Add 2 sandwiches to pan. Place a cast-iron or other heavy skillet on top of sandwiches; press gently to flatten. Cook 3 minutes on each side or until bread is lightly toasted (leave pan on sandwiches while they cook). Repeat with remaining sandwiches. Sprinkle evenly with sugar. **YIELD:** 4 servings (serving size: 1 sandwich).

CALORIES 243; **FAT** 8.5g (sat 4.8g, mono 2.7g, poly 0.5g); **PROTEIN** 9.8g; **CARB** 33.1g; **FIBER** 2.5g; **CHOL** 13mg; **IRON** 2.2mg; **SODIUM** 326mg; **CALC** 78mg

FAST & FRESH SALADS

4

Give it some crunch.

For crunch, add 2 tablespoons toasted chopped nuts per serving. You can use any you choose, from shelled pistachios to cashews, pecans to walnuts—but look for unsalted roasted nuts to keep the sodium in check. Or skip the nuts altogether, and add a few crunchy croutons, preferably ones you make yourself from day-old cubed bread in a dry skillet over medium heat. Dot these all around the plates.

6

Drizzle the dressing.

Drizzle two or three tablespoons of your favorite salad dressing over each salad. We've got several good candidates on pages 34-43. Or you might have a bottled favorite you like to use. Just read the label, and make sure you're using a low-sodium dressing.

7

Add the seasoning.

Add several grinds of black pepper to each plate, and you're ready to enjoy a tasty, easy meal.

5

Get Cheesy.

If you'd like, add 1 ounce shredded, shaved, or crumbled cheese per person—blue cheese, Parmesan, cheddar, Gouda, fresh goat cheese, or another of your favorites. Sprinkle the cheese over the plates.

Enlightened Greek Salad

The classic salad is often a heavy thing, way too oily, not nearly fresh enough for a satisfying meal—which is really too bad because a Greek salad can be a simple but healthy dinner, stocked with veggies, laced with feta, and tossed with a less oily version of the classic Greek dressing. There's really not much more you need—except a piece of crunchy baguette to soak up the remaining dressing on your plate.

8 cups torn romaine lettuce

1 cup halved cherry tomatoes

¾ cup (⅛-inch-thick) red onion slices, separated into rings

½ cup sliced pitted ripe olives

½ cup (2 ounces) crumbled feta cheese

8 drained canned artichoke hearts, rinsed and halved

1 English cucumber, quartered lengthwise and sliced

Enlightened Greek Dressing (page 34)

1. Combine first 7 ingredients in a large bowl. Drizzle lettuce mixture with Enlightened Greek Dressing; toss gently. **YIELD:** 4 servings (serving size: 3¼ cups).

CALORIES 243; FAT 16g (sat 4g, mono 7.2g, poly 1.2g); PROTEIN 10.1g; CARB 15.6g; FIBER 5.1g; CHOL 38mg; IRON 2mg; SODIUM 683mg; CALC 164mg

QUICK TIP: You can find almost all of these fresh ingredients on a well-stocked salad bar at your supermarket. They might even have the artichoke hearts!

Spinach Salad with Canadian Bacon and a Poached Egg

This is a cross of sorts—between the traditional spinach salad with chopped hard-cooked egg and the French classic, *salade aux lardons*, with a poached egg on top. The yolk melts into the warm skillet dressing, making it even more irresistible.

4 large eggs

Cooking spray

8 cups packed baby spinach leaves

1 tablespoon olive oil

1 (6-ounce) package Canadian bacon, diced

¾ cup diced red onion

2 teaspoons Dijon mustard

1 teaspoon Worcestershire sauce

3 tablespoons white balsamic vinegar

¼ teaspoon freshly ground black pepper

1. In a 12-inch skillet, bring a 2-inch layer of water (about 4 cups) to a low boil. Break an egg into a 6-ounce custard cup. Gently slip egg into water. Repeat procedure with remaining eggs. Turn off heat; cover and let stand 3 minutes or until desired degree of doneness. Remove eggs from pan with a slotted spoon; transfer to a plate coated with cooking spray. Cover and keep warm.

2. Place spinach in a large bowl.

3. Heat oil in a large nonstick skillet over medium-high heat. Add Canadian bacon; cook 4 minutes, stirring often, or until browned. Remove from pan with a slotted spoon, reserving drippings in pan; drain on paper towels.

4. Cook onion in drippings 3 minutes or until tender. Stir in mustard and Worcestershire sauce; cook 30 seconds. Stir in vinegar. Pour over spinach; toss well.

5. Divide spinach mixture evenly among 4 plates. Top each serving with an egg; sprinkle evenly with Canadian bacon and pepper. **YIELD:** 4 servings (serving size: 2 cups salad, 1 egg, and ¼ cup bacon).

CALORIES 197; **FAT** 10.8g (sat 2.8g, mono 5.7g, poly 1.3g); **PROTEIN** 15g; **CARB** 11.5g; **FIBER** 2.8g; **CHOL** 232mg; **IRON** 3mg; **SODIUM** 658mg; **CALC** 72mg

savvy IN A SNAP

White balsamic vinegar is a sweeter, lighter vinegar than aged, syrupy balsamic vinegar, although it's made from the same Trebbiano grapes. For white balsamic, the must (that is, the grape pressings) is simmered at a low temperature with white wine vinegar. The resulting concoction has a brighter, spikier, but still sweet taste.

Start with 1½ cups of fresh mixed greens. Add a tablespoon of your favorite vinaigrette. Then pile on the good stuff.

Protein-Packed

2 tablespoons edamame +
1 tablespoon crunchy
Chinese noodles + 2 tablespoons
mandarin orange segments +
1 tablespoon chopped
roasted peanuts

Californian

3 tablespoons cubed
avocado + 1 slice center-cut
bacon, crumbled +
1 tablespoon shredded
cheddar cheese

Classic Caprese

2 plum tomatoes +
2 tablespoons chopped
fresh basil + 1 ounce
fresh mozzarella

Nuts, Berries & Blue

1 tablespoon crumbled
blue cheese + 1 tablespoon
sweetened dried cranberries +
1 tablespoon chopped
toasted walnuts

Southwestern

2 tablespoons rinsed and
drained black beans +
2 tablespoons sweet yellow corn +
2 tablespoons crumbled
queso fresco +
2 tablespoons cubed avocado

Perfect Pear Up

½ ounce goat cheese +
1 tablespoon chopped
toasted walnuts +
¼ cup fresh pear slices

Greek

¼ cup sliced red bell pepper +
2 tablespoons crumbled
feta cheese + ¼ cup chopped
fresh cucumber +
4 sliced kalamata olives

THE ENTRÉE OPTION

Double the greens
and dressing, pick
your favorite flavor
booster, and then
add extra protein
for a super salad
supper that clocks
in under 400
calories.

- **Flank steak**
  (3 ounces broiled)
  375 calories

- **Chicken breast**
  (3 ounces roasted)
  360 calories

- **Shrimp**
  (¼ pound grilled)
  345 calories

Grilled Salad

Here's a surprise: Lettuce takes on a sweet smokiness when it caramelizes in a grill pan over high heat. In minutes, you have terrific flavor without a lot of fuss—plus, the residual oil on the leaves becomes part of the salad's dressing. If you've got a little more time on your hands, you can grill the cut lettuces on an outdoor grill preheated to high heat.

2 tablespoons olive oil

2 heads romaine lettuce, halved lengthwise

1 head radicchio, halved lengthwise

2 tablespoons balsamic vinegar

¼ teaspoon salt

¼ teaspoon freshly ground black pepper

⅓ cup chopped pecans

¼ cup (1 ounce) grated fresh Parmigiano-Reggiano cheese

1. Heat a seasoned cast-iron grill pan over high heat until smoking. Brush oil evenly on cut sides of romaine and radicchio. Place greens, cut sides down, on grill pan in 3 batches. Cook 4 minutes or until lightly charred and beginning to wilt, turning after 2 minutes.

2. While greens cook, combine vinegar, salt, and pepper in a large bowl, stirring with a whisk. Cut greens into bite-sized pieces; add to vinegar mixture. Add pecans and cheese; toss well. **YIELD:** 6 servings (serving size: 1½ cups).

CALORIES 135; **FAT** 9.8g (sat 1.3g, mono 5.8g, poly 2.2g); **PROTEIN** 4.1g; **CARB** 10.6g; **FIBER** 5.4g; **CHOL** 1mg; **IRON** 3mg; **SODIUM** 129mg; **CALC** 94mg

MORE CHOICES: For a full meal, add protein to the salad: precooked peeled and deveined shrimp; shredded skinless, boneless rotisserie chicken; or crumbled feta or blue cheese with some crunchy bacon bits from your supermarket's salad bar.

ALL ABOUT *greens*

BUYING: We prefer to use fresh heads rather than bagged greens because the heads stay crisper longer. However, bagged greens are a great quick solution when time is of the essence. Choose greens with fresh-looking, brightly colored leaves with no sign of wilting. Avoid any that are spotted, limp, or yellowing. A brown core does not necessarily indicate poor quality. If buying bagged salad greens, check the expiration date, and choose the freshest.

CLEANING: Wash all greens with cold water. Leafy greens like spinach can harbor sand and other debris; to clean, dunk them in a large bowl, pot, or clean sink filled with cold water. The dirt will sink to the bottom while the greens float to the top. Remove the greens by hand, pour out the water, and repeat the procedure until the water is free of debris. Drain greens on paper towels or with a salad spinner.

STORING: Store washed greens in your refrigerator crisper drawer in zip-top plastic bags with a paper towel to absorb moisture; squeeze out air before sealing. Use within a day or two (use firm lettuces, such as iceberg, within a week).

MEASURING: When measuring greens, don't pack the leaves too tightly in the measuring cup. Instead, place them in the cup, and lightly pat down.

Farmers' markets and good supermarkets are offering more and more greens. Here's a glossary of the essential greens and lettuces for great salads.

ARUGULA: This peppery green's assertive flavor is widely used in Italian cuisine. It's slightly bitter and has a hint of mustard. The prime season for arugula is spring, when its leaves are tender and less bitter. Spinach makes a milder substitute.

BELGIAN ENDIVE: This endive variety grows in a compact cylindrical shape with a tapered end. Its pale leaves are slightly bitter with red or pale yellow-green tips.

BUTTER LETTUCE: Named for its buttery-textured leaves, this lettuce has a slightly sweet flavor. Handle the leaves gently; they bruise easily. Varieties include Boston lettuce and the slightly smaller Bibb lettuce.

ICEBERG LETTUCE: This cool, crunchy head lettuce can hold its texture for hours in a heavy dressing, so it's ideal for make-ahead layered salads. When stored properly, it can keep in the refrigerator for up to a week—much longer than its high-end lettuce cousins.

LEAF LETTUCE (green, red, and oak leaf): This variety has leaves that splay from a central root. The most common are green leaf; red leaf, with its distinctive burgundy tinge; and oak leaf, which is so named because its shape is similar to that of an oak leaf. Leaf lettuce tends to be more perishable than head lettuce.

RADICCHIO: Also known as Italian chicory, this bitter pepper-flavored plant has stark white veins and dramatic coloring that ranges from magenta to maroon. Depending on the variety, it can grow in a small rounded head or have narrow leaves that taper.

CURLY ENDIVE: This lettuce-like endive has an off-white, compact center and loose, lacy green-rimmed outer leaves that curl at the tips. It has a prickly texture and a slightly bitter taste.

ESCAROLE: The mildest of the endive varieties, escarole has broad bright leaves that curl slightly. Escarole has only a hint of the bitterness that is characteristic of Belgian and curly endives.

FRISÉE: A member of the chicory family, this green has slender, featherlike leaves that range from almost white to yellow-green. It has a mildly bitter taste and adds delicate visual interest to a salad.

ROMAINE: Romaine leaves grow in heads and range in color from dark-green outer leaves to a yellowish-green heart in the center. The lettuce of choice for Caesar salads, romaine adds crisp texture to any lettuce mix.

SPINACH: Choose spinach leaves that are crisp and dark green with a fresh fragrance. We like baby spinach because its mild, tender leaves are prime for enjoying raw in salads, and there's no need to trim the stems.

WATERCRESS: This member of the mustard family has small, crisp, dark-green leaves with a sharp, peppery flavor. Pungent-flavored arugula makes a good substitute. If you don't care for the sharp flavor, you can use spinach.

Pesto Caesar Salad

Purchased pesto can be very oily. And there's no need to weigh down the fresh flavors of high-quality ingredients. If yours has a film of oil on top, pour it off, rather than just stirring it in. The lighter pesto will then really shine in this simple salad with crunchy, homemade croutons.

3 ounces French bread baguette, cut into ½-inch cubes

1½ teaspoons extra-virgin olive oil

Cooking spray

2 ounces Parmigiano-Reggiano cheese

¼ cup organic canola mayonnaise

3 tablespoons purchased pesto

4 teaspoons water

2 teaspoons fresh lemon juice

1 teaspoon anchovy paste

½ teaspoon Worcestershire sauce

½ teaspoon Dijon mustard

⅛ teaspoon hot pepper sauce

1 garlic clove, minced

12 cups torn romaine lettuce

1. Preheat oven to 400°.

2. Place bread in a large bowl; drizzle with oil. Toss to coat. Arrange bread in a single layer on a baking sheet coated with cooking spray. Bake at 400° for 10 minutes or until golden, turning once. Set aside.

3. Grate 2 tablespoons cheese; shave remaining cheese to equal about 6 tablespoons. Set shaved cheese aside.

4. Combine grated cheese, mayonnaise, and next 8 ingredients (through garlic) in a medium bowl, stirring with a whisk. Combine croutons and lettuce in a large bowl. Drizzle mayonnaise mixture over lettuce mixture; toss to coat.

5. Place 1⅓ cups salad on each of 6 plates; top each serving with 1 tablespoon shaved cheese. **YIELD:** 6 servings.

CALORIES 202; **FAT** 14.3g (sat 2.3g, mono 6.2g, poly 5.4g); **PROTEIN** 6.2g; **CARB** 13.6g; **FIBER** 2.9g; **CHOL** 15mg; **IRON** 1.9mg; **SODIUM** 331mg; **CALC** 131mg

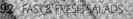

Gazpacho Panzanella

This colorful salad combines the best of the classic Spanish soup, gazpacho, and the Italian bread salad, panzanella. Chop the vegetables, and toast the bread cubes ahead of time, but assemble the salad right before serving because the bread will soak up the juices and become soggy if it sits too long. If you prefer a drier panzanella, add less dressing.

Salad:

4 ounces French bread, cut into ½-inch cubes

Olive oil–flavored cooking spray

3½ cups chopped seeded tomato (about 2 pounds)

2 cups chopped skinless, boneless rotisserie chicken breast

1¾ cups chopped seeded cucumber (about 1 pound)

1 cup chopped green bell pepper

½ cup thinly sliced red onion

¼ cup chopped fresh flat-leaf parsley

Dressing:

½ cup low-sodium vegetable juice

¼ cup red wine vinegar

1 tablespoon olive oil

1 tablespoon water

2 garlic cloves, minced

½ teaspoon salt

⅛ teaspoon freshly ground black pepper

1. Preheat oven to 350°.

2. To prepare salad, arrange bread cubes in a single layer on a baking sheet. Lightly coat bread cubes with cooking spray. Bake at 350° for 15 minutes or until golden brown, stirring once. Set aside.

3. Place tomato, chicken, cucumber, bell pepper, onion, and parsley in a large bowl; toss gently to combine.

4. To prepare dressing, combine juice and next 6 ingredients (through pepper), stirring with a whisk. Drizzle over salad, tossing gently to coat. Stir in bread cubes; let stand 5 minutes. Serve immediately. **YIELD:** 4 servings (serving size: 2½ cups).

CALORIES 294; FAT 7.7g (sat 1.5g, mono 4.1g, poly 1.4g); PROTEIN 26.9g; CARB 29.6g; FIBER 4.4g; CHOL 60mg; IRON 3mg; SODIUM 553mg; CALC 68mg

MORE CHOICES:
Substitute chopped, precooked, peeled and deveined shrimp for the chicken.

Arugula, Italian Tuna, and White Bean Salad

Here's a classic—and it's even a no-cook dinner, packed with colorful vegetables. What's more, it gets a flavor kick from a zesty vinaigrette.

3 tablespoons fresh lemon juice

1½ tablespoons extra-virgin olive oil

½ teaspoon minced garlic

¼ teaspoon kosher salt

¼ teaspoon freshly ground black pepper

¼ teaspoon Dijon mustard

1 cup grape tomatoes, halved

1 cup vertically sliced red onion

2 (6-ounce) cans Italian tuna packed in olive oil, drained and broken into chunks

1 (15-ounce) can cannellini beans or other white beans, rinsed and drained

1 (5-ounce) package baby arugula

2 ounces Parmigiano-Reggiano cheese, shaved

1. Combine first 6 ingredients in a large bowl, stirring with a whisk. Add tomatoes and next 4 ingredients (through arugula); toss. Top with cheese. **YIELD:** 4 servings (serving size: 2¼ cups).

CALORIES 301; FAT 14.5g (sat 4.1g, mono 6.7g, poly 2.8g); PROTEIN 27.5g; CARB 15g; FIBER 3.8g; CHOL 21mg; IRON 2.5mg; SODIUM 709mg; CALC 263mg

savvy IN A SNAP

Italian canned tuna is often cooked only once, not twice like regular canned tuna. It's then hand-packed in olive oil. Although often still labeled "Italian" tuna, it's now made in many Mediterranean countries.

Southeast Asian Cabbage and Shrimp Salad

Fresh mint adds a cooling balance to this spicy salad. However, if you're the type who likes more heat, keep the seeds in the jalapeño pepper.

Dressing:

½ cup lime juice

⅓ cup chopped fresh cilantro

¼ cup water

3 tablespoons brown sugar

2 tablespoons minced seeded jalapeño pepper

2 tablespoons thinly sliced fresh mint

1½ tablespoons fish sauce

1 garlic clove, minced

Salad:

6 cups thinly sliced napa (Chinese) cabbage

1½ cups shredded carrot

1½ cups loosely packed fresh mint leaves

1 cup vertically sliced red onion

1½ pounds precooked, peeled and deveined medium shrimp

1 English cucumber, halved lengthwise and sliced (about 1½ cups)

6 tablespoons chopped unsalted, dry-roasted peanuts

Mint sprigs (optional)

1. To prepare dressing, combine first 8 ingredients, stirring with a whisk until sugar dissolves.

2. To prepare salad, combine cabbage and next 5 ingredients (through cucumber) in a large bowl. Drizzle dressing over salad, and toss well to coat. Sprinkle with peanuts; garnish with mint sprigs, if desired. Serve immediately. **YIELD:** 6 servings (serving size: 2 cups salad and 1 tablespoon peanuts).

CALORIES 252; FAT 6.7g (sat 1g, mono 2.6g, poly 2.3g); PROTEIN 27.5g; CARB 21.6g; FIBER 3.8g; CHOL 172mg; IRON 3.7mg; SODIUM 553mg; CALC 170mg

QUICK TIP: Did you know that many butchers at supermarkets will sharpen a knife or two for you if they have the time while you shop? And a sharp knife is a quick cook's best tool!

Crab and Grilled Corn Salad

This savory, summery salad can also be rolled up in those Boston lettuce leaves, turning it into a wrap-snack-on-the-go to take in the cooler on car trips or to the kids' ball games.

6 ears shucked corn

1 cup finely chopped celery

1 cup chopped bottled roasted red bell peppers, rinsed and drained

½ cup chopped fresh cilantro

⅓ cup thinly sliced green onions

12 ounces lump crabmeat, shell pieces removed

¼ cup fresh lime juice

3 tablespoons canola mayonnaise

½ teaspoon freshly ground black pepper

⅛ teaspoon salt

⅛ teaspoon ground red pepper

12 Boston lettuce leaves

1. Heat a large grill pan over medium-high heat. Place corn in pan; cook 8 minutes or until slightly charred, turning frequently. Cool slightly. Cut kernels from ears of corn; place in a large bowl. Add celery and next 4 ingredients (through crabmeat) to corn; toss gently to combine.

2. Combine lime juice, mayonnaise, black pepper, salt, and ground red pepper in a small bowl, stirring well with a whisk. Pour dressing over crab mixture; toss gently to coat. Serve salad over lettuce leaves. **YIELD:** 6 servings (serving size: 1⅓ cups salad and 2 lettuce leaves).

CALORIES 249; FAT 8.3g (sat 0.6g, mono 2.4g, poly 4.7g); PROTEIN 16.8g; CARB 31g; FIBER 4.9g; CHOL 59mg; IRON 1.9mg; SODIUM 475mg; CALC 90mg

EVEN *faster*

Use 3 cups frozen corn kernels, thawed. To give them a more sophisticated taste, cook 2 to 3 minutes in a skillet sprayed with cooking spray and set over medium heat, stirring often.

Chicken-Fruit Salad

To add even more Mediterranean flavor in this simple salad, buy a rotisserie chicken with lots of oregano and rosemary in the rub.

1 (10-ounce) package Italian-blend salad greens (about 6 cups)

2 cups chopped skinless, boneless rotisserie chicken breast

1 cup blueberries

1 cup quartered strawberries

1 cup sliced banana

1 cup sliced peeled kiwifruit (about 3 kiwifruit)

2 tablespoons pine nuts, toasted

2 tablespoons herbed goat cheese

Creamy Raspberry Dressing (page 35)

1. Arrange 1½ cups salad greens on each of 4 plates. Divide remaining ingredients except Creamy Raspberry Dressing equally among 4 plates. Drizzle each serving with 3 tablespoons Creamy Raspberry Dressing. **YIELD:** 4 servings (serving size: 1 salad).

CALORIES 332; FAT 8.8g (sat 2.4g, mono 3.3g, poly 2.1g); PROTEIN 15.9g; CARB 53.3g; FIBER 5.9g; CHOL 32mg; IRON 2.7mg; SODIUM 699mg; CALC 114mg

MORE CHOICES: Add up to 2 cups quickly blanched green beans or sugar snap peas with the fruit and chicken.

Asian Edamame and Chicken Salad

This bright, fresh salad will keep in a sealed container in the fridge for up to 3 days. Look for frozen shelled edamame (that is, green, immature soybeans) in the freezer case of most supermarkets, often in the organic section.

Asian Ginger-Carrot Dressing (page 39)

2 cups shredded rotisserie chicken breast (8 ounces)

1 (10-ounce) package frozen shelled edamame (green soybeans), thawed

¾ cup diced red bell pepper

1. Place Asian Ginger-Carrot Dressing in a large bowl. Add chicken and remaining ingredients; toss well. **YIELD:** 4 servings (serving size: 1 cup).

CALORIES 227; **FAT** 5.1g (sat 0.6g, mono 0.7g, poly 0.5g); **PROTEIN** 27g; **CARB** 13.5g; **FIBER** 4.2g; **CHOL** 48mg; **IRON** 3mg; **SODIUM** 442mg; **CALC** 50mg

Curried Chicken Salad

Stuff this chicken salad along with a crunchy lettuce leaf into whole-wheat pita pockets for a quick, on-the-go lunch.

¼ cup plain low-fat yogurt

¼ cup cranberry chutney

3 tablespoons light mayonnaise

1½ teaspoons curry powder

2½ cups chopped rotisserie chicken breast (about 12 ounces)

1¼ cups finely chopped celery

⅓ cup minced red onion

1. Combine first 4 ingredients in a medium bowl, stirring with a whisk. Add chicken and remaining ingredients; toss well. Store, covered, in refrigerator for up to 3 days.

YIELD: 4 servings (serving size: about ¾ cup).

CALORIES 209; **FAT** 7.3g (sat 1.5g, mono 2.2g, poly 2.3g); **PROTEIN** 26g; **CARB** 10g; **FIBER** 1.4g; **CHOL** 81mg; **IRON** 1.7mg; **SODIUM** 424mg; **CALC** 99mg

QUICK TIP: Many supermarkets' prepared-food counters sell roasted chicken breasts. Buying these will save you the trouble of skinning and deboning that rotisserie bird.

Warm Bow Tie Pasta Salad

Adding pasta is an easy way to bulk up a salad. Make sure you cook the pasta al dente—that is, just until there's a little chew left in each piece. Rinse it under warm water so that the pieces don't clump on the plate.

8 ounces uncooked farfalle (bow tie pasta)

2 tablespoons olive oil, divided

1⅓ cups julienne-cut red bell pepper (about 1 large pepper)

1 cup sliced cremini mushrooms (about 2 ounces)

1 cup thinly sliced shiitake mushroom caps (about 2 ounces)

3 garlic cloves, minced

3 tablespoons balsamic vinegar

1 tablespoon Dijon mustard

¼ teaspoon salt

6 cups gourmet salad greens

½ cup (2 ounces) finely grated Asiago cheese

Freshly ground black pepper (optional)

1. Cook pasta according to package directions, omitting salt and fat.

2. While pasta is cooking, heat 1 tablespoon oil in a large nonstick skillet over medium heat. Add bell pepper, mushrooms, and garlic, and sauté 10 minutes. Combine remaining 1 tablespoon oil, vinegar, mustard, and salt in a large bowl.

3. Drain pasta. Add pasta, salad greens, and mushroom mixture to bowl; toss well. Serve topped with cheese and, if desired, black pepper. **YIELD:** 4 servings (serving size: 2 cups pasta salad and 2 tablespoons cheese).

CALORIES 360; **FAT** 12.1g (sat 3.5g, mono 6.4g, poly 1.3g); **PROTEIN** 14.1g; **CARB** 48.6g; **FIBER** 3.6g; **CHOL** 15mg; **IRON** 4mg; **SODIUM** 441mg; **CALC** 198mg

MORE CHOICES:
For even more texture and flavor, choose whole-wheat farfalle.

savvy IN A SNAP

Here's the quickest way to **core a bell pepper:** Stand it stem up on your work surface, and slice down around the core, taking large strips of the flesh away from the fruit, leaving the core standing in the center as you work your way around the pepper.

Pasta Fagioli Salad

Pasta and beans—they're a classic combination in Italian cooking, savory and sweet all together. This quick pasta salad is based on that pairing. The dressing uses a basil-infused oil; look for it among the flavored and nut oils at your supermarket. Best of all, the salad can be stored in the refrigerator in a sealed container for up to four days, ready when you are.

8 ounces uncooked penne (tube-shaped pasta)

¼ cup balsamic vinegar

3 tablespoons basil-flavored olive oil

1 teaspoon salt

1 teaspoon freshly ground black pepper

4 teaspoons minced garlic

2 teaspoons Worcestershire sauce

1 (15.5-ounce) can cannellini beans or other white beans, rinsed and drained

1 (12-ounce) package frozen green beans, thawed and cut into 1-inch pieces

1¼ cups diced tomato

¼ cup thinly sliced fresh basil

2 tablespoons minced red onion

1. Cook pasta according to package directions, omitting salt and fat. Drain; rinse under cold running water until cool. Drain.

2. Combine vinegar and next 5 ingredients (through Worcestershire sauce) in a large bowl, stirring with a whisk. Add pasta, beans, and remaining ingredients. Toss until coated. **YIELD:** 8 servings (serving size: 1 cup).

CALORIES 219; **FAT** 6.2g (sat 0.8g, mono 3.8g, poly 0.8g); **PROTEIN** 6.8g; **CARB** 33g; **FIBER** 3.7g; **CHOL** 0mg; **IRON** 1mg; **SODIUM** 365mg; **CALC** 45mg

savvy IN A SNAP

Infused olive oils are a great way to add lots of flavor to dishes in no time. Ever had smoked olive oil? It's amazing!

Couscous Salad with Chickpeas and Tomatoes

Quick and easy to make, this salad keeps well and tastes best at room temperature. Toss in leftover chicken or shrimp to boost protein, and create an ideal weekday lunch. Pack it along with cut-up fresh pineapple and biscotti.

6 tablespoons vegetable broth

6 tablespoons water

¾ cup uncooked couscous

¾ cup canned chickpeas (garbanzo beans), rinsed and drained

⅓ cup chopped seeded plum tomato

6 tablespoons (1½ ounces) feta cheese, crumbled

2 tablespoons chopped pitted kalamata olives

2 tablespoons minced red onion

2 tablespoons chopped fresh parsley

1 tablespoon red wine vinegar

1 tablespoon fresh lemon juice

1 tablespoon olive oil

⅛ teaspoon salt

Dash of freshly ground black pepper

1. Bring vegetable broth and 6 tablespoons water to a boil in a medium saucepan; gradually stir in couscous. Remove from heat; cover and let stand 10 minutes. Fluff with a fork.

2. Combine cooked couscous and remaining ingredients in a large bowl. **YIELD:** 6 servings (serving size: ¾ cup).

CALORIES 181; **FAT** 6.2g (sat 1.7g, mono 3.5g, poly 0.7g); **PROTEIN** 5.5g; **CARB** 25.8g; **FIBER** 2.7g; **CHOL** 6mg; **IRON** 0.9mg; **SODIUM** 373mg; **CALC** 56mg

QUICK TIP: Although canned beans and chickpeas are a boon to a quick cook, always take an extra minute or two to rinse them in a colander set in the sink to get rid of excess sodium.

Lemony Orzo-Veggie Salad with Chicken

This easy pasta salad is ready in minutes and stocked with fresh veggies and lots of flavor. The goat cheese gives it a little creaminess—but you could also substitute a shaved or grated hard cheese, like Parmigiano-Reggiano or aged Gouda.

¾ cup uncooked orzo (rice-shaped pasta)

¼ teaspoon grated lemon rind

3 tablespoons fresh lemon juice

1 tablespoon extra-virgin olive oil

½ teaspoon kosher salt

½ teaspoon minced garlic

¼ teaspoon honey

⅛ teaspoon freshly ground black pepper

1 cup shredded skinless, boneless rotisserie chicken breast

½ cup diced English cucumber

½ cup prechopped red bell pepper

⅓ cup thinly sliced green onions

1 tablespoon chopped fresh dill

½ cup (2 ounces) crumbled goat cheese

1. Cook orzo according to package directions, omitting salt and fat. Drain and rinse with cold water; drain and place in a large bowl.

2. While orzo cooks, combine lemon rind and next 6 ingredients (through black pepper), stirring well with a whisk. Drizzle juice mixture over orzo; toss to coat. Add chicken and next 4 ingredients (through dill); toss gently to combine. Sprinkle with cheese.

YIELD: 4 servings (serving size: about 1¼ cups).

CALORIES 275; **FAT** 9.7g (sat 3.8g, mono 3.9g, poly 0.9g); **PROTEIN** 18.2g; **CARB** 28g; **FIBER** 1.8g; **CHOL** 41mg; **IRON** 0.9mg; **SODIUM** 338mg; **CALC** 60mg

savvy IN A SNAP

Orzo is a small pasta, about the size of puffed rice grains. Because it's small, it cooks quickly. You can turn almost any pasta salad into a quick-cook dish by substituting orzo.

Cuban Beans and Rice Salad

This salad has a lot of textures—from the creamy avocado to the chewy beans, not to mention the rice and tomatoes. Plus, there's cooked shrimp, which you can find on ice at almost every supermarket's fish counter. In the end, all these add up to lots of satiety. For even more, try it with long-grain brown rice, which is loaded with fiber.

½ cup diced peeled avocado

2 tablespoons balsamic vinegar

1 tablespoon olive oil

1 teaspoon ground cumin

½ teaspoon salt

¼ teaspoon black pepper

3 cups cooked white rice

1 cup chopped seeded plum tomato
(about 3 tomatoes)

¼ cup minced fresh parsley

1 (15-ounce) can black beans, rinsed and
drained

6 ounces medium chopped cooked shrimp

2 tablespoons minced fresh cilantro
(optional)

1. Combine first 6 ingredients in a bowl, and toss gently. Add rice, next 4 ingredients (through shrimp), and, if desired, cilantro; toss well. **YIELD:** 6 servings (serving size: 1 cup).

CALORIES 184; **FAT** 4.6g (sat 0.7g, mono 3g, poly 0.5g); **PROTEIN** 4.9g; **CARB** 32.8g; **FIBER** 4g; **CHOL** 0mg; **IRON** 2.3mg; **SODIUM** 421mg; **CALC** 36mg

EVEN *faster*

Cook the rice the night before for a quick prep the next day. Or stop at a Chinese restaurant and buy cooked rice.

Mexican Bulgur Salad with Citrus-Jalapeño Vinaigrette

Salads like this one are a boon to busy lives. Make it on the weekend, and then have it for lunch over the next few days—perhaps with some purchased baba ghanoush or hummus on the side for a lovely contrast.

1 cup uncooked fine-grain bulgur or cracked wheat

1 cup boiling water

1½ cups diced zucchini

1 cup fresh corn kernels (about 2 ears)

¾ cup (3 ounces) diced Monterey Jack cheese with jalapeño peppers

3 tablespoons minced fresh cilantro

1 (15-ounce) can black beans, rinsed and drained

¼ cup fresh orange juice

¼ cup fresh lime juice

2 tablespoons minced seeded jalapeño pepper

1 tablespoon olive oil

¼ teaspoon salt

¼ teaspoon ground cumin

Lime wedges (optional)

1. Combine bulgur and 1 cup boiling water in a large bowl. Cover; let stand 30 minutes or until liquid is absorbed. Add zucchini and next 4 ingredients (through black beans); stir gently.

2. Combine orange juice and next 5 ingredients (through cumin) in a small bowl, stirring with a whisk. Pour over bulgur mixture; toss gently. Serve salad at room temperature or chilled. Garnish with lime wedges, if desired. **YIELD:** 4 servings (serving size: 1½ cups).

CALORIES 371; FAT 11.4g (sat 4.8g, mono 4.6g, poly 1.1g); PROTEIN 17.6g; CARB 55.1g; FIBER 11g; CHOL 17mg; IRON 3.2mg; SODIUM 413mg; CALC 207mg

MORE CHOICES: Use any kind of beans you prefer: pink, kidney, white, or even chickpeas. For more protein, stir in up to 2 cups chopped, skinned, and boned rotisserie chicken breast.

Goat Cheese, Apple, and Lentil Salad

Make sure you use brown lentils for this savory, healthy salad. They'll soften more quickly than the green lentils and offer a great earthy, almost musky contrast to the spiky goat cheese. Consider this a make-ahead lunch: It'll keep several days in a sealed container in the refrigerator.

1½ cups dried lentils

1¼ cups chopped peeled Granny Smith apple

¾ cup shredded carrot

½ cup thinly sliced celery

¼ cup minced shallot (1 small)

3 tablespoons cider vinegar

2 tablespoons toasted walnut oil

2 teaspoons minced fresh thyme

½ teaspoon salt

½ teaspoon freshly ground black pepper

¾ cup (3 ounces) crumbled goat cheese

1. Sort and wash lentils; drain. Place lentils in a large saucepan; cover with water to 2 inches above lentils. Bring to a boil over high heat; reduce heat, and simmer, uncovered, 15 minutes or until tender. Drain and place in a large bowl. Cool. Add apple and next 3 ingredients (through shallot).

2. Combine vinegar and next 4 ingredients (through pepper) in a small bowl, stirring with a whisk; add to lentil mixture, and toss gently. Sprinkle with goat cheese (do not stir).

YIELD: 4 servings (serving size: 1½ cups).

CALORIES 437; **FAT** 10.1g (sat 3.5g, mono 1.5g, poly 5.1g); **PROTEIN** 25.2g; **CARB** 61g; **FIBER** 13.1g; **CHOL** 15mg; **IRON** 7.2mg; **SODIUM** 520mg; **CALC** 241mg

QUICK TIP: If you're going to the trouble to make lentils, cook a double batch. Cover the rest, and save them in the fridge to toss into salads, stir into soups, or add to wraps all week.

Zucchini and Quinoa Salad

Everyone wants to eat more whole grains. But who knew they were also a part of a quick cook's repertoire? Quinoa, done in minutes, is a protein-rich whole grain that'll keep you satisfied for hours without the temptation to snack. As a bonus, this lemony vinaigrette is a great addition to almost any green or grain salad.

1 cup uncooked quinoa

2 cups water

3 cups shredded zucchini (about 2 medium), squeezed dry

¼ cup sliced almonds

¼ cup (1 ounce) finely grated Parmigiano-Reggiano cheese

1 tablespoon grated lemon rind

1 tablespoon minced fresh dill

3 tablespoons fresh lemon juice

2 tablespoons olive oil

¼ teaspoon salt

¼ teaspoon freshly ground black pepper

1. Place quinoa in a fine sieve; place sieve in a large bowl. Cover quinoa with water. Using your hands, rub grains together for 30 seconds; rinse and drain. Repeat procedure twice. Drain well. Combine 2 cups water and quinoa in a medium saucepan; bring to a boil. Cover, reduce heat, and simmer 20 minutes or until liquid is absorbed. Remove from heat; fluff with a fork. Cool.

2. Combine quinoa and zucchini in a large bowl. Stir in almonds and cheese.

3. Combine lemon rind and next 5 ingredients (through pepper); pour over quinoa mixture, and toss well. **YIELD:** 4 servings (serving size: about 1 cup).

CALORIES 274; **FAT** 12.7g (sat 1.7g, mono 7.4g, poly 2.9g); **PROTEIN** 9g; **CARB** 33g; **FIBER** 5g; **CHOL** 1mg; **IRON** 2.7mg; **SODIUM** 165mg; **CALC** 75mg

savvy IN A SNAP

A lot of recipes call for **toasting quinoa** before it's cooked. While doing so increases its nutty taste, it's not a necessary step. For more flavor without toasting, search for red or black varieties of quinoa.

Farro Salad with White Beans and Artichokes

Farro, sometimes called "emmer wheat," is a high-protein grain with a mellow nutty flavor, prized in Italian cooking. Some versions are sold as "pearled" or "perlato," meaning parts of the bran have been scored or removed to promote faster cooking—a real gift to us quick cooks. This salad is nice chilled or at room temperature. Include a cluster of red grapes and crusty Italian bread to round out your meal.

1¼ cups uncooked pearled (or perlato) farro, rinsed and drained

⅓ cup chopped fresh mint

⅓ cup chopped fresh parsley

¼ cup minced red onion

3 tablespoons fresh lemon juice

2 tablespoons olive oil

¼ teaspoon salt

⅛ teaspoon freshly ground black pepper

1 (15-ounce) can navy beans, rinsed and drained

1 (14-ounce) can artichoke hearts, drained and chopped

2 ounces slivered almonds, toasted

1. Place farro in a medium saucepan. Fill saucepan two-thirds with water; bring to a boil. Cover, reduce heat, and simmer 30 minutes or until tender. Drain in a fine-mesh sieve or colander set in the sink; rinse with cool water, and drain thoroughly.

2. Combine cooked farro, mint, and remaining ingredients in a large bowl, stirring well. Cover and store in refrigerator. **YIELD:** 5 servings (serving size: 1 cup).

CALORIES 204; **FAT** 6.5g (sat 0.8g, mono 4g, poly 0.9g); **PROTEIN** 7.4g; **CARB** 30.7g; **FIBER** 4.9g; **CHOL** 0mg; **IRON** 3.2mg; **SODIUM** 437mg; **CALC** 40mg

MORE CHOICES:
Substitute quinoa for the farro, cooking 1¼ cups in a large saucepan of boiling water for just 12 minutes before draining in a fine-mesh sieve or colander.

Prosciutto and Melon Pasta Salad

Prosciutto crudo is a salted, dried, Italian ham. For the best taste, have the butcher slice it fresh for you at the deli counter, rather than buying packaged, sliced strips. Substitute whole-wheat pasta, if you like.

8 ounces uncooked legume-based farfalle pasta

1½ tablespoons fresh lemon juice

1½ tablespoons white wine vinegar

¼ teaspoon Dijon mustard

¼ teaspoon salt

¼ teaspoon black pepper

⅛ teaspoon ground red pepper

1 garlic clove, coarsely chopped

2½ tablespoons extra-virgin olive oil

1 cup baby arugula

¾ cup diced cantaloupe

¼ cup thinly vertically sliced shallots

2 tablespoons torn mint leaves

2 ounces thinly sliced prosciutto, cut into 2-inch-long strips

1 ounce shaved Parmigiano-Reggiano cheese

1. Cook pasta according to package directions, omitting salt and fat. Drain; cool to room temperature.

2. Combine lemon juice and next 6 ingredients (through garlic) in a food processor; process to blend. With processor on, slowly pour olive oil through food chute; process for 15 seconds or until blended.

3. Combine cooled pasta, arugula, cantaloupe, shallots, mint, and prosciutto in a large bowl. Drizzle the dressing over salad just before serving, and toss gently to coat. Top salad with cheese. **YIELD:** 4 servings (serving size: 1¼ cups).

CALORIES 357; **FAT** 12.8g (sat 2.9g, mono 7.5g, poly 1.6g); **PROTEIN** 16.8g; **CARB** 44.3g; **FIBER** 4.7g; **CHOL** 13mg; **IRON** 2.5mg; **SODIUM** 518mg; **CALC** 134mg

EVEN *faster*

Look for cubed cantaloupe in the refrigerator case of your supermarket's produce section. Simply dice these cubes into smaller bits. Can't find cantaloupe? Try watermelon.

NO-SHOPPING SUPPERS

Dinner Without Going to the Store

NOTHING'S MORE COMFORTING THAN A WELL-STOCKED LARDER—except those meals that come from it!

All the recipes in this chapter can be made straight out of our quick-cook pantry (see pages 16-17). Frankly, the range you can create in minutes from what you have on hand is surprising: spaghetti to skillet sautés, oven-fried fish to oatmeal-crusted chicken. It's also surprising how much family-friendly comfort food you can make: loaded potatoes, meat loaf, meatballs, chili, even pork chops. Having one of these meals for dinner one night might convince even the hesitant among us to keep the pantry up to date and ready to go at a moment's notice.

One of the best ways to stock up is to buy when you spot sales. But to do so, you need to keep an up-to-date list of what needs restocking.

What's more, if you keep that list on your smartphone or nearby while you're reading the morning paper, you'll be able to take advantage of lower prices when you peruse the ads. Having that list at hand when you're shopping can really be a money-saver now and a time-saver later on. Maybe you don't need frozen shrimp or canned beans right now—but they're on sale, and you might as well stock up. You're saving yourself the time of a future trip to the super-market right now!

While you're at it, stock up on sealable containers and bags. Keep flour and sugar in airtight containers and open boxes of pasta in zip-top plastic bags.

After that, there's not much else to do except get dinner on the table. What are you waiting for? You already have it on hand.

Lemon Pepper Shrimp Scampi

Shrimp are a quick dinner any night of the week. They're done when they're pink and firm, in a few minutes at most. Don't overcook them, or they'll turn rubbery. Serve with roasted asparagus to round out your meal.

1 cup uncooked orzo (rice-shaped pasta)

2 tablespoons chopped fresh parsley

½ teaspoon salt, divided

7 teaspoons unsalted butter, divided

1½ pounds peeled and deveined jumbo shrimp

2 teaspoons bottled minced garlic

2 tablespoons fresh lemon juice

¼ teaspoon black pepper

1. Cook orzo according to package directions, omitting salt and fat. Drain. Place orzo in a medium bowl. Stir in parsley and ¼ teaspoon salt; cover and keep warm.

2. While orzo cooks, melt 1 tablespoon butter in a large nonstick skillet over medium-high heat. Sprinkle shrimp with remaining ¼ teaspoon salt. Add half of shrimp to pan; sauté 2 minutes or until almost done. Transfer shrimp to a plate. Melt 1 teaspoon butter in pan. Add remaining shrimp to pan; sauté 2 minutes or until almost done. Transfer to plate.

3. Melt remaining 1 tablespoon butter in pan. Add garlic to pan; cook 30 seconds, stirring constantly. Stir in shrimp, juice, and pepper; cook 1 minute or until shrimp are done. **YIELD:** 4 servings (serving size: ½ cup orzo mixture and about 7 shrimp).

CALORIES 403; **FAT** 10.4g (sat 4.8g, mono 2.2g, poly 1.4g); **PROTEIN** 40.1g; **CARB** 34.7g; **FIBER** 1.7g; **CHOL** 276mg; **IRON** 4.3mg; **SODIUM** 549mg; **CALC** 97mg

savvy IN A SNAP

Remember: **Dried herbs** are pantry staples. A well-stocked spice cabinet means you don't need to go to the store for meals like this one. In general, use half the amount of dried herbs that you would use for fresh.

Garlic-Lover's Shrimp

There's a lot of garlic here, although you can adjust the amount to suit your taste. Serve this dish with lots of crusty French bread to soak up the sauce.

1 tablespoon olive oil

¼ teaspoon crushed red pepper

8 teaspoons bottled minced garlic

1 bay leaf

1½ pounds peeled and deveined large shrimp

¼ teaspoon salt

½ cup dry vermouth

2 tablespoons minced fresh parsley

¼ teaspoon dried thyme

1. Heat oil in a large nonstick skillet over medium-high heat. Add pepper, garlic, and bay leaf; sauté 30 seconds. Add shrimp and salt; sauté 3 minutes. Remove shrimp from pan. Add wine, parsley, and thyme; bring to a boil, and cook until reduced to ¼ cup (about 1 minute). Return shrimp to pan; toss to coat. Discard bay leaf. **YIELD:** 4 servings.

CALORIES 177; **FAT** 5.6g (sat 0.9g, mono 2.8g, poly 1.2g); **PROTEIN** 26.4g; **CARB** 3.8g; **FIBER** 0.2g; **CHOL** 194mg; **IRON** 3.5mg; **SODIUM** 340mg; **CALC** 84mg

savvy IN A SNAP

Avoid so-called **"cooking wines,"** which are often loaded with sodium and sometimes even artificial flavors. Use a flavorful, but inexpensive wine for cooking—or dry vermouth. Dry vermouth has a long shelf life—at least 1 year if stored in a cool, dry place.

6 MEALS WITH *frozen shrimp*

1
Lemon Shrimp Sauté

Melt 1 tablespoon unsalted butter in a large skillet over medium heat. Add 1 pound thawed, peeled, and deveined frozen medium shrimp. Cook 5 minutes, turning once; add 2 tablespoons lemon juice. Increase heat to medium-high, boil 30 seconds, and then season with ½ teaspoon freshly ground black pepper. Top each of the 4 servings with 1 tablespoon chopped fresh herbs like parsley, thyme, and/or oregano.

CALORIES 149; **FAT** 4.9g (sat 2.2g, mono 1g, poly 0.9g); **PROTEIN** 23.2g; **CARB** 1.9g; **FIBER** 0.1g; **CHOL** 180mg; **IRON** 2.9mg; **SODIUM** 169mg; **CALC** 63mg

3
Shrimp Tacos

For 4 servings, coat 1 pound thawed, peeled, and deveined frozen medium shrimp with 1 tablespoon chili powder and 1 tablespoon vegetable oil. Cook in a heated grill pan over high heat 6 minutes, turning occasionally, until done. Serve with 8 warmed 6-inch corn tortillas, 2 cups shredded lettuce, 1 cup diced tomato, ½ cup shredded reduced-fat cheese, ½ cup bottled salsa, and ¼ cup minced fresh cilantro.

CALORIES 352; **FAT** 10.7g (sat 2.5g, mono 3.2g, poly 3.4g); **PROTEIN** 29.8g; **CARB** 34.4g; **FIBER** 3.5g; **CHOL** 182mg; **IRON** 3.2mg; **SODIUM** 551mg; **CALC** 279mg

2
Asian-Style Skewered Shrimp

For 4 servings, thread 1 pound thawed, peeled, and deveined frozen medium shrimp onto water-soaked bamboo skewers. Mix 2 tablespoons hoisin sauce with 2 teaspoons rice vinegar; brush over the shrimp. Cook in a preheated grill pan, turning once, 6 minutes or until done.

CALORIES 138; **FAT** 2.2g (sat 0.4g, mono 0.4g, poly 0.9g); **PROTEIN** 23.3g; **CARB** 4.6g; **FIBER** 0.2g; **CHOL** 173mg; **IRON** 2.8mg; **SODIUM** 297mg; **CALC** 62mg

4
Roasted Shrimp

Place 2 tablespoons olive oil and 2 sprigs rosemary in a 13 x 9–inch glass or ceramic baking dish. Set in a cool oven; heat oven to 400°. When oven has heated, add 1 pound thawed, peeled, and deveined frozen medium shrimp, toss well, and bake 10 minutes, tossing once. Remove from oven. Sprinkle 1 tablespoon red wine vinegar over hot shrimp, and stir well to make 4 servings.

CALORIES 181; **FAT** 8.7g (sat 1.3g, mono 5.2g, poly 1.5g); **PROTEIN** 23g; **CARB** 1.1g; **FIBER** 0g; **CHOL** 172mg; **IRON** 2.8mg; **SODIUM** 168mg; **CALC** 60mg

5
Easy Shrimp Stir-Fry

Heat 2 teaspoons vegetable oil in a large wok over medium-high heat. Add 3 minced green onions, 1 tablespoon bottled minced ginger, and 1 teaspoon bottled minced garlic. Stir-fry 30 seconds, and then add 1 cup diced red bell pepper, 1 cup thinly sliced celery, and 1 pound thawed, peeled, and deveined frozen medium shrimp. Stir-fry 2 minutes or until shrimp are done. Pour in ⅓ cup fat-free, lower-sodium chicken broth; 1 tablespoon rice vinegar; ½ tablespoon oyster sauce; and ½ tablespoon lower-sodium soy sauce. Bring to a full boil, tossing over the heat 1 minute. Makes 4 servings.

CALORIES 171; **FAT** 4.6g (sat 0.7g, mono 1.3g, poly 1.8g); **PROTEIN** 24.1g; **CARB** 5.9g; **FIBER** 1.4g; **CHOL** 172mg; **IRON** 3.1mg; **SODIUM** 362mg; **CALC** 82mg

6
No-Beach-Necessary Shrimp Bake

For 4 servings, set a bamboo steamer over a saucepan of simmering water or a vegetable steamer in a saucepan with about 1 inch of simmering water. Add 8 small red potatoes; cover and steam 10 minutes. Add 4 ears shucked corn and 1 pound thawed, peeled, and deveined frozen shrimp. Cover and steam 10 minutes.

CALORIES 421; **FAT** 3.3g (sat 0.6g, mono 0.6g, poly 1.4g); **PROTEIN** 31.8g; **CARB** 69g; **FIBER** 7.8g; **CHOL** 172mg; **IRON** 5.6mg; **SODIUM** 199mg; **CALC** 94mg

Spaghetti with Spicy Red Clam Sauce

Canned clams make this no-fuss spaghetti and sauce recipe supereasy. Use less crushed red pepper, or omit it altogether, if you prefer a milder sauce. Serve with garlic bread and a tossed green salad.

1 (9-ounce) package whole-wheat spaghetti

1 tablespoon olive oil

½ cup chopped onion

1 tablespoon bottled minced garlic

½ teaspoon crushed red pepper

2 tablespoons no-salt-added tomato paste

1 (14.5-ounce) can no-salt-added diced tomatoes, undrained

2 (6.5-ounce) cans minced clams, undrained

2 tablespoons chopped fresh parsley

1 tablespoon chopped fresh basil

1 tablespoon chopped fresh oregano

1. Cook pasta according to package directions, omitting salt and fat. Drain.

2. Heat olive oil in a large nonstick skillet over medium-high heat. Add onion, garlic, and pepper to pan; sauté 3 minutes or until onion is lightly browned. Stir in tomato paste and tomatoes; cook 2 minutes or until thick, stirring constantly. Stir in clams; cook 2 minutes or until thoroughly heated. Remove from heat; stir in parsley, basil, and oregano. Serve with pasta. **YIELD:** 4 servings (serving size: 1 cup pasta and about 1 cup sauce).

CALORIES 337; **FAT** 4.7g (sat 0.7g, mono 2.6g, poly 0.8g); **PROTEIN** 17.5g; **CARB** 59g; **FIBER** 9.7g; **CHOL** 17mg; **IRON** 4.5mg; **SODIUM** 630mg; **CALC** 58mg

MORE CHOICES: You can also use fresh littleneck clams, if you prefer. Add them with the tomatoes, and cook until the shells open; discard any unopened shells.

QUICK TIP: If you have frozen chopped onions, you don't even need to thaw them—just toss them right into the hot skillet.

Oatmeal-Crusted Chicken Tenders

Oatmeal-crusted chicken tenders are delightfully crunchy and sure to be a hit with adults and children alike. Serve them with Roasted Red Bell Pepper Aioli (page 50), Chimichurri Sauce (page 49), or a commercial honey mustard or light ranch dressing for dipping.

1 cup old-fashioned rolled oats

¾ cup (3 ounces) grated Parmigiano-Reggiano cheese

1 teaspoon chopped fresh thyme

½ teaspoon salt

¼ teaspoon freshly ground black pepper

1 pound chicken breast tenders

Cooking spray

1. Preheat oven to 450°.

2. Place oats in a food processor, and process 20 seconds or until coarsely ground. Add cheese, thyme, salt, and pepper. Pulse to combine, and place in a shallow bowl.

3. Place each chicken breast tender between 2 sheets of heavy-duty plastic wrap; pound to ¼-inch thickness using a meat mallet or small heavy skillet. Coat both sides of tenders with cooking spray, and dredge tenders in oat mixture. Place tenders on a baking sheet coated with cooking spray. Bake at 450° for 15 minutes or until browned. **YIELD:** 4 servings (serving size: about 4 ounces).

CALORIES 266; **FAT** 7.4g (sat 3.2g, mono 2.1g, poly 1g); **PROTEIN** 34.4g; **CARB** 14.2g; **FIBER** 2.1g; **CHOL** 79mg; **IRON** 2mg; **SODIUM** 593mg; **CALC** 180mg

Oven-Fried Tilapia

Although this is a three-bowl technique, it's worth the extra mess to have such crunchy, delicate fish hot from the oven.

1.1 ounces all-purpose flour (about ¼ cup)

¼ cup fat-free milk

6 tablespoons yellow cornmeal

1½ teaspoons no-salt-added lemon pepper seasoning

4 (6-ounce) tilapia fillets

Cooking spray

¼ teaspoon salt

1. Place a large jelly-roll pan in oven.

2. Preheat oven to 450°.

3. Weigh or lightly spoon flour into a dry measuring cup; level with a knife. Place flour in a shallow bowl; pour milk into another shallow bowl. Combine cornmeal and lemon pepper seasoning in a third shallow bowl.

4. Dredge fillets in flour, shaking off excess. Dip into milk; dredge in cornmeal mixture. Place fillets on a wire rack. Remove jelly-roll pan from oven. Coat pan with cooking spray. Transfer fillets on wire rack to prepared pan. Coat fillets with cooking spray.

5. Bake at 450° for 18 minutes or until desired degree of doneness. Sprinkle fillets evenly with salt. **YIELD:** 4 servings (serving size: 1 fillet).

CALORIES 254; **FAT** 3.2g (sat 1.2g, mono 1g, poly 0.8g); **PROTEIN** 36.4g; **CARB** 18.7g; **FIBER** 0.6g; **CHOL** 85mg; **IRON** 1.7mg; **SODIUM** 240mg; **CALC** 37mg

QUICK TIP: Remember to keep tilapia fillets on hand in your "freezer" pantry. Thaw them on a plate in the fridge all day for a supper that's ready when you are.

Whether stocking your kitchen from scratch or paring down to the basics, here are the tools and equipment we recommend.

1

Chef's Knife

The chef's knife (along with a cutting board) is the workhorse of the *Cooking Light* Test Kitchens. It's ideal for chopping herbs, onions, garlic, fruits, and vegetables and for cutting boneless meats (it even cuts through small bones, such as those of chicken and fish), slicing and dicing, and general cutting tasks.

2

Colanders/ Strainers

We use both metal and plastic colanders in varying sizes. A large colander works well for draining pasta and salad greens and rinsing vegetables. A small strainer is great for separating fruit juice or pulp from seeds. Mesh strainers are the most versatile because only liquid can get through the holes.

3

Cutting Boards

We use both wooden and plastic cutting boards. Whichever you choose, wash the board thoroughly to avoid food contamination. Wipe wooden boards with diluted bleach, and wash thoroughly; sanitize plastic ones in the dishwasher.

4

Food Scales

To measure the correct amount of cheese or to make sure that pieces of meat, poultry, and fish are the specified size, use a scale. A digital scale is small, lightweight, and accurate. A food service balance scale also works well.

5

Instant-Read Thermometer

Use an instant-read thermometer to check meringues, meat, and poultry to be sure they're cooked to the correct temperature. Don't leave the thermometer in the oven while the food is cooking; remove it from the food once you've read the temperature.

6

Kitchen Shears

Keep kitchen shears handy to mince small amounts of herbs, chop canned tomatoes, trim fat from meat and skin from poultry, and make slits in bread dough.

7

Measuring Cups

Dry measuring cups, available in metal or plastic, are flat across the rim and used for ingredients like flour, grains, and cereals. We use a 1, ½, ⅓, and ¼ nest of cups. Liquid measuring cups, sized from 1 cup to 4 cups, are available in clear glass or plastic so that you can see the level of liquid through the cup.

 8

Measuring Spoons

Sometimes adding a "pinch of this" and a "dash of that" results in less flavor than desired—or more. Measuring spoons ensure that your recipes come out just right.

9

Peeler

A peeler removes the skin from both vegetables and fruits. Select one with a comfortable grip and tip to remove potato eyes and other blemishes on vegetables and fruits. It's also handy for making Parmesan cheese shavings or chocolate curls.

10

Pepper Mill

Give your food a bit of pungent flavor by sprinkling it with cracked or freshly ground pepper from a pepper mill. Many are now available in the spice section of supermarkets or in the kitchenwares department of discount stores.

 11

Stainless-Steel Box Grater

A box-style grater gives you a choice of hole sizes. Use the smallest holes for grating hard cheese or chocolate and the largest holes for shredding foods like cheddar cheese or carrots.

12

Whisks

Whisks in assorted sizes are ideal for beating eggs and egg whites, blending salad dressings, and dissolving solids in liquids. We consider them essential for making creamy sauces. Whisks are available in both stainless steel and nylon; the nylon ones won't scratch nonstick surfaces.

Chicken and Apricot Skillet Sauté

This is a simple skillet dinner, full of fresh flavors from only pantry staples and some frozen chicken breasts that you've thawed. There's not much more you need—except maybe mashed potatoes on the side.

1 cup boiling water

8 dried apricots, quartered

½ cup fat-free, lower-sodium chicken broth

2 tablespoons low-sugar apricot preserves

1 tablespoon white wine vinegar

1 teaspoon fresh thyme

½ teaspoon honey

4 (6-ounce) skinless, boneless chicken
 breast halves

¼ teaspoon salt

¼ teaspoon freshly ground black pepper

2 teaspoons olive oil

2 teaspoons unsalted butter

¼ cup frozen chopped onion

1. Combine 1 cup boiling water and apricots in a small bowl; let stand 10 minutes.

2. Combine broth and next 4 ingredients (through honey) in a small bowl. Sprinkle chicken evenly with salt and pepper.

3. Heat oil in a large nonstick skillet over medium heat. Add chicken to pan. Cook 6 minutes on each side or until done. Place 1 chicken breast half on each of 4 serving plates.

4. Melt butter in pan. Add onion; sauté 1 minute. Drain apricots, discarding liquid. Add apricots to onion; sauté 1 minute. Stir in broth mixture, scraping pan to loosen browned bits. Bring to a boil; boil 2 minutes or until reduced to ⅔ cup. Pour sauce evenly over chicken. **YIELD:** 4 servings (serving size: 1 chicken breast half and about 3 tablespoons apricot sauce).

CALORIES 281; **FAT** 6.3g (sat 2.1g, mono 2.7g, poly 0.8g); **PROTEIN** 40g; **CARB** 13g; **FIBER** 0.8g; **CHOL** 104mg; **IRON** 2mg; **SODIUM** 315mg; **CALC** 29mg

savvy IN A SNAP

Jarred all-fruit preserves are excellent pantry staples! They can add a little zip to sauces or marinades—or here, to an easy skillet sauté.

1
Italian Omelet

For 2 servings, place ¼ cup lower-sodium marinara sauce in a small bowl, and microwave at HIGH 2 minutes. Spoon the sauce into a 2-whole-eggs-plus-2-egg-whites omelet just before you flip it closed and slip it out of the skillet. Top with 1 tablespoon grated Parmigiano-Reggiano.

PER SERVING: CALORIES 117;
FAT 6.8g (sat 2.1g); **SODIUM** 202mg

3
Baked Fish Fillets

To make 4 servings, pour 3 cups lower-sodium marinara sauce into a large glass or ceramic baking dish, and top with 4 (6-ounce) skinless halibut, snapper, or bass fillets. Bake in a preheated 350° oven 20 minutes, basting once or twice, until desired degree of doneness.

PER SERVING: CALORIES 307;
FAT 9.9g (sat 0.6g); **SODIUM** 467mg

2
No-Fuss
Chicken Cacciatore

For 4 servings, coat a large, deep skillet with cooking spray, and then dice and brown 6 skinless, bone-in chicken thighs over medium heat, turning occasionally. Add 1 cup frozen bell pepper strips and 1 (6-ounce) package sliced button or cremini mushrooms; cook 2 minutes. Pour in 2 cups bottled lower-sodium marinara sauce, cover, and simmer 40 minutes or until the chicken is tender.

PER SERVING: CALORIES 221;
FAT 8.3g (sat 1g); **SODIUM** 481mg

4
Quick Minestrone

Mix 2 cups lower-sodium marinara sauce with 2 cups fat-free, lower-sodium chicken broth; 1 (15-ounce) can drained and rinsed kidney beans; and 2 cups frozen chopped vegetables in a large saucepan. Bring to a simmer over medium heat. Cover and simmer 5 to 10 minutes to make 4 servings.

PER SERVING: CALORIES 143; **FAT** 4.4g (sat 0.1g); **SODIUM** 663mg

5
Mussels Fra Diavolo

For 4 servings, place 1 cup lower-sodium marinara sauce and ½ teaspoon crushed red pepper in a large saucepan; bring to a simmer over medium heat. Add 2 pounds cleaned and debearded mussels; bring back to a simmer. Cover and cook until mussels open, about 6 minutes. Discard any unopened shells.

PER SERVING: CALORIES 236; **FAT** 7.1g (sat 1g); **SODIUM** 774mg

6
Vegetables Marinara

For 2 servings, cut zucchini, summer squash, seeded bell peppers, and/or eggplant into ¼-inch slices (1 cup each). Plan on 2 cups sliced vegetables for each serving. Place these in a large saucepan, and add 1 cup lower-sodium marinara sauce. Bring to a simmer over medium heat, cover, and cook 20 minutes or until the vegetables are tender.

PER SERVING: CALORIES 123; **FAT** 4.4g (sat 0.1g); **SODIUM** 260mg

Chicken Paprikash–Topped Potatoes

The traditional Hungarian dish of chicken and onion in creamy paprika sauce makes a hearty topping for baked potatoes. Serve the dish alongside wedges of iceberg lettuce dressed with Maple-Mustard Dressing (page 37).

4 baking potatoes (about 1½ pounds)

2 tablespoons all-purpose flour

2 teaspoons paprika

¾ teaspoon salt

¼ teaspoon ground red pepper

4 skinless, boneless chicken thighs (about 12 ounces), cut into bite-sized pieces

1 tablespoon butter

½ cup coarsely chopped onion

2 teaspoons bottled minced garlic

1 (8-ounce) package presliced mushrooms

½ cup fat-free, lower-sodium chicken broth

¼ cup reduced-fat sour cream

2 tablespoons chopped fresh parsley

1. Pierce potatoes with a fork; arrange in a circle on paper towels in a microwave oven. Microwave at HIGH 16 minutes or until done, rearranging potatoes after 8 minutes. Let stand 5 minutes.

2. Combine flour, paprika, salt, and pepper in a large zip-top plastic bag; add chicken. Seal and shake to coat.

3. Melt butter in a large nonstick skillet over medium-high heat. Add chicken mixture, onion, garlic, and mushrooms; sauté 5 minutes. Add broth; bring to a boil. Cook 6 minutes or until chicken is done and sauce thickens, stirring frequently. Remove from heat; stir in sour cream.

4. Split potatoes open with a fork; fluff pulp. Divide chicken mixture evenly over potatoes; sprinkle with parsley. **YIELD:** 4 servings (serving size: 1 potato and ½ cup chicken mixture).

CALORIES 311; **FAT** 8.6g (sat 3.9g, mono 1.9g, poly 1.2g); **PROTEIN** 22.9g; **CARB** 36.3g; **FIBER** 3.4g; **CHOL** 86mg; **IRON** 2.6mg; **SODIUM** 619mg; **CALC** 56mg

QUICK TIP: If you keep frozen skinless, boneless chicken thighs and prechopped onion in your "freezer" pantry, you may find you need to go to the store only once a week!

Chicken Puttanesca with Fettuccine

We added olives, capers, crushed red pepper, and fresh basil to bottled pasta sauce for this quick variation on a classic recipe.

8 ounces uncooked refrigerated fettuccine

2 teaspoons olive oil

4 (6-ounce) frozen skinless, boneless chicken breast halves

2 cups tomato-basil pasta sauce

¼ cup coarsely chopped pitted kalamata olives

2 teaspoons capers

¼ teaspoon crushed red pepper

¼ cup (1 ounce) shaved Parmigiano-Reggiano cheese

Chopped fresh basil or basil sprigs (optional)

1. Cook pasta according to package directions, omitting salt and fat. Drain and keep warm.

2. Heat oil in a large nonstick skillet over medium-high heat. Cut chicken into 1-inch pieces. Add chicken to pan. Cook chicken 5 minutes or until lightly browned, stirring occasionally. Stir in pasta sauce, olives, capers, and pepper; bring to a simmer. Cook 5 minutes or until chicken is done, stirring frequently. Arrange 1 cup pasta on each of 4 plates; top with 1½ cups chicken mixture. Sprinkle each serving with 1 tablespoon cheese. Garnish with basil, if desired. **YIELD:** 4 servings.

CALORIES 457; **FAT** 9.4g (sat 2g, mono 4.4g, poly 1.1g); **PROTEIN** 48.1g; **CARB** 38g; **FIBER** 2.8g; **CHOL** 103mg; **IRON** 2.3mg; **SODIUM** 538mg; **CALC** 88mg

QUICK TIP: While this dish is great with fresh pasta, it's a no-shopping supper if you have dried pasta in your pantry. You can even substitute spaghetti for linguine if that's what you have on hand.

A well-tended pantry is such a convenient, comforting storehouse of good-for-you treasures. Here's how to keep it tip-top.

1. TAKE STOCK NOW

Know what you have, when to use it, and when to toss it.

Good for 6 months

Baking soda and baking powder: Both of these leavening agents typically last up to 6 months, but there is a way to see if they're still active: For baking soda, mix ¼ teaspoon with 2 teaspoons of vinegar. For baking powder, mix 1 teaspoon with ½ cup hot water. The mixtures should bubble immediately; if not, replace.

Brown rice: Because it's richer in oil than white rice, brown rice is more susceptible to rancidity. Store in an airtight container for up to 6 months.

Nuts: Presuming your pantry is cool, dark, and dry, nuts stored in an airtight container should be fine for 6 months. Or freeze them for up to 1 year.

Oil: Turns rancid quickly, so keep it away from heat and light. Unopened containers last up to 6 months; once opened, use within 3 months. Buy small bottles of seldom-used oils.

Peanut butter: Store natural peanut butters, which often separate, in the refrigerator. The regular kind will be fine in your pantry for up to 6 months after opening.

Good for 1 year

Flour: If stored properly in an airtight container, flour can last up to 1 year. One exception: Flours with high fat content, such as whole-wheat flour, should be stored in a tightly sealed container in the refrigerator or freezer and used within 6 months.

Grains: Prevent spoilage in products like barley, rolled oats, and quinoa by storing them in airtight containers.

Good for more than 1 year

Canned goods: High-acid items, like fruits, can be stored for up to 18 months; low-acid foods, like meats and vegetables, can last 2 to 5 years. Discard if the can has leaks, rust, cracks, or large dents.

Dried beans: Store at room temperature indefinitely.

Honey: Best if used within 2 years. **NOTE:** Honey can crystallize, a natural process in which its sugar solidifies. To remedy, remove the lid from the glass jar, and place the jar in a pan of simmering water over low heat until it decrystallizes.

Sugar: Sealed tightly and away from moisture, granulated sugar will last up to 2 years. Brown sugar, however, should be used within 6 months.

Vinegar: Because of its acidic nature, unopened vinegar can be kept indefinitely. Once opened, plan to use within 6 months. As with wine, settling may occur. Strain particles away when pouring.

Put your pantry in order

If you heed only one piece of advice, make sure it's this: first in, first out. If pasta is on sale and you buy two extra boxes of penne, store them behind the penne already in your pantry. That way, you'll use the older items first.

(continued on page 134)

2. UPGRADE YOUR INGREDIENTS

Small changes have big nutritional payoffs.

100% whole-grain or legume-based pasta: Legume-based pastas (made from chickpeas or lentils) and 100% whole-grain pastas have more nutrients and fiber than plain pastas. Legume-based pastas cook in a similar amount of time; whole-grain varieties take a little bit longer and often have a heartier flavor and texture.

Brown rice: Unlike white rice, which loses nutrients in processing, brown rice counts as a serving of whole grain. Its nutty flavor is more assertive than that of white rice but still complements a variety of dishes.

Whole-wheat white flour: All-purpose white flour is stripped of nutrients and then enriched. Whole-wheat white flour, available from most grocers, is simply a mild-flavored flour made from naturally pale-colored wheat. It has all the natural goodness of the whole grain.

Corn tortillas: Try standard 6-inch corn tortillas on taco night, and you'll cut about half the fat and calories and one-fourth the sodium found in flour tortillas.

Canola oil: Among vegetable oils, mild-flavored canola has the lowest amount of saturated fat. Also, it has a high smoke point so you can use it for nearly anything.

Nuts for snacking: The calories in a handful of nuts come with good-for-you fats, protein, fiber, vitamins, and minerals. Chips can't say the same—they're calories, fat, salt, and little else.

Fat-free, lower-sodium chicken broth: By using fat-free, lower-sodium broth, you'll avoid saturated fat and a whopping 1,210 milligrams of sodium per can than regular. By starting with less, you can better control the amount that goes into your dish.

No-salt-added diced canned tomatoes: Again, why let the manufacturer decide? You'll save about 350 milligrams of sodium per can.

3. BUILD A COLLECTION OF ESSENTIAL SPICES

Although hundreds are available, these are the 8 we reach for regularly.

Ground red pepper: Also known as cayenne, a little (⅛ to ¼ teaspoon) lends kick to anything from deviled eggs to roasted root vegetables.
TIP: Use within 6 months because it loses potency.

Oregano: We usually prefer fresh herbs, but dried oregano is often a key component in long-simmering pasta sauces, soups, and stews.
TIP: Add it early in the cooking process to draw out flavor.

Black peppercorns: When freshly ground, they have much more flavor than pre-ground.
TIP: Adjust the coarseness of your grind for textural variety in pan sauces and spice rubs.

Nutmeg: A pungent, versatile spice for use in both sweet and savory dishes.
TIP: Use a Microplane® to grate fresh, and add small amounts to milk-based sauces, cheesy gratins, and braised meat dishes.

Cumin seeds: Evoke an earthy, pleasantly musty taste that's integral to many cuisines.
TIP: Because the seeds are tough, pulverize using a coffee or spice grinder.

Cinnamon: A must-have for its sweetness and warmth.
TIP: Works well in savory applications, too. Use part of a stick to infuse stews or chilis with complexity, or grind a bit into Asian or Middle Eastern dishes.

Fennel seeds: Their slightly sweet, anise-like taste complements pork, fish, and Mediterranean dishes.
TIP: Lightly crush with a mortar and pestle so seeds retain some texture.

Coriander seeds: Bring slightly sour, almost citrus-like flavor to Mediterranean, Latin American, or Middle Eastern dishes.
TIP: Intensify flavor by toasting before grinding.

Flavors worth the splurge

Flake sea salt: These delicate grains add crunch and light, clean flavor. Sprinkle on garlic bread, grilled fish or meats, or green salads.

Truffle oil: A splash of this heady, aromatic oil can make a good dish exquisite. Stir into mashed potatoes or scrambled eggs, or drizzle over steamed fresh asparagus. White truffle oil packs more flavor than black.

Extra-virgin olive oil: Some markets allow you to sample before you buy. Shop around to find one that suits you. Flavors vary widely—some are fruity, some grassy, some bitter and pungent.

QUICK TIP: Frozen ground beef and ground sirloin should definitely be part of your freezer pantry. Thaw overnight in the fridge on a plate, and you have dinner the next day without ever going to the store.

◀ Barbecued Meatballs

Although it takes a little extra time to brown the meatballs before you add the sauce, the enhanced flavor is well worth the effort. Here, the sauce is simply commercial barbecue sauce. Pick your favorite—but avoid any sauce that is too sweet and sticky. Try Garlic-Roasted Kale (page 299) for a crunchy and flavorful side dish.

½ (1-ounce) slice whole-wheat bread, crumbled

⅓ cup fat-free milk

1 large egg

1½ pounds ground sirloin

1 teaspoon ground cumin

1 teaspoon dried rubbed sage

1 teaspoon mild smoked paprika

½ teaspoon celery seeds

½ teaspoon salt

¼ teaspoon garlic powder

1 tablespoon olive oil

¾ cup lower-sodium barbecue sauce

1. Place bread in a large bowl; pour milk over bread. Let stand 10 minutes. Add egg, stirring with a whisk until blended. Add beef and next 6 ingredients (through garlic powder) to bread mixture. Using hands, gently mix just until blended. With moist hands, shape mixture into 16 meatballs.

2. Heat oil in a large nonstick skillet over medium-high heat. Add meatballs to pan. Cook 8 to 9 minutes or until browned, turning often; stir in barbecue sauce. Bring to a boil; cover, reduce heat, and simmer 20 minutes or until meatballs are done. **YIELD:** 4 servings (serving size: 4 meatballs and 2 tablespoons sauce).

CALORIES 332; **FAT** 12.6g (sat 3.9g, mono 6.1g, poly 1.4g); **PROTEIN** 36.4g; **CARB** 19.8g; **FIBER** 1g; **CHOL** 143mg; **IRON** 4.7mg; **SODIUM** 457mg; **CALC** 172mg

Southwestern Meat Loaf and Baked Potatoes

Although a meat loaf is hardly a 20-minute dinner, there's not much to do after it's in the oven. Besides, we couldn't resist the notion of such comfort food right out of our quick-cooking pantry.

1 pound ground sirloin

1 cup frozen whole-kernel corn

½ cup picante sauce

⅓ cup old-fashioned rolled oats

¼ cup minced fresh cilantro

1 tablespoon chili powder

1½ teaspoons ground cumin

1 large egg white

Cooking spray

¼ cup ketchup

4 medium baking potatoes (about 1½ pounds)

½ cup fat-free sour cream

1. Preheat oven to 375°.

2. Combine first 8 ingredients in a large bowl; stir well. Shape meat mixture into a 9 x 4–inch loaf on a broiler pan coated with cooking spray. Brush ketchup over meat loaf. Arrange potatoes around meat loaf on broiler pan.

3. Bake at 375° for 50 minutes. Let meat loaf stand 10 minutes before slicing. Split potatoes in half lengthwise; top with sour cream. **YIELD:** 4 servings (serving size: 2 slices meat loaf, 1 potato, and 2 tablespoons sour cream).

CALORIES 374; **FAT** 6.8g (sat 2.4g, mono 2.4g, poly 0.9g); **PROTEIN** 30.1g; **CARB** 51.7g; **FIBER** 5.4g; **CHOL** 63mg; **IRON** 4.1mg; **SODIUM** 535mg; **CALC** 77mg

savvy IN A SNAP

To prepare the meat loaf in advance, shape the ground beef mixture into a loaf, wrap in heavy-duty plastic wrap, and freeze. Thaw overnight in refrigerator; bake as directed.

Parmesan-Crusted Pork Chops

These easy baked chops have a crunchy, cheesy coating that makes them irresistible. Buy a wedge of Parmigiano-Reggiano cheese, and grate it yourself with the small holes of a box grater or using a Microplane®.

Cooking spray

6 tablespoons whole-wheat panko (Japanese breadcrumbs)

¼ cup (1 ounce) finely grated Parmigiano-Reggiano cheese

1 teaspoon chopped fresh oregano

1 teaspoon chopped fresh rosemary

½ teaspoon salt

½ teaspoon freshly ground black pepper

4 (4-ounce) boneless center-cut loin pork chops

4 lemon wedges

1. Preheat oven to 425°.

2. Place a wire rack coated with cooking spray in a large jelly-roll pan lined with foil. Combine breadcrumbs and next 5 ingredients (through pepper) in a shallow bowl. Dredge pork in crumb mixture, pressing to adhere. Place pork on prepared rack.

3. Bake at 425° for 20 minutes or until done. Serve with lemon wedges. **YIELD:** 4 servings (serving size: 1 chop and 1 lemon wedge).

CALORIES 200; **FAT** 6.8g (sat 2.8g, mono 2.1g, poly 0.5g); **PROTEIN** 28g; **CARB** 6.5g; **FIBER** 1g; **CHOL** 79mg; **IRON** 1.5mg; **SODIUM** 382mg; **CALC** 80mg

Loin Pork Chops with Peppers and Vinegar

There's no need to thaw the frozen bell pepper strips in this quick skillet sauce—just make sure you cook them long enough so they release some of their pent-up moisture and it boils away without waterlogging the sauce.

4 (4-ounce) boneless center-cut loin pork chops, trimmed

½ teaspoon salt

½ teaspoon ground black pepper

1 tablespoon olive oil

2 teaspoons bottled minced garlic

½ teaspoon crushed red pepper

2 cups frozen bell pepper stir-fry

1½ tablespoons red wine vinegar

½ teaspoon dried oregano

1. Sprinkle pork with salt and black pepper. Heat oil in a large nonstick skillet over medium heat. Add pork to pan. Cook 3 minutes on each side or until pork is done. Place 1 chop on each of 4 serving plates.

2. Add garlic and crushed red pepper to pan; cook 20 seconds. Add stir-fry; sauté 3 minutes or until liquid evaporates. Stir in vinegar and oregano; cook 1 minute. Spoon sauce evenly over chops. **YIELD:** 4 servings (serving size: 1 chop and ¼ cup bell pepper sauce).

CALORIES 213; **FAT** 9g (sat 2.3g, mono 4.5g, poly 0.8g); **PROTEIN** 25g; **CARB** 5.4g; **FIBER** 1.7g; **CHOL** 75mg; **IRON** 1.7mg; **SODIUM** 346mg; **CALC** 13mg

MORE CHOICES: Frozen pork chops are a quick cook's dream! Substitute frozen corn kernels or lima beans for the bell pepper strips, if desired.

QUICK TIP: Keep bottled lemon juice in your pantry—or once opened, in your fridge. You'll always have a splash of flavor to perk up soups and dishes like this one. Figure about 1 teaspoon lemon juice per wedge.

Barley Pilaf with Artichoke Hearts

A serving of this meatless main dish offers nearly a third of an adult's suggested daily requirement of fiber. Serve with halved cherry tomatoes tossed with a bottled vinaigrette.

2 cups warm water

1 cup uncooked quick-cooking barley

¼ teaspoon salt

1 tablespoon olive oil

1 (14-ounce) can quartered artichoke hearts packed in water, rinsed and drained

1 teaspoon bottled minced garlic

2 tablespoons commercial pesto

1 tablespoon lemon juice

1 (15-ounce) can no-salt-added chickpeas (garbanzo beans), rinsed and drained

½ cup (2 ounces) shaved or grated Parmigiano-Reggiano cheese

1. Combine first 3 ingredients in a medium saucepan. Bring to a boil; cook 3 minutes. Cover, reduce heat, and simmer 8 minutes or until tender.

2. While barley cooks, heat oil in a large nonstick skillet over medium-high heat; add artichokes and garlic. Sauté 3 minutes.

3. Stir pesto, lemon juice, and chickpeas into cooked barley. Serve artichoke mixture over barley; top with cheese. **YIELD:** 4 servings (serving size: 1 cup barley mixture, ¼ cup artichoke mixture, and 2 tablespoons cheese).

CALORIES 334; **FAT** 11.5g (sat 3.6g, mono 3.3g, poly 0.5g); **PROTEIN** 13.5g; **CARB** 46.3g; **FIBER** 6.5g; **CHOL** 9mg; **IRON** 3mg; **SODIUM** 528mg; **CALC** 139mg

QUICK TIP: If you're grating fresh Parmigiano-Reggiano, grate more than you need for another meal. Store it in a zip-top plastic bag in the fridge for up to 2 weeks.

Mexican Black-Bean Chili

If you're looking for an easy chili recipe, check out this Mexican-inspired black bean chili that features ground sirloin, onion, bell pepper, and traditional spices. Best of all, it can be made right from your pantry.

1 cup frozen chopped onion, thawed

1 cup frozen bell pepper strips, thawed and chopped

1 pound ground sirloin

1½ cups fat-free, lower-sodium beef broth

1 tablespoon chili powder

1½ teaspoons ground cumin

¾ teaspoon dried oregano

½ teaspoon salt

⅛ teaspoon pepper

3 garlic cloves, crushed

2 (14.5-ounce) cans no-salt-added diced tomatoes, undrained

2 (15-ounce) cans no-salt-added black beans, drained

6 tablespoons light sour cream

1. Place a large nonstick skillet over medium-high heat until hot. Add first 3 ingredients; cook until browned, stirring to crumble meat. Drain well; return meat mixture to pan. Add broth and next 8 ingredients (through black beans); bring to a boil.

2. Reduce heat; simmer 15 minutes or until slightly thick, stirring occasionally. Ladle chili into soup bowls; top with sour cream. **YIELD:** 6 servings (serving size: 1½ cups chili and 1 tablespoon sour cream).

CALORIES 230; FAT 4.5g (sat 2.1g, mono 1.6g, poly 0.4g); PROTEIN 22.7g; CARB 26.3g; FIBER 7.6g; CHOL 45mg; IRON 3.4mg; SODIUM 435mg; CALC 102mg

savvy IN A SNAP

Quick cooks always use **lower-sodium canned (or boxed) broth.** It takes far less time to open a can than it does to dissolve a bouillon cube!

MORE CHOICES: Substitute store-bought coleslaw for the lettuce leaves.

Black Bean Burgers

2 tablespoons olive oil, divided

½ cup frozen chopped onion

1 cup fresh salsa, divided

½ cup old-fashioned rolled oats

⅓ cup pecan pieces

2 tablespoons whole-wheat flour

1 tablespoon bottled chili sauce

½ teaspoon ground cumin

½ teaspoon chipotle chile powder

½ teaspoon freshly ground black pepper

1 (15-ounce) can no-salt-added black beans, rinsed and drained

1 large egg white

6 green leaf lettuce leaves

6 (1.8-ounce) white-wheat hamburger buns

1. Heat 1 tablespoon oil in a large nonstick skillet over medium heat. Add onion; cook 3 minutes or until tender, stirring often.

2. Place onion in a food processor, reserving drippings in pan. Add ¼ cup salsa and next 9 ingredients (through egg white). Pulse 5 times or until a coarse paste forms, scraping sides. With moist hands, shape bean mixture into 6 (3-inch) patties.

3. Add 1½ teaspoons oil to drippings in pan. Cook 3 patties in hot oil over medium-high heat 2 minutes and 30 seconds on each side or until firm and brown. Remove patties from pan; keep warm.

4. Repeat procedure with remaining 1½ teaspoons oil and remaining patties.

5. Place 1 lettuce leaf on each bun bottom; top each with 1 patty, 2 tablespoons remaining salsa, and a bun top. **YIELD:** 6 servings (serving size: 1 burger).

CALORIES 256; **FAT** 8.5g (sat 1.2g, mono 3.7g, poly 2.7g); **PROTEIN** 10.5g; **CARB** 39g; **FIBER** 9.7g; **CHOL** 0mg; **IRON** 4.3mg; **SODIUM** 440mg; **CALC** 292mg

QUICK TIP: For a no-shopping supper, freeze hamburger buns for up to 6 months; thaw on the counter for 6 to 8 hours.

CONVENIENCE COOKING

Let the Supermarket Do the Work

A LOT OF US FEEL A TWINGE WHEN WE CONSIDER THE SUPERMARKET: It represents all the work we have to do to get dinner on the table.

Sometimes it's hard to remember what a revolution the modern supermarket was. No more going from this store to that to collect the bits and pieces of a meal. It changed the way we think about food.

And it's still our best ally. Think about it: We've been given a kitchen staff! Sometimes we think we have to negotiate and even "trick" the supermarket if we want to be quick cooks. Far from it! In fact, the supermarket is a place where so much is already done for us that we can assemble meals in no time.

For instance, the butcher is not only our best source of information for what's fresh, but he or she is also a real helper in the kitchen. The butcher can tie roasts, trim fat, pound chicken breasts, and grind meat. The butcher is like a personal sous chef!

In the produce section, we can find chopped butternut squash, matchstick carrots, and stemmed green beans, ready to steam or microwave. There are also frozen versions of many of these chopped or diced vegetables—and these are often more economical.

The salad bar, often set in the produce section or near the prepared foods, has chopped carrots, celery sticks, and other veggies ripe for the picking.

So here are 24 meals from that salad bar, from the deli case, and from other convenience products scattered around the market. If that's not the very definition of quick cooking, we don't know what is.

Antipasto Plate

An antipasto platter isn't just a great first course; beefed up a little, it can be a full meal, and especially fast since the supermarket can provide the protein and a host of bottled conveniences. Here, a creamy pepper dip and sweet-savory caponata spread are paired with crackers and thinly sliced prosciutto from the deli case. Serve with grapes to round out the plate.

Dip:

2 tablespoons golden raisins

2 tablespoons balsamic vinegar

3 tablespoons part-skim ricotta cheese

2 tablespoons chopped fresh parsley

2 tablespoons chopped fresh basil

2 tablespoons ⅓-less-fat cream cheese

¾ teaspoon honey

1 (5½-ounce) bottle roasted red bell peppers, rinsed and drained

Spread:

4 plum tomatoes, quartered and seeded

2 garlic cloves, peeled

1 medium eggplant (about 1 pound), cubed

½ medium onion, peeled and cut into 4 wedges

1 teaspoon olive oil

2 tablespoons chopped fresh basil

2 tablespoons balsamic vinegar

¼ teaspoon anchovy paste

Remaining Ingredients:

16 water crackers

2 ounces very thin slices prosciutto

1. To prepare dip, combine raisins and 2 tablespoons vinegar in a microwave-safe bowl. Microwave at HIGH 45 seconds. Let stand 10 minutes; drain. Place raisins, ricotta, and next 5 ingredients (through roasted red peppers) in a food processor; pulse until well combined.

2. Preheat oven to 450°.

3. To prepare spread, combine tomatoes, garlic, eggplant, and onion on a foil-lined jelly-roll pan; toss gently to combine. Drizzle with oil. Toss to coat. Arrange vegetables in a single layer on pan. Bake at 450° for 20 minutes or until vegetables are lightly blistered and eggplant is tender, stirring after 10 minutes. Cool slightly. Place vegetable mixture, 2 tablespoons basil, 2 tablespoons vinegar, and anchovy paste in a food processor; pulse until combined. Serve dip and spread with crackers and prosciutto slices. **YIELD:** 4 servings (serving size: 3 tablespoons dip, 3 tablespoons spread, 4 crackers, and ½ ounce prosciutto).

CALORIES 211; **FAT** 8.1g (sat 3.7g, mono 1.9g, poly 0.4g); **PROTEIN** 9.6g; **CARB** 27.7g; **FIBER** 3.5g; **CHOL** 25mg; **IRON** 1.2mg; **SODIUM** 656mg; **CALC** 75mg

savvy IN A SNAP

Part of being a quick cook is finding recipes that allow you to make bits and pieces of a larger meal during the day when you have a gap in your schedule. In this case, **both the dip and the spread can be made and refrigerated up to a day in advance;** serve them chilled or at room temperature.

Tabbouleh with Chicken and Red Bell Pepper

As any quick cook knows, a rotisserie chicken from the supermarket is a treasure indeed! Here's a recipe that'll let you use a little bit of it tonight and save some for tomorrow's lunch. If you're making this easy grain salad in advance, store the cucumber and tomato separately, and add them close to serving time to keep the salad at its best.

½ cup uncooked bulgur

½ cup boiling water

1½ cups diced plum tomato

¾ cup shredded skinless, boneless
   rotisserie chicken breast

¾ cup minced fresh flat-leaf parsley

½ cup finely chopped red bell pepper

½ cup diced English cucumber

¼ cup minced fresh mint

1½ tablespoons fresh lemon juice

1 tablespoon extra-virgin olive oil

½ teaspoon salt

¼ teaspoon freshly ground black pepper

1. Combine bulgur and ½ cup boiling water in a large bowl. Cover and let stand 15 minutes or until bulgur is tender. Drain well; return bulgur to bowl. Cool.

2. Add tomato and remaining ingredients; toss well. **YIELD:** 4 servings (serving size: 1¼ cups).

CALORIES 150; **FAT** 4.7g (sat 0.8g, mono 2.9g, poly 0.7g); **PROTEIN** 11.2g; **CARB** 16.9g; **FIBER** 4.5g; **CHOL** 22mg; **IRON** 1.6mg; **SODIUM** 326mg; **CALC** 33mg

ON THE SIDE: Round out the meal with some purchased hummus, sometimes available on the salad bar at your supermarket but usually in small tubs in the produce section or dairy aisle. Add some toasted whole-wheat pita chips on the side for a little crunch.

Superfast Chicken Posole

Posole is a hominy stew, popular in Mexico and the American Southwest. It usually cooks for hours on the stove, but here's a streamlined version—a nice warm-up on a chilly day.

1 tablespoon olive oil

1 teaspoon dried oregano

¾ teaspoon ground cumin

½ teaspoon chili powder

2 garlic cloves, minced

1 (8-ounce) package prechopped onion and celery mix

4 canned tomatillos, drained and coarsely chopped

2 (14-ounce) cans fat-free, lower-sodium chicken broth

1 (15-ounce) can white hominy, rinsed and drained

2 cups chopped skinless, boneless rotisserie chicken breast

1 tablespoon lime juice

¼ teaspoon salt

¼ teaspoon black pepper

½ ripe peeled avocado, diced

4 radishes, thinly sliced

Cilantro leaves (optional)

1. Heat olive oil in a large saucepan over medium-high heat. Add oregano and next 4 ingredients (through onion and celery mix); sauté 2 minutes. Stir in tomatillos; cook 1 minute. Add broth and hominy; cover and bring to a boil. Uncover and cook 8 minutes. Stir in chicken; cook 1 minute or until thoroughly heated. Remove from heat; stir in lime juice, salt, and pepper. Divide evenly among 4 bowls. Top evenly with avocado and radish. Garnish with cilantro, if desired. **YIELD:** 4 servings (serving size: 1½ cups soup, 2 tablespoons avocado, and 1 radish).

CALORIES 290; **FAT** 11.2g (sat 2.2g, mono 5.9g, poly 2g); **PROTEIN** 28.2g; **CARB** 20.2g; **FIBER** 4.5g; **CHOL** 60mg; **IRON** 2.4mg; **SODIUM** 452mg; **CALC** 62mg

savvy IN A SNAP

Tomatillos are a green fruit in the tomato family, related to Cape gooseberries, which have the same papery hulls. Look for canned tomatillos in the Mexican or Southwestern section of your supermarket.

Thai Chicken Roll-Ups

Rather than a rotisserie chicken, use the house-roasted chicken or turkey breasts available at the deli counter of your supermarket. For the best taste, skip the extruded, rolled meat, and get the real thing.

2 tablespoons lime juice

2 tablespoons light mayonnaise

1 tablespoon reduced-fat peanut butter

1 teaspoon bottled minced garlic

½ teaspoon ground ginger

⅛ teaspoon ground red pepper

4 (10-inch) flour tortillas

4 large napa (Chinese) cabbage leaves

6 ounces thinly sliced deli-roasted chicken or turkey breast

1 cup red bell pepper strips

½ cup chopped fresh basil

1. Combine first 6 ingredients in a bowl; stir well with a whisk.

2. Spread each tortilla with 1 tablespoon mayonnaise mixture. Top each tortilla with 1 cabbage leaf, one-fourth of chicken, ¼ cup bell pepper strips, and 2 tablespoons basil; roll up. Wrap in plastic wrap; chill. **YIELD:** 4 servings (serving size: 1 roll-up).

CALORIES 319; FAT 10.3g (sat 1.8g, mono 3.9g, poly 4g); PROTEIN 15.9g; CARB 39.8g; FIBER 2.4g; CHOL 2mg; IRON 2.8mg; SODIUM 763mg; CALC 98mg

QUICK TIP: If you want to take these roll-ups on a picnic and plan on staying outside for longer than 2 hours, place a blue chill pack in the cooler along with them to keep the filling at a safe temperature.

Summer Crab Rolls

Here's a New England classic, ready for your table! You can even make these crab rolls ahead and take them on a picnic. Look for 12-pack dinner rolls in the bakery section of your local supermarket.

¼ cup finely chopped Vidalia or other sweet onion

¼ cup reduced-fat mayonnaise

2 tablespoons chopped fresh chives

1 tablespoon Dijon mustard

1 teaspoon fresh lemon juice

½ teaspoon hot pepper sauce

1 pound lump crabmeat, drained and shell pieces removed

1½ tablespoons butter, softened

12 (1-ounce) dinner rolls, cut in half horizontally

12 Boston lettuce leaves (about 1 small head)

6 plum tomatoes, each cut into 4 slices

1. Combine first 7 ingredients in a large bowl; toss well.

2. Spread butter evenly onto cut sides of rolls. Heat a large nonstick skillet over medium heat. Place 6 roll halves, cut sides down, in pan; cook 1 minute or until toasted. Repeat procedure with remaining roll halves. Spoon ¼ cup crab mixture onto each roll bottom. Place 1 lettuce leaf and 2 tomato slices on crab mixture; top with remaining roll halves.

YIELD: 6 servings (serving size: 2 rolls).

CALORIES 320; **FAT** 8.3g (sat 2g, mono 1.2g, poly 3.2g); **PROTEIN** 22.2g; **CARB** 40.8g; **FIBER** 2.9g; **CHOL** 83mg; **IRON** 3.4mg; **SODIUM** 696mg; **CALC** 132mg

MORE CHOICES: Substitute cooked lobster meat or chopped cocktail shrimp for crab.

Turkey Reuben Sandwiches

Quick cooks know that sandwiches are not just for lunch. They're an easy meal any night of the week. Smoked turkey stands in for corned beef in this lightened variation on a deli favorite. Serve with chips and a pickle spear, if desired.

2 tablespoons Dijon mustard

8 (1¼-ounce) slices rye bread

4 (1-ounce) slices reduced-fat, reduced-sodium Swiss cheese

8 ounces deli-smoked turkey, thinly sliced

⅔ cup sauerkraut, rinsed and drained

¼ cup fat-free Thousand Island dressing

1 tablespoon canola oil, divided

1. Spread about ¾ teaspoon mustard over each bread slice. Place 1 cheese slice on each of 4 bread slices. Divide turkey evenly over cheese. Top each serving with 2½ tablespoons sauerkraut and 1 tablespoon dressing. Top each serving with 1 bread slice, mustard side down.
2. Heat 1½ teaspoons oil in a large nonstick skillet over medium-high heat. Add 2 sandwiches to pan. Cook 3 minutes on each side or until golden; remove sandwiches from pan, and keep warm. Repeat procedure with remaining oil and sandwiches. **YIELD:** 4 servings (serving size: 1 sandwich).

CALORIES 255; **FAT** 10.7g (sat 4.8g, mono 3.9g, poly 1.5g); **PROTEIN** 19.6g; **CARB** 18.9g; **FIBER** 3.4g; **CHOL** 44mg; **IRON** 0.7mg; **SODIUM** 865mg; **CALC** 311mg

QUICK TIP: Skip the overly salty sauerkraut in cans, and instead look for bags of sauerkraut in the deli case at your supermarket.

Moo Shu Shrimp Roll-Ups

We've taken the flavors of this Chinese take-out favorite and blended them with bagged slaw mix to make a simple, on-the-go roll-up that's great for lunches or snacks.

1 tablespoon dark sesame oil

1 (16-ounce) package cabbage-and-carrot coleslaw

½ pound peeled and deveined cooked shrimp, chopped

2 tablespoons lower-sodium soy sauce

1½ tablespoons hoisin sauce

¼ teaspoon freshly ground black pepper

8 (6-inch) flour tortillas

1. Heat oil in a large nonstick skillet over medium heat. Add coleslaw; cook 4 minutes or until wilted, stirring occasionally.

2. Stir in shrimp and next 3 ingredients (through pepper). Cook 1 minute or until bubbly. Spoon ½ cup coleslaw mixture down center of each tortilla; roll up. Serve immediately.

YIELD: 4 servings (serving size: 2 roll-ups).

CALORIES 336; **FAT** 9.3g (sat 1.6g, mono 3.8g, poly 2.5g); **PROTEIN** 21g; **CARB** 41g; **FIBER** 4.7g; **CHOL** 115mg; **IRON** 3.9mg; **SODIUM** 855mg; **CALC** 175mg

savvy IN A SNAP

Hoisin sauce is a sweet condiment used in traditional moo shu dishes and Peking duck. You can find bottles of it in the Asian aisle of most supermarkets.

QUICK TIP: If your pitas are a bit stale and don't roll up well, cut them into half circles, and stuff the pita pockets with the chicken mixture.

◀ Roasted Chicken Pitas with Cumin-Lemon Dressing

Admittedly, this quick dish is best made when the rotisserie chicken is still warm, just home from the store. Otherwise, consider heating the meat in the microwave for 30 seconds or so to make sure it's moist and flavorful.

3 cups shredded skinless, boneless rotisserie chicken

1 cup cubed seeded peeled cucumber (about 1 cucumber)

⅓ cup fresh lemon juice (about 2 lemons)

¾ teaspoon salt

2 tablespoons extra-virgin olive oil

2 teaspoons cumin seeds

4 teaspoons bottled minced garlic

6 (6-inch) pitas

1 cup mixed salad greens (optional)

1. Preheat oven to 375°.

2. Combine first 4 ingredients in a large bowl, tossing to coat. Heat oil in a small skillet over medium heat. Add cumin and garlic; cook 1 minute or until toasted, stirring frequently. Pour cumin mixture over chicken mixture; toss well to combine.

3. Wrap pitas in foil; bake at 375° for 10 minutes or until thoroughly heated. Spoon ⅔ cup chicken mixture onto each pita; top each pita evenly with mixed greens, if desired, and roll up. **YIELD:** 6 servings (serving size: 1 pita roll).

CALORIES 333; **FAT** 10.1g (sat 2g, mono 5.2g, poly 1.9g); **PROTEIN** 23.4g; **CARB** 36g; **FIBER** 1.6g; **CHOL** 53mg; **IRON** 3mg; **SODIUM** 671mg; **CALC** 74mg

Salad Bar Soft Tacos

If you have a good salad bar at your supermarket, and if your market also sells rotisserie chicken, you can have soft tacos for dinner in minutes when you get home tonight.

8 (6-inch) corn tortillas

2 cups shredded skinless, boneless rotisserie chicken breast

1¼ cups fresh salsa, divided

1 teaspoon ground cumin

2 cups shredded iceberg lettuce

½ cup diced tomato

½ cup rinsed and drained canned black beans

½ cup rinsed and drained canned yellow corn

½ cup shredded reduced-fat sharp cheddar cheese

½ cup reduced-fat sour cream

1. Warm tortillas according to package directions; keep warm.

2. Combine chicken, ¼ cup salsa, and cumin in a microwave-safe bowl. Microwave at HIGH 2 minutes or until warm.

3. Top each tortilla with ¼ cup lettuce, ¼ cup chicken mixture, and 1 tablespoon each tomato, beans, corn, and cheese. Fold tortillas over filling. Serve with remaining 1 cup salsa and sour cream. **YIELD:** 4 servings (serving size: 2 tacos, ¼ cup salsa, and 2 tablespoons sour cream).

CALORIES 392; **FAT** 11.1g (sat 5g, mono 1.3g, poly 1.2g); **PROTEIN** 32.1g; **CARB** 41g; **FIBER** 6g; **CHOL** 85mg; **IRON** 2.4mg; **SODIUM** 545mg; **CALC** 376mg

MORE CHOICES: Use any salsa you like, even salsa verde. Or try a spicy-sweet peach salsa.

◀ Ancho Chicken Tacos with Cilantro Slaw and Avocado Cream

Create authentic Mexican-style tacos by cooking the chicken in a mixture of ancho chili powder and cumin and serving over corn tortillas topped with slaw and avocado cream.

1 pound skinless, boneless chicken breasts, cut into ¼-inch strips

¾ teaspoon ancho chile powder

½ teaspoon garlic salt

¼ teaspoon ground cumin

Cooking spray

⅛ teaspoon grated lime rind

2 tablespoons fresh lime juice, divided

¼ cup light sour cream

2 tablespoons 1% low-fat milk

½ ripe peeled avocado, diced

2 cups packaged angel hair slaw

½ cup thinly sliced green onions

¼ cup chopped fresh cilantro

1 tablespoon canola oil

¼ teaspoon salt

8 (6-inch) corn tortillas

1. Heat a large skillet over high heat. Sprinkle chicken evenly with chile powder, garlic salt, and cumin. Coat pan with cooking spray. Add chicken to pan; cook 4 minutes, stirring frequently. Remove chicken from pan.

2. Combine rind, 1 tablespoon juice, and next 3 ingredients (through avocado) in a blender or food processor; process until smooth.

3. Combine remaining 1 tablespoon juice, slaw, onions, cilantro, oil, and salt, tossing to coat.

4. Heat tortillas according to directions. Divide chicken mixture evenly among tortillas. Top each tortilla with about 1 tablespoon avocado mixture and ¼ cup slaw mixture.

YIELD: 4 servings (serving size: 2 tacos).

CALORIES 319; **FAT** 11.6g (sat 2.3g, mono 5.5g, poly 2.4g); **PROTEIN** 30g; **CARB** 25.3g; **FIBER** 5.1g; **CHOL** 72mg; **IRON** 1.3mg; **SODIUM** 385mg; **CALC** 80mg

Herbed Chicken Salad Sandwiches

Not only is a cool sandwich heaven on a hot summer night, but it's also a welcome treat on a winter evening alongside a cup of soup.

1 tablespoon finely chopped fresh tarragon

3 tablespoons canola mayonnaise

3 tablespoons plain 2% reduced-fat Greek yogurt

1 tablespoon fresh lemon juice

⅛ teaspoon kosher salt

2 cups chopped skinless, boneless rotisserie chicken breast

¼ cup minced sweet onion

8 (1½-ounce) slices rye sandwich bread

4 red leaf lettuce leaves

1 cup bagged microgreens or arugula

1. Combine first 5 ingredients in a large bowl. Stir in chicken and onion. Top each of 4 bread slices with 1 lettuce leaf, about ½ cup packed chicken salad, ¼ cup microgreens, and 1 bread slice.

YIELD: 4 servings (serving size: 1 sandwich).

CALORIES 382; **FAT** 9g (sat 1.4g, mono 3.9g, poly 2.4g); **PROTEIN** 30.2g; **CARB** 42.9g; **FIBER** 5.1g; **CHOL** 60mg; **IRON** 3.2mg; **SODIUM** 745mg; **CALC** 89mg

Salad Bar Pizza

Look for pliable sun-dried tomatoes on the salad bar or in the produce section of your supermarket, rather than the bottled ones packed in oil. If your market's salad bar doesn't have artichoke hearts, buy a can of artichokes packed in water. If you want to cut down on the heat of this pie, use only 1 or 2 pepperoncini.

1 (12-inch) ready-to-bake whole-wheat pizza crust

¼ cup commercial pesto

¾ cup (3 ounces) shredded provolone cheese

16 sun-dried tomatoes packed without oil, chopped

1 cup chopped drained quartered artichoke hearts

4 pickled pepperoncini peppers, drained, stemmed, and chopped

2 tablespoons sliced pitted ripe olives

¼ cup finely grated Parmigiano-Reggiano cheese

1. Preheat oven to 450°.

2. Place crust on a large baking sheet. Spread pesto over crust to within ½ inch of edge. Sprinkle provolone cheese and remaining ingredients over pesto in the order given.

3. Bake at 450° for 12 minutes or until crust is crisp. Cool 5 minutes; cut into 6 wedges.

YIELD: 6 servings (serving size: 1 wedge).

CALORIES 289; **FAT** 13.6g (sat 6.1g, mono 1.6g, poly 0.2g); **PROTEIN** 12.1g; **CARB** 32g; **FIBER** 6g; **CHOL** 13mg; **IRON** 1.2mg; **SODIUM** 813mg; **CALC** 155mg

ON THE SIDE: Bring home sliced cucumbers from the salad bar at your supermarket, and dress them with rice vinegar and a little salt. Some sesame seeds sprinkled on top are a nice garnish.

Pear and Prosciutto Pizza

Prebaked pizza crusts come in all sorts of flavors. For a pizza with flavors as complex as these, make sure you get a plain crust—no herbs or cheese added. You don't want anything to get in the way of that great combo of peppery arugula and creamy, sweet, caramelized onion.

2 teaspoons olive oil

2 cups vertically sliced sweet onion

1 (12-ounce) prebaked pizza crust

½ cup (2 ounces) shredded provolone cheese

1 medium pear, thinly sliced

2 ounces prosciutto, cut into thin strips

Dash of freshly ground black pepper

2 tablespoons chopped walnuts, toasted

1½ cups baby arugula leaves

1 teaspoon sherry vinegar

1. Preheat oven to 450°.

2. Heat oil in a large nonstick skillet over medium-high heat. Add onion to pan; cover and cook 3 minutes. Uncover and cook 10 minutes or until golden brown, stirring frequently.

3. Place pizza crust on a baking sheet. Top evenly with onion mixture; sprinkle with cheese. Top evenly with pear and prosciutto. Sprinkle with pepper. Bake at 450° for 12 minutes or until cheese melts. Sprinkle with nuts. Place arugula in a medium bowl. Drizzle vinegar over greens; toss gently to coat. Top pizza evenly with arugula mixture. Cut pizza into 8 wedges. **YIELD:** 4 servings (serving size: 2 wedges).

CALORIES 446; **FAT** 18.8g (sat 4.9g, mono 5.1g, poly 7.3g); **PROTEIN** 16.6g; **CARB** 55.5g; **FIBER** 3.8g; **CHOL** 17mg; **IRON** 3.6mg; **SODIUM** 664mg; **CALC** 221mg

savvy IN A SNAP

Keep the kitchen sink full of **soapy water;** as you work, toss in used utensils for easy cleanup later.

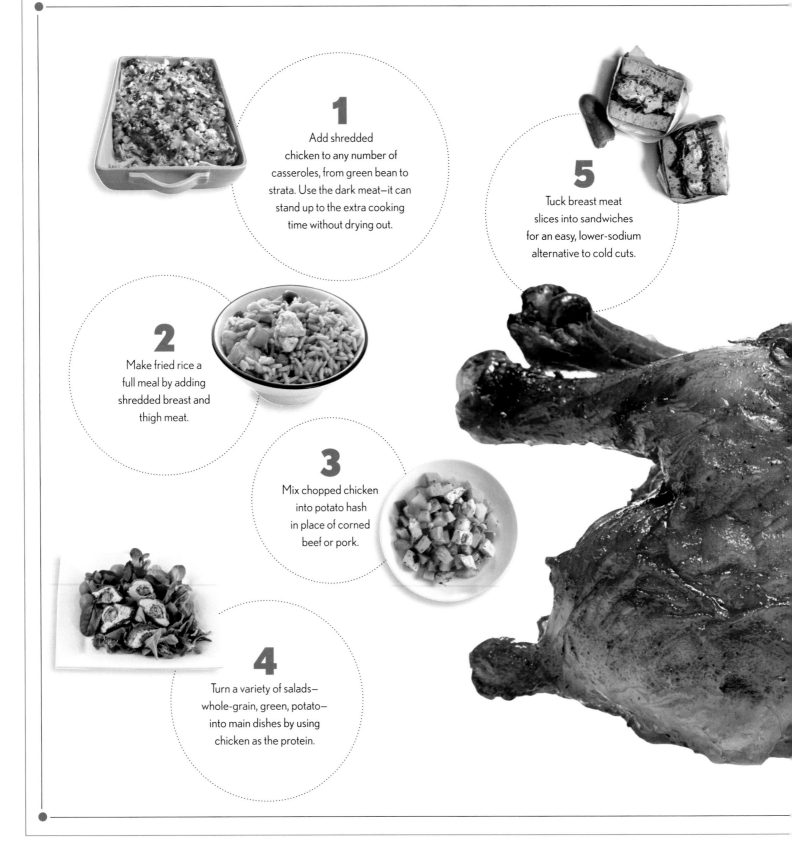

1

Add shredded chicken to any number of casseroles, from green bean to strata. Use the dark meat—it can stand up to the extra cooking time without drying out.

2

Make fried rice a full meal by adding shredded breast and thigh meat.

3

Mix chopped chicken into potato hash in place of corned beef or pork.

4

Turn a variety of salads— whole-grain, green, potato— into main dishes by using chicken as the protein.

5

Tuck breast meat slices into sandwiches for an easy, lower-sodium alternative to cold cuts.

6

Use whenever a recipe calls for cooked chicken, and save all that cooking time.

7

Toss chicken chunks with bottled salsa verde and preshredded Mexican blend cheese for a quick and easy filling for enchiladas, quesadillas, or tacos.

8

Combine shredded chicken with a mix of bottled barbecue sauce and light ranch dressing, and top a baked potato.

9

Stir chopped or shredded breast meat into chilis, stews, and soups.

10

Make a simple chicken salad by adding canola mayonnaise, prechopped celery and onion, chopped walnuts, and halved red grapes.

Chicken, Red Grape, and Pesto Pizza

Romano cheese, similar to Parmigiano-Reggiano, offers a tangy contrast to the grapes in this simple pie.

1 (11-ounce) can refrigerated thin-crust pizza crust dough

Cooking spray

⅓ cup commercial pesto

1½ cups seedless red grapes, halved

8 ounces shredded skinless, boneless rotisserie chicken breast

3 garlic cloves, thinly sliced

4 ounces fresh mozzarella cheese, thinly sliced

3 tablespoons grated Romano cheese

¼ teaspoon black pepper

¼ cup sliced green onions

1. Preheat oven to 425°.

2. On a lightly floured surface, pat dough into a 12-inch circle; gently place dough on a pizza pan coated with cooking spray. Spread pesto evenly over dough to within ½ inch of edge. Arrange grapes evenly over dough; top evenly with chicken. Top with garlic and mozzarella; sprinkle with Romano and pepper. Bake at 425° for 20 minutes or until crust is golden brown. Sprinkle with onions. Cut into 12 wedges. **YIELD:** 6 servings (serving size: 2 wedges).

CALORIES 364; **FAT** 14.4g (sat 4.8g, mono 6.3g, poly 1.4g); **PROTEIN** 22.6g; **CARB** 34.6g; **FIBER** 1.7g; **CHOL** 55mg; **IRON** 2.5mg; **SODIUM** 562mg; **CALC** 191mg

STORE-BOUGHT *shortcuts*

If you can't make homemade dough the night before, here are some ways to get a jump start on the pizza-making process.

Store-bought crusts, prebaked items from makers such as Boboli and Mama Mary's, will cut significant time from your prep work. Our toppings will still taste great on these crusts. A couple of tips: They may be higher in sodium than homemade crusts, so if sodium is a concern, decrease the amount of salt called for in the recipe. They will also likely require a different baking time and temperature, so heed the package guidelines.

Refrigerated canned dough from makers like Pillsbury is also an option, and fresh pizza dough is available at many supermarkets (ask for it in the bakery section). You can also sometimes buy pizza dough from pizzerias. Check out the smaller neighborhood pizzerias, rather than nationwide chains. Many will sell you dough balls for about $3 to $5 that will make 14- to 16-inch pizzas. Because that's bigger than our pizzas, you can freeze leftover uncooked dough to make smaller pizzas another time.

In reality, regardless of crust shortcuts, some nights frozen pizza might be all you have time for. No worries: There are actually some nutritionally sound options. Our picks help you avoid freezer burn. Both pass muster for decent nutrition—with regard to sodium, saturated fat, and calories (and no trans fats)—plus, they satisfied a tasting panel of food editors and Test Kitchens chefs.

- **MADE IN NATURE ORGANIC GOURMET THREE CHEESE PIZZA ($8)**
  The thick crust and melty cheeses made this one a winner.
  1 serving: 330 calories, 5 grams saturated fat, and 490 milligrams sodium

- **WHOLE FOODS 365 CHICKEN CAESAR PIZZA ($5)**
  We liked the crispy crust and Caesar flavor profile.
  1 serving: 340 calories, 6 grams saturated fat, and 580 milligrams sodium

Pizza Provençal

Remember: A prebaked crust isn't the only way to make a pie. A loaf of Italian bread is a great base for this fresh, quick meal. A food processor makes fast work of the homemade sauce.

¼ cup niçoise olives, pitted

3 tablespoons fresh basil leaves

3 tablespoons drained oil-packed sun-dried tomatoes

1 teaspoon grated lemon rind

2 tablespoons fresh lemon juice

1½ teaspoons minced fresh garlic

1 teaspoon water

1 (16-ounce) loaf Italian bread, split in half horizontally

2 cups thinly sliced roasted skinless, boneless chicken breast (about 6 ounces)

¾ cup (3 ounces) crumbled goat cheese

2 tablespoons chopped fresh basil

1. Preheat oven to 450°.

2. Combine first 7 ingredients in a food processor; process until smooth. Place bottom half of bread, cut side up, on a baking sheet (reserve top half for another use). Spread olive mixture over bread. Arrange chicken over bread; sprinkle with cheese. Bake at 450° for 10 minutes or until thoroughly heated. Sprinkle with chopped basil. Cut into 4 pieces. **YIELD:** 4 servings (serving size: 1 piece).

CALORIES 330; **FAT** 10.7g (sat 4.4g, mono 3.8g, poly 1.6g); **PROTEIN** 23.2g; **CARB** 34.4g; **FIBER** 2.3g; **CHOL** 46mg; **IRON** 3mg; **SODIUM** 595mg; **CALC** 98mg

savvy IN A SNAP

A lot of people are surprised when super-fast recipes call for **fresh herbs.** But when you're using convenience products and canned alternatives to get a meal on the table in minutes, you need to pump up the flavor with the bright taste of fresh herbs.

Barbecued Chicken Pizza

Here's a real crowd-pleaser, perfect for any weeknight with a vinegary salad alongside. If you have young kids, you might want to buy a mild barbecue sauce—although many teenagers and adults will go for far more fiery concoctions.

1 (10-ounce) whole-wheat thin Italian pizza crust

6 tablespoons bottled barbecue sauce

1 cup shredded skinless, boneless rotisserie chicken breast

¾ cup (3 ounces) shredded smoked Gouda cheese

½ cup diced red onion

½ teaspoon dried oregano

½ teaspoon crushed red pepper

¼ cup (1 ounce) freshly grated Parmigiano-Reggiano cheese

1. Preheat oven to 450°.

2. Place crust on a large baking sheet. Spread barbecue sauce over crust to within ½ inch of edge. Sprinkle with chicken, Gouda, onion, oregano, crushed red pepper, and Parmigiano-Reggiano cheese.

3. Bake at 450° for 16 minutes or until cheese melts and crust is golden. Cool 5 minutes. Cut pizza into 6 wedges. **YIELD:** 6 servings (serving size: 1 wedge).

CALORIES 263; FAT 8.3g (sat 4.6g, mono 2.5g, poly 0.4g); PROTEIN 18.5g; CARB 7.3g; FIBER 4.5g; CHOL 41mg; IRON 1.5mg; SODIUM 568mg; CALC 194mg

QUICK TIP: If you can't find smoked Gouda at your market, use regular Gouda, and sprinkle the pie with ½ teaspoon smoked paprika along with the oregano and crushed red pepper.

Quick Chicken and Dumplings ▶

In this recipe, flour tortillas stand in for the traditional biscuit dough, while rotisserie chicken breast completes the dish in a jiffy.

1 tablespoon butter

½ cup prechopped frozen onion

2 cups chopped skinless, boneless rotisserie chicken breast

1 (10-ounce) package frozen mixed vegetables, thawed

1½ cups water

1 tablespoon all-purpose flour

1 (14-ounce) can fat-free, lower-sodium chicken broth

¼ teaspoon salt

¼ teaspoon black pepper

1 bay leaf

8 (6-inch) flour tortillas, cut into ½-inch-wide strips

1 tablespoon chopped fresh parsley

1. Melt butter in a large saucepan over medium-high heat. Add onion; sauté 5 minutes or until tender. Stir in chicken and vegetables; cook 3 minutes or until thoroughly heated, stirring constantly.

2. While chicken mixture cooks, combine 1½ cups water, flour, and broth. Gradually stir broth mixture into chicken mixture. Stir in salt, pepper, and bay leaf; bring to a boil. Reduce heat, and simmer 3 minutes. Stir in tortilla strips, and cook 2 minutes or until tortilla strips soften. Remove from heat; stir in parsley. Discard bay leaf. Serve immediately. **YIELD:** 4 servings (serving size: about 1½ cups).

CALORIES 366; **FAT** 9.3g (sat 3.1g, mono 3.9g, poly 1.4g); **PROTEIN** 29.8g; **CARB** 40.3g; **FIBER** 5.3g; **CHOL** 67mg; **IRON** 3.4mg; **SODIUM** 652mg; **CALC** 104mg

Thai Shrimp Pizza

Bottled Thai peanut sauces run the gamut from tooth-achingly sweet to piercingly hot. Look for one that's more balanced in its approach: a little hot, a little sweet, even a little sour—a better foil for the green onions and peanuts in this "nouveau" pizza favorite.

1 (10-ounce) whole-wheat thin Italian pizza crust

6 tablespoons bottled Thai peanut sauce

1½ cups (6 ounces) shredded part-skim mozzarella cheese

2 cups frozen broccoli florets, thawed

6 ounces chopped cooked shrimp

¾ cup thinly sliced green onions (6 medium)

2 tablespoons chopped unsalted, dry-roasted peanuts

1. Preheat oven to 450°.

2. Place crust on a large baking sheet. Spread peanut sauce over crust to within ½ inch of edge. Sprinkle with cheese, broccoli, shrimp, green onions, and peanuts.

3. Bake at 450° for 16 minutes. Cool 5 minutes. Cut into 6 wedges. **YIELD:** 6 servings (serving size: 1 wedge).

CALORIES 315; **FAT** 12g (sat 3.4g, mono 4.8g, poly 2.7g); **PROTEIN** 21g; **CARB** 7g; **FIBER** 5.6g; **CHOL** 57mg; **IRON** 2mg; **SODIUM** 695mg; **CALC** 88mg

> **MORE CHOICES:** You can also grill a pizza. Set up the grill for indirect cooking, and preheat the grill to high heat. Set the pizza on the unheated section of the rack, cover, and grill for about the same amount of time you would bake the pizza in the oven.

MORE CHOICES: Customize the veggies to suit your taste: frozen lima beans, frozen pearl onions, frozen bell pepper strips, or a combination of all three!

6 MEALS WITH *frozen mixed vegetables*

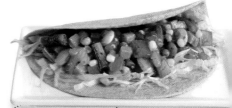

1
Fast Vegetable Soup

To make 4 servings, combine 1 quart fat-free, lower-sodium chicken broth, 1 (16-ounce) bag frozen mixed vegetables, 1 (15-ounce) can drained and rinsed white beans, 1 teaspoon dried thyme, and 1 teaspoon dried sage in a large saucepan. Bring to a low simmer over medium heat. Simmer, covered, 5 minutes, stirring once or twice.

CALORIES 160; **FAT** 0.8g (sat 0.3g); **SODIUM** 622mg

3
Vegetable Tacos

For 4 servings, combine 1 (16-ounce) bag frozen mixed vegetables and 1 cup bottled salsa in a medium saucepan. Heat over medium heat, stirring occasionally. Serve in fat-free whole-wheat tortillas with shredded lettuce and chopped tomatoes.

CALORIES 239; **FAT** 2.3g (sat 0g); **SODIUM** 755mg

2
Vegetable Stir-Fry

For 4 servings, toss 1 (16-ounce) bag frozen mixed vegetables, preferably an Asian blend, into a hot wok with 3 tablespoons of your favorite bottled Asian stir-fry sauce. Toss and stir over medium-high heat 1 minute. Sprinkle with 1 teaspoon dark sesame oil and 2 teaspoons rice vinegar just before serving.

CALORIES 105; **FAT** 1.2g (sat 0.2g); **SODIUM** 184mg

4
Stuffed Baked Potatoes

For 4 servings, bake or microwave 4 russet potatoes until tender. Cut in half lengthwise; scoop the creamy white flesh into a large bowl. Use a fork to mash the potato with ⅓ cup 1% low-fat milk, ¼ cup reduced-fat shredded cheddar cheese, and half of 1 (16-ounce) bag frozen mixed vegetables. Season with salt and pepper, and then pile the filling back into the potato skins. Bake at 400° for 5 minutes or until thoroughly heated.

CALORIES 251; **FAT** 1.9g (sat 1.2g); **SODIUM** 242mg

5
Vegetable Singapore Mai Fun

To make 4 servings, spray a large skillet with cooking spray, and set over medium heat. Add 1 tablespoon bottled minced ginger and 1 teaspoon bottled minced garlic; cook 1 minute. Add 1 (16-ounce) bag frozen mixed vegetables; cook 3 minutes or until tender. Add ½ cup light coconut milk and 2 teaspoons curry powder. Toss in a large bowl with cooked and drained angel hair pasta.

CALORIES 301; **FAT** 2.1g (sat 0.6g); **SODIUM** 54mg

6
Pasta Primavera

For a family-sized meal, 6 servings, combine 1 (28-ounce) jar marinara sauce and 1 (16-ounce) bag frozen mixed vegetables in a large saucepan; simmer over medium heat. Meanwhile, cook 1 pound whole-wheat spaghetti in a second saucepan according to package directions, omitting salt and fat; drain in a colander in the sink. Mix the pasta into the sauce, and stir in 2 tablespoons freshly grated Parmigiano-Reggiano cheese.

CALORIES 396; **FAT** 2.9g (sat 0.5g); **SODIUM** 487mg

Chicken Chilaquiles

Chilaquiles are a traditional breakfast or brunch dish in Mexico, often a way to use the previous day's leftover tortillas. The tortillas are simmered in a sauce before eggs or shredded chicken are added. Here, we've revamped the dish for dinner, making it a quick supper casserole. If you want more heat in the dish, add ¼ teaspoon ground red pepper to the tomatillo mixture.

2 cups shredded skinless, boneless rotisserie chicken breast

½ cup chopped green onions

½ cup (2 ounces) shredded Monterey Jack cheese with jalapeño peppers, divided

2 tablespoons freshly grated Parmigiano-Reggiano cheese

1 teaspoon chili powder

¼ teaspoon salt

¼ teaspoon black pepper

¾ cup 1% low-fat milk

¼ cup chopped fresh cilantro

1 (11-ounce) can tomatillos, drained

1 (4.5-ounce) can chopped green chiles, drained

12 (6-inch) corn tortillas

Cooking spray

1. Preheat oven to 375°.

2. Combine chicken, green onions, ¼ cup Monterey Jack cheese, Parmigiano-Reggiano cheese, chili powder, salt, and pepper in a medium bowl. Place milk and next 3 ingredients (through green chiles) in a food processor or blender; process until smooth.

3. Warm tortillas according to package directions. Pour ⅓ cup tomatillo mixture into an 11 x 7–inch glass or ceramic baking dish coated with cooking spray. Arrange 4 tortillas in dish, and top with half of chicken mixture. Repeat layers with remaining tortillas and chicken mixture, ending with tortillas.

4. Pour remaining 1½ cups tomatillo mixture over tortillas; sprinkle with remaining ¼ cup Monterey Jack cheese. Bake at 375° for 20 minutes or until bubbly. **YIELD:** 4 servings (serving size: 1½ cups).

CALORIES 347; **FAT** 10.9g (sat 4.5g, mono 2.9g, poly 1.9g); **PROTEIN** 30.9g; **CARB** 33.3g; **FIBER** 5.9g; **CHOL** 79mg; **IRON** 1.5mg; **SODIUM** 560mg; **CALC** 272mg

QUICK TIP: Substitute frozen chopped onions for the chopped green onions, if desired.

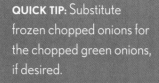

North African Chicken and Couscous

Couscous is a traditional whole-grain dish from North Africa often served with lamb and vegetables, a sort of one-pot comfort food. We've taken those traditional flavors and revamped the recipe for our speedier kitchens, turning this all-day affair into a weeknight dinner.

2 cups water

1½ cups uncooked couscous

½ cup golden raisins

½ cup thawed orange juice concentrate, undiluted

⅓ cup lemon juice

2 tablespoons water

2 tablespoons olive oil

2 teaspoons ground cumin

½ teaspoon salt

¼ teaspoon black pepper

3 cups chopped cooked chicken breast (about 3 breasts)

2 cups chopped peeled cucumber

1 cup chopped red bell pepper

¼ cup thinly sliced green onions

½ cup chopped fresh cilantro

Sliced green onions (optional)

1. Bring 2 cups water to a boil in a medium saucepan, and gradually stir in couscous and raisins. Remove from heat. Cover; let stand 5 minutes. Fluff with a fork.

2. Combine orange juice and next 6 ingredients (through black pepper); stir well with a whisk.

3. Combine couscous mixture, juice mixture, chicken, and remaining ingredients except additional green onions in a large bowl, and toss well. Garnish with additional green onions, if desired. **YIELD:** 6 servings (serving size: 2 cups).

CALORIES 332; FAT 6.6g (sat 1.2g, mono 3.9g, poly 0.9g); PROTEIN 19.6g; CARB 51.2g; FIBER 3.3g; CHOL 35mg; IRON 2.8mg; SODIUM 498mg; CALC 51mg

ON THE SIDE: Slice cherry tomatoes in half, hollow them out with a melon baller, and fill them with purchased hummus.

ON THE SIDE: If you're hankering for a vinegary salad to cut through bolder flavors, make one that will last for weeks. Place sliced cucumbers and onions in a large bowl; add 1 cup white vinegar, 2 teaspoons sugar, and 1 teaspoon salt. Fill the bowl with water to cover the vegetables. Cover and store in the refrigerator for up to 2 weeks, spooning out the veggies when you want them. For more flavor, add some fresh dill fronds or crushed red pepper.

Rotisserie Chicken Shepherd's Pie

Use premade mashed potatoes for the topping of this easy casserole. Look for them in a refrigerator case, usually near the produce section or the deli counter. Buy a brand that's not stocked with lots of additives and additional flavors. Simple is best for this family favorite.

1¼ cups fat-free, lower-sodium chicken broth

1½ tablespoons all-purpose flour

2 cups chopped skinless, boneless rotisserie chicken breast (about 6 ounces)

1 teaspoon dried thyme

1 (16-ounce) package frozen mixed vegetables

Cooking spray

1 (24-ounce) package country-style refrigerated mashed potatoes

1 large egg, lightly beaten

¼ teaspoon freshly ground black pepper

1. Preheat oven to 375°.

2. Combine broth and flour in a medium saucepan, stirring with a whisk. Stir in chicken, thyme, and vegetables; cook over medium-high heat 5 minutes or until mixture thickens. Pour chicken mixture into an 8-inch square glass or ceramic baking dish coated with cooking spray.

3. Combine potatoes and egg in a large bowl; spread over chicken mixture. Sprinkle with pepper.

4. Bake, uncovered, at 375° for 20 minutes or until puffed and lightly browned. **YIELD:** 6 servings (serving size: 1 cup).

CALORIES 251; **FAT** 6g (sat 3.1g, mono 1g, poly 0.5g); **PROTEIN** 21g; **CARB** 27g; **FIBER** 3.7g; **CHOL** 88mg; **IRON** 1.8mg; **SODIUM** 335mg; **CALC** 53mg

◄ Quick Barbecued Beef Potpie

1 (17-ounce) package prepared beef roast au jus

¾ cup lower-sodium barbecue sauce

2 tablespoons chopped fresh cilantro

1½ tablespoons all-purpose flour

1 teaspoon ground cumin

1 (15¼-ounce) can 50%-less-sodium whole-kernel corn, drained

1 (15-ounce) can no-salt-added black beans, rinsed and drained

1 (4.5-ounce) can chopped green chiles, undrained

Cooking spray

½ cup (2 ounces) reduced-fat shredded extrasharp cheddar cheese

1 sheet frozen puff pastry dough, thawed

1. Preheat oven to 450°.

2. Heat beef roast according to package directions. Drain and reserve ¼ cup au jus from beef roast, reserving remaining beef juices for another use. Pull beef into large pieces. Combine beef, reserved ¼ cup jus, barbecue sauce, and next 6 ingredients (through green chiles) in a large bowl. Pour beef mixture into an 8-inch square glass or ceramic baking dish coated with cooking spray. Sprinkle beef mixture with cheese.

3. Place pastry on top of casserole, folding under edges. Bake at 450° for 27 minutes or until crust is golden. **YIELD:** 6 servings (serving size: ⅙ of casserole).

CALORIES 276; **FAT** 8g (sat 3.1g, mono 0g, poly 0.1g); **PROTEIN** 21g; **CARB** 31g; **FIBER** 3.4g; **CHOL** 45mg; **IRON** 2.4mg; **SODIUM** 489mg; **CALC** 54mg

savvy IN A SNAP

Nothing slows you down like **washing cutting boards.** Buy two or three, so you can stash a dirty one in the dishwasher and use another without stopping to clean.

Chicken and Black Bean-Stuffed Burritos ▶

These skillet-grilled burritos come together in a flash thanks to store-bought rotisserie chicken. Keep this meal light by serving with a fresh green salad.

¼ cup water

2 tablespoons fresh lime juice

½ teaspoon chili powder

¼ teaspoon ground cumin

¼ teaspoon black pepper

⅛ teaspoon ground red pepper

2 cups shredded rotisserie chicken breast

¼ cup thinly sliced green onions

¾ cup canned black beans, rinsed and drained

½ cup refrigerated fresh salsa

4 (8-inch) flour tortillas

½ cup shredded Monterey Jack cheese

Cooking spray

1. Bring first 6 ingredients to a boil in a small saucepan. Stir in shredded chicken and green onions.

2. Combine beans and salsa. Spoon ¼ cup bean mixture and ½ cup chicken mixture down center of each tortilla; sprinkle with 2 tablespoons cheese. Roll up.

3. Heat a large skillet over medium-high heat. Coat pan with cooking spray. Add 2 burritos. Place a cast-iron or other heavy skillet on top of burritos, and cook for 3 minutes on each side. Remove from pan, and repeat procedure with the remaining 2 burritos. **YIELD:** 4 servings (serving size: 1 burrito).

CALORIES 353; **FAT** 9.8g (sat 4.1g, mono 3.6g, poly 1.3g); **PROTEIN** 30.9g; **CARB** 33.1g; **FIBER** 2.4g; **CHOL** 72mg; **IRON** 1.6mg; **SODIUM** 595mg; **CALC** 137mg

Speedy Chicken and Cheese Enchiladas

Enchiladas are usually a time-consuming meal to prepare, mostly because of the sauce. But there are so many bottled sauces now on the market that you can try out several over a couple of weeks with this casserole to determine your favorite. Always select the lower-sodium or even no-salt options because many products are loaded with too much salt and other sodium preservatives.

Cooking spray

1 cup prechopped onion

1 cup prechopped bell pepper

1 (10-ounce) can enchilada sauce

2 cups chopped skinless, boneless rotisserie chicken breast (about 8 ounces)

1 cup (4 ounces) preshredded reduced-fat Mexican blend cheese, divided

½ teaspoon ground cumin

8 (6-inch) corn tortillas

¼ cup fat-free sour cream

¼ cup chopped fresh cilantro

1. Preheat broiler.

2. Heat a large nonstick skillet over medium-high heat. Coat pan with cooking spray. Add onion and bell pepper; sauté 2 minutes or until crisp-tender. Add enchilada sauce; bring to a boil. Cover, reduce heat, and simmer 5 minutes.

3. Combine chicken, ¾ cup cheese, and cumin, tossing well.

4. Wrap tortillas in paper towels; microwave at HIGH 30 seconds or until warm. Spoon ¼ cup chicken mixture down center of each tortilla; roll up. Place tortillas, seam sides down, in an 11 x 7–inch glass or ceramic baking dish coated with cooking spray. Pour sauce mixture over enchiladas; broil 3 minutes or until thoroughly heated. Sprinkle remaining ¼ cup cheese evenly over enchiladas, and broil 1 minute or until cheese melts. Serve with sour cream and cilantro. **YIELD:** 4 servings (serving size: 2 enchiladas, 1 table-spoon sour cream, and 1 tablespoon cilantro).

CALORIES 364; **FAT** 10.9g (sat 4.9g, mono 2.9g, poly 1.4g); **PROTEIN** 29.7g; **CARB** 37.2g; **FIBER** 4.1g; **CHOL** 70mg; **IRON** 1.7mg; **SODIUM** 701mg; **CALC** 339mg

ON THE SIDE: Start with some purchased guacamole, a real time-saver found in your supermarket's produce section. Check the ingredient list to make sure it contains only what you'd put in it if you were making it from scratch.

WEEKNIGHT DINNERS

Fast & Healthy—Monday to Friday

HERE IS A SET OF 36 WEEKNIGHT RECIPES. Most clock in at under 15 minutes of prep time. Only a few require the oven.

Some are made under the broiler, but most are stove-top dinners, quick sautés, hearty sandwiches, and fast main-course salads.

Sure, some of these meals use rotisserie chicken, frozen mixed vegetables, and the like; but a surprising number are made with fresh ingredients, even fresh vegetables and leafy herbs. Some, like the scaloppine recipes or the broiled fish entrées, could even do double duty as dinner-party fare. Elegance does not require complexity. You can make a sophisticated dinner on a busy weeknight, too!

In some ways, this chapter is the heart of this book: good nutrition, big flavors, just a few minutes to bring it together. Set the table, and you're ready to eat. It's as good as a big pot of stew on the weekend. And much faster.

MORE CHOICES: For a nonalcoholic alternative to the mirin, use 2 tablespoons unsweetened apple juice and 1 teaspoon sugar.

◀ Seared Salmon with Jalapeño Ponzu

Ponzu is a traditional citrus-based Japanese sauce. This version would also make a great mop for chicken, fish, or shellfish on the grill.

3 tablespoons lower-sodium soy sauce

2 tablespoons fresh orange juice

2 tablespoons mirin (sweet rice wine)

1 tablespoon fresh lemon juice

1 tablespoon dark sesame oil

4 (6-ounce) salmon fillets

1 large jalapeño pepper, cut crosswise into thin slices

1. Combine first 4 ingredients in a small bowl; mix well.

2. Heat oil in a large nonstick skillet over medium-high heat. Add fillets, skin sides down; cook 4 minutes on each side or until desired degree of doneness. Arrange 1 fillet on each of 4 plates. Top fillets evenly with jalapeño slices. Spoon about 2 tablespoons soy sauce mixture over each fillet; let stand 10 minutes before serving. **YIELD:** 4 servings (serving size: 1 fillet and 2 tablespoons sauce).

CALORIES 333; **FAT** 16.6g (sat 3.6g, mono 7.2g, poly 4.7g); **PROTEIN** 37.2g; **CARB** 5g; **FIBER** 0.3g; **CHOL** 87mg; **IRON** 0.9mg; **SODIUM** 477mg; **CALC** 24mg

Honey-Glazed Salmon ▼

Brush heart-healthy salmon with a mixture of honey and Dijon mustard for a quick and easy dinner.

2 tablespoons minced shallots

1 tablespoon chopped fresh or 1 teaspoon dried thyme

3 tablespoons honey

1 tablespoon Dijon mustard

½ teaspoon salt

¼ teaspoon ground red pepper

4 (6-ounce) salmon fillets (about 1 inch thick)

Cooking spray

Thyme sprigs (optional)

Lemon wedges (optional)

1. Preheat grill or broiler.

2. Combine first 6 ingredients in a small bowl. Brush honey mixture over skinless side of fish. Place fish, coated sides up, on grill rack or broiler pan coated with cooking spray; cook 6 minutes or until desired degree of doneness. Garnish with thyme and lemon, if desired. **YIELD:** 4 servings (serving size: 1 fillet).

CALORIES 334; **FAT** 14.4g (sat 2.5g, mono 6.8g, poly 3.1g); **PROTEIN** 35.1g; **CARB** 14.4g; **FIBER** 0.1g; **CHOL** 111mg; **IRON** 0.9mg; **SODIUM** 490mg; **CALC** 15mg

MORE CHOICES: You can add complexity to the flavor of a dish that uses honey by selecting from any number of specialty honeys, wildflower to chestnut, star thistle to eucalyptus.

Mojo Bass

Mojo sauce is a staple in the Canary Islands, often served on fish. For even cooking, choose fillets with a uniform thickness.

1 tablespoon fresh orange juice

1 tablespoon fresh lime juice

1 teaspoon ground coriander

1 teaspoon bottled minced garlic

1 teaspoon olive oil

½ teaspoon ground cumin

**4 (6-ounce) striped bass fillets
(about 1 inch thick)**

Cooking spray

1. Preheat broiler.

2. Combine first 6 ingredients, stirring with a whisk.

3. Arrange fish, skin sides down, on a foil-lined baking sheet coated with cooking spray. Brush half of orange juice mixture over fish; broil 4 minutes. Brush with remaining orange juice mixture; broil 4 minutes or until desired degree of doneness. **YIELD:** 4 servings (serving size: 1 fillet).

CALORIES 183; **FAT** 5.3g (sat 1g, mono 2g, poly 1.5g); **PROTEIN** 30.4g; **CARB** 1.5g; **FIBER** 0.5g; **CHOL** 136mg; **IRON** 1.6mg; **SODIUM** 409mg; **CALC** 35mg

ON THE SIDE : Serve this quick main course alongside a simple salad of diced tomatoes and diced peeled cucumbers, dressed with our Essential Lemon Dressing (page 43) or a purchased low-fat, lower-sodium vinaigrette.

Seared Halibut with Garlic Sauce

This is sort of an East-meets-West dish, a more traditional French technique with flavors inspired by the Chinese take-out favorite and all gussied up with fresh, modern ingredients. When you're at the fish counter, always remember the rule: If it doesn't smell fresh, it probably isn't.

1 (1-pound) halibut fillet (about 2 inches thick)

2 teaspoons olive oil

¼ cup water

¼ cup dry vermouth

¼ teaspoon salt

¼ teaspoon freshly ground black pepper

4 garlic cloves, minced

2 tablespoons chopped fresh parsley

Lemon wedges (optional)

1. Cut fish crosswise into 4 equal pieces. Heat oil in a large nonstick skillet over medium-high heat. Add fish, and cook 1 minute. Turn fish over; gradually add ¼ cup water and next 4 ingredients (through garlic) to pan. Cover, reduce heat to medium, and cook 3 minutes or until desired degree of doneness.

2. Remove fish from pan, set aside, and keep warm. Cook vermouth mixture over medium-high heat 1 minute or until slightly thickened. Pour over fish; sprinkle with parsley. Garnish with lemon wedges, if desired. **YIELD:** 4 servings (serving size: 3 ounces).

CALORIES 166; **FAT** 4.9g (sat 0.7g, mono 2.5g, poly 1.1g); **PROTEIN** 23.9g; **CARB** 1.2g; **FIBER** 0.2g; **CHOL** 36mg; **IRON** 1.1mg; **SODIUM** 212mg; **CALC** 62mg

QUICK TIP: Consider giving the kids a small chore or a quick task before you start cooking. You'll be able to concentrate on the preparation of your quick meal—and enjoy the fruits of your creativity even more.

Greek Tuna Steaks

The combination of Mediterranean flavors works well not only with the tuna steaks in this recipe, but also with striped bass or red snapper fillets. Serve with couscous mixed with feta cheese, sliced ripe olives, and chopped tomato.

1½ teaspoons chopped fresh oregano

1 teaspoon olive oil

¾ teaspoon chopped fresh thyme

½ teaspoon salt

¼ teaspoon black pepper

4 (6-ounce) tuna steaks (about ¾ inch thick)

Cooking spray

4 lemon wedges

1. Combine first 5 ingredients in a small bowl, and rub evenly over fish. Cover and marinate in refrigerator 15 minutes.

2. Heat a large grill pan over medium-high heat. Coat pan with cooking spray. Add fish, and cook 5 minutes on each side or until desired degree of doneness. Serve with lemon wedges. **YIELD:** 4 servings (serving size: 1 tuna steak and 1 lemon wedge).

CALORIES 250; FAT 9.7g (sat 2.3g, mono 3.6g, poly 2.7g); PROTEIN 38.2g; CARB 0.2g; FIBER 0.1g; CHOL 63mg; IRON 1.8mg; SODIUM 357mg; CALC 4mg

Seared Tuna Sandwich with Balsamic Onions

Stock up on frozen tuna steaks when they go on sale at your supermarket. Thaw them during the day on a plate in the fridge.

2 teaspoons butter

2 cups vertically sliced onion

1½ tablespoons balsamic vinegar

¼ teaspoon dried thyme

1 tablespoon all-purpose flour

½ teaspoon salt

¼ teaspoon garlic powder

¼ teaspoon black pepper

4 (6-ounce) tuna steaks (about ½ inch thick)

Cooking spray

4 teaspoons Dijon mustard

4 (2-ounce) whole-wheat hamburger buns

4 curly leaf lettuce leaves

4 (¼-inch-thick) slices tomato

1. Melt butter in a medium skillet over medium-high heat. Add onion; sauté 5 minutes. Stir in vinegar and thyme; cover and cook 5 minutes, stirring occasionally.

2. While onion cooks, combine flour, salt, garlic powder, and pepper in a shallow dish. Dredge fish in flour mixture. Heat a large nonstick skillet over medium-high heat. Coat pan with cooking spray Add fish; cook 3 minutes on each side or until desired degree of doneness.

3. Spread 1 teaspoon mustard inside top half of each bun. Layer 1 lettuce leaf, 1 fish steak, 1 tomato slice, and ¼ cup onion mixture on bottom half of each bun. Top with top halves of buns. **YIELD:** 4 servings (serving size: 1 sandwich).

CALORIES 402; **FAT** 7.8g (sat 2.5g, mono 2.8g, poly 1.4g); **PROTEIN** 46.2g; **CARB** 35.5g; **FIBER** 3.8g; **CHOL** 2mg; **IRON** 4mg; **SODIUM** 701mg; **CALC** 158mg

EVEN *faster*

Use frozen chopped onions. The dish won't be as toothsome, but the preparation will go more quickly. Do not thaw the onions; cook them just until soft, about 2 minutes, before adding the vinegar and thyme.

ON THE SIDE: Serve these tasty fillets with cooked jasmine rice and steamed green beans. Look for packages of green beans that you can pop in the microwave to steam right in the bag.

Snapper with Basil-Mint Sauce

You'll make more sauce than you need with this easy supper—but not to worry: It's great drizzled over baked potatoes, tossed in grain salads, or mixed into reduced-fat mayo for a tasty spread on sandwiches. Store the extra, covered, in the refrigerator for up to 2 days. The herbs may brown a bit in the mix, but they'll still be fresh and tasty.

4 (6-ounce) red snapper fillets

Cooking spray

¼ teaspoon salt

⅛ teaspoon freshly ground black pepper

1 cup basil leaves

¼ cup mint leaves

2 tablespoons chopped seeded jalapeño pepper

2 tablespoons olive oil

2 tablespoons water

2 teaspoons fresh lime juice

⅛ teaspoon salt

1 garlic clove, chopped

1. Preheat broiler.

2. Arrange fish in a single layer on a broiler pan lightly coated with cooking spray. Sprinkle fish with ¼ teaspoon salt and black pepper. Broil 6 minutes or until desired degree of doneness.

3. Combine basil and next 7 ingredients (through garlic) in a food processor; process 1 minute or until smooth. Spoon 1 tablespoon sauce over each fillet. Cover and reserve remaining sauce in refrigerator. **YIELD:** 4 servings (serving size: 1 fillet and about 1 tablespoon sauce).

CALORIES 237; **FAT** 9.1g (sat 1.4g, mono 5.4g, poly 1.6g); **PROTEIN** 35.3g; **CARB** 1.4g; **FIBER** 0.7g; **CHOL** 63mg; **IRON** 0.8mg; **SODIUM** 328mg; **CALC** 77mg

EVEN *faster*

When you cook, tuck a clean kitchen towel into your waistband. You won't need to search for it to wipe up spills, which in turn won't morph over time into gunky blobs in need of a more deliberate scrubbing.

10 QUICK SIDES to round out your *weeknight meals*

 1   **2**   **3**   **4** **5**

1. Sautéed Spinach with Garlic and Red Pepper

Heat 1 tablespoon olive oil and 2 teaspoons butter in a Dutch oven over medium-low heat. Add ¼ teaspoon crushed red pepper and 5 thinly sliced garlic cloves; cook 5 minutes, stirring occasionally. Increase heat to medium-high. Gradually add 2 (9-ounce) packages fresh spinach, tossing constantly until spinach wilts (about 2 minutes). Stir in ⅛ teaspoon kosher salt. **YIELD:** 4 servings (serving size: about ¾ cup).

CALORIES 82; **FAT** 5.8g (sat 1.8g); **SODIUM** 175mg

2. Quinoa Salad with Peaches

Bring 1½ cups water to a boil in a medium saucepan; add ¾ cup uncooked quinoa. Cover, reduce heat, and simmer 20 minutes. Cool quinoa slightly. Stir in ¼ cup minced red bell pepper, ¼ cup chopped green onions, 3 tablespoons fresh lemon juice, 1½ tablespoons olive oil, ½ teaspoon kosher salt, 1½ teaspoons honey, ¼ teaspoon black pepper, and 1 sliced ripe peach. **YIELD:** 4 servings (serving size: about 1 cup).

CALORIES 196; **FAT** 7.1g (sat 0.9g); **SODIUM** 245mg

3. Pan-Grilled Corn with Chipotle-Lime Butter

Heat a grill pan over medium-high heat. Coat pan with cooking spray. Add 4 ears shucked corn to pan; cook 8 minutes, turning frequently. Place 1 tablespoon butter in a microwave-safe dish. Microwave at HIGH 30 seconds or until butter melts. Stir in ½ teaspoon chipotle chile powder, ½ teaspoon grated lime rind, ¼ teaspoon freshly ground black pepper, and ⅛ teaspoon salt. Brush butter mixture over corn. **YIELD:** 4 servings (serving size: 1 ear).

CALORIES 103; **FAT** 3.9g (sat 2g); **SODIUM** 115mg

4. Tomato-Dill Couscous

Heat a small saucepan over medium-high heat. Add 1 tablespoon olive oil to pan. Stir in 1 cup uncooked couscous; sauté 1 minute. Add 1 cup plus 2 tablespoons fat-free, lower-sodium chicken broth and ⅛ teaspoon salt; bring to a boil. Cover, remove from heat, and let stand 5 minutes. Fluff with a fork. Stir in ½ cup quartered cherry tomatoes, ¼ cup finely chopped red onion, and 2 tablespoons chopped fresh dill. **YIELD:** 4 servings (serving size: ¾ cup).

CALORIES 201; **FAT** 3.7g (sat 0.5g); **SODIUM** 149mg

5. Roasted Curried Cauliflower

Preheat oven to 475°. Combine 6 cups cauliflower florets (about 1 medium head), 1½ tablespoons olive oil, ½ teaspoon Madras curry powder, and ¼ teaspoon kosher salt on a baking sheet; toss to coat. Bake at 475° for 18 minutes or until browned and crisp-tender, stirring occasionally. **YIELD:** 4 servings (serving size: about 1¼ cups).

CALORIES 82; **FAT** 5.2g (sat 0.7g); **SODIUM** 159mg

6

Roasted Carrots with Fennel Seeds

Preheat oven to 425°. Toss 2 cups (2-inch) diagonally cut carrot with 2 teaspoons olive oil, ½ teaspoon crushed fennel seeds, ¼ teaspoon salt, and ¼ teaspoon black pepper. Arrange carrots on a baking sheet. Roast at 425° for 15 minutes or until tender. Stir in ¼ cup chopped fresh parsley. **YIELD:** 4 servings (serving size: ½ cup).

CALORIES 46; **FAT** 2.4g (sat 0.3g); **SODIUM** 188mg

7

Greek Orzo Salad

Cook ¾ cup uncooked orzo (rice-shaped pasta) according to package directions, omitting salt and fat. Drain and rinse under cold water; drain well. Stir in ⅓ cup sliced feta cheese, 3 tablespoons chopped pitted kalamata olives, 1 tablespoon extra-virgin olive oil, 1 tablespoon fresh lemon juice, 1½ teaspoons chopped fresh oregano, ½ teaspoon freshly ground black pepper, and ⅛ teaspoon salt. **YIELD:** 4 servings (serving size: about ¾ cup).

CALORIES 202; **FAT** 8.1g (sat 2.3g); **SODIUM** 266mg

8

Green Apple Slaw

Combine 2 tablespoons cider vinegar, 1 tablespoon extra-virgin olive oil, 1½ teaspoons sugar, ¼ teaspoon kosher salt, and ¼ teaspoon freshly ground black pepper in a medium bowl; stir until sugar dissolves. Add 3 cups thinly sliced fennel bulb (about 1 large), 2 cups thinly sliced Granny Smith apple (1 large), ¼ cup fresh flat-leaf parsley leaves, and ¼ cup slivered red onion; toss to coat. **YIELD:** 4 servings (serving size: about 1 cup).

CALORIES 91; **FAT** 3.6g (sat 0.5g); **SODIUM** 155mg

9

Roasted Potatoes with Thyme and Garlic

Preheat broiler. Combine 1 (20-ounce) package refrigerated potato wedges, 2 tablespoons olive oil, ¼ teaspoon kosher salt, and ¼ teaspoon freshly ground black pepper on a baking sheet. Broil 12 minutes, stirring after 6 minutes. Stir in 1 tablespoon minced garlic; broil 2 minutes or until potatoes are tender. Remove from oven; sprinkle with 2 teaspoons chopped fresh thyme. **YIELD:** 4 servings (serving size: about ¾ cup).

CALORIES 151; **FAT** 6.8g (sat 0.9g); **SODIUM** 265mg

10

Green Beans with Browned Butter and Lemon

Cook 1 pound trimmed green beans in boiling water 5 minutes or until crisp-tender. Drain and plunge beans into ice water; drain well. Melt 1½ tablespoons butter in a large skillet over medium-high heat; cook 2 minutes or until browned. Add beans to pan; cook 1 minute or until thoroughly heated, stirring frequently. Stir in ½ teaspoon grated lemon rind, 1 teaspoon fresh lemon juice, ¼ teaspoon kosher salt, and ¼ teaspoon freshly ground black pepper. **YIELD:** 4 servings (serving size: about 1 cup).

CALORIES 74; **FAT** 4.4g (sat 2.7g); **SODIUM** 155mg

◀ Spicy Chipotle Shrimp Salad

Shrimp salad is an easy make-ahead meal. For a kid-friendly twist, substitute diced red bell pepper for the chipotle chile.

1½ pounds peeled and deveined large shrimp

⅛ teaspoon salt

⅛ teaspoon freshly ground black pepper

Cooking spray

¼ cup finely chopped celery

2 tablespoons finely chopped red onion

2 tablespoons chopped fresh cilantro

3 tablespoons canola mayonnaise

1 tablespoon chopped chipotle chile, canned in adobo sauce

2 teaspoons fresh lime juice

½ teaspoon ground cumin

8 Boston lettuce leaves

1. Heat a grill pan over medium-high heat. Sprinkle shrimp with salt and black pepper. Coat pan with cooking spray. Add half of shrimp to pan; cook 2 minutes on each side or until done. Remove shrimp from pan; repeat procedure with remaining shrimp. Cool shrimp 5 minutes.

2. Place shrimp in a medium bowl; stir in celery and next 6 ingredients (through cumin). Arrange 2 lettuce leaves on each of 4 plates; top each serving with ¾ cup shrimp mixture. **YIELD:** 4 servings (serving size: 2 lettuce leaves and ¾ cup shrimp mixture).

CALORIES 235; **FAT** 10.9g (sat 0.9g, mono 3g, poly 6.2g); **PROTEIN** 29.2g; **CARB** 3.2g; **FIBER** 0.8g; **CHOL** 219mg; **IRON** 3.8mg; **SODIUM** 400mg; **CALC** 87mg

EVEN *faster*

Your favorite music can make you more relaxed and even speed up your pace as your work to the rhythm.

Sautéed Asparagus and Shrimp with Gremolata

Sauté the two main ingredients separately to avoid overcrowding the pan. Gremolata is a fresh lemon-herb topping that rounds out the flavors in this entrée.

Gremolata:

¼ cup finely chopped fresh flat-leaf parsley

2 teaspoons grated lemon rind

⅛ teaspoon salt

⅛ teaspoon freshly ground black pepper

3 garlic cloves, minced

Shrimp:

4 teaspoons olive oil, divided

3 cups (1½-inch) sliced asparagus (about ½ pound)

1½ pounds peeled and deveined medium shrimp

⅛ teaspoon salt

⅛ teaspoon freshly ground black pepper

1. To prepare gremolata, combine first 5 ingredients; set aside.

2. To prepare shrimp, heat a large nonstick skillet over medium-high heat. Add 2 teaspoons oil to pan, swirling to coat; heat 20 seconds. Add asparagus; sauté 3 minutes. Remove asparagus from pan; keep warm.

3. Add remaining 2 teaspoons oil to pan, swirling to coat; heat 20 seconds. Add shrimp to pan; cook 3 minutes or until done, stirring occasionally. Add asparagus, ⅛ teaspoon salt, and ⅛ teaspoon pepper to pan; sauté 1 minute or until thoroughly heated. Sprinkle evenly with gremolata. **YIELD:** 4 servings (serving size: 1½ cups).

CALORIES 240; **FAT** 7.6g (sat 1.2g, mono 3.7g, poly 1.7g); **PROTEIN** 36.1g; **CARB** 5.2g; **FIBER** 1.6g; **CHOL** 259mg; **IRON** 5.6mg; **SODIUM** 403mg; **CALC** 115mg

MORE CHOICES: You can make this same recipe with broccoli florets and chopped skinless, boneless chicken breasts.

Hoisin-Glazed Chicken Breasts

Adding the remaining glaze to the chicken after broiling intensifies the flavor. Be sure to use a clean spoon or brush when adding the final amount of hoisin mixture. You don't want it to come into contact with any utensils that touched raw chicken.

¼ cup hoisin sauce

1 tablespoon fresh lime juice

1 tablespoon lower-sodium soy sauce

2 teaspoons bottled minced garlic

2 teaspoons dark sesame oil

¾ teaspoon bottled minced fresh ginger

Cooking spray

4 (6-ounce) skinless, boneless chicken breast halves

4 lime wedges

1. Preheat broiler.

2. Combine first 6 ingredients. Remove 2 tablespoons hoisin mixture, and reserve to brush on cooked chicken. Line a shallow roasting pan with foil; coat foil with cooking spray. Place chicken on prepared pan. Brush 2 tablespoons hoisin mixture evenly over chicken; broil 5 minutes. Turn chicken over; brush with 2 tablespoons hoisin mixture. Broil 5 minutes or until chicken is done. Spoon reserved 2 tablespoons hoisin mixture over cooked chicken. Serve with lime wedges. **YIELD:** 4 servings (serving size: 1 chicken breast half and 1 lime wedge).

CALORIES 249; **FAT** 4.9g (sat 1g, mono 1.6g, poly 1.7g); **PROTEIN** 40.2g; **CARB** 8.4g; **FIBER** 0.5g; **CHOL** 99mg; **IRON** 1.4mg; **SODIUM** 520mg; **CALC** 26mg

Quick Chef Salad ▶

Start with a bag of prechopped romaine lettuce and a rotisserie chicken from the grocery store for an easy, healthy dinner any night of the week. Serve with a crusty multigrain baguette.

10 cups torn or chopped romaine lettuce

1 cup shredded skinless, boneless rotisserie chicken breast

½ cup thinly sliced onion

⅓ cup shaved carrot

1 sliced peeled avocado

3 tablespoons crumbled blue cheese

½ cup Easy Herb Vinaigrette (page 40)

1. Arrange 2½ cups lettuce on each of 4 plates. Top lettuce evenly with chicken, onion, carrot, avocado, and blue cheese. Drizzle each serving with 2 tablespoons Easy Herb Vinaigrette; serve immediately. **YIELD:** 4 servings.

CALORIES 367; **FAT** 28.2g (sat 3.4g, mono 15g, poly 6.2g); **PROTEIN** 18.5g; **CARB** 12.6g; **FIBER** 4.6g; **CHOL** 43mg; **IRON** 2mg; **SODIUM** 451mg; **CALC** 66mg

EVEN *faster*

Just use clean hands to shred rotisserie chicken—or pork, or even beef, for that matter. The two-fork method can take forever.

ON THE SIDE: Try this chicken supper with Buttery Lemon Broccolini (page 296) or Herbed Couscous Pilaf (page 317).

MORE CHOICES: For a fancier meal, omit the greens; serve the chicken and sauce over creamy polenta.

◀ Grilled Chicken with Mustard-Tarragon Sauce

A tangy sauce enlivens simple grilled chicken breasts; a hint of sugar balances the flavors.

4 (6-ounce) skinless, boneless chicken breast halves

½ teaspoon salt, divided

¼ teaspoon black pepper, divided

Cooking spray

3 tablespoons minced shallots

3 tablespoons Dijon mustard

2 tablespoons red wine vinegar

2 tablespoons water

1 tablespoon extra-virgin olive oil

1 teaspoon chopped fresh tarragon

½ teaspoon sugar

4 cups gourmet salad greens

1. Heat a grill pan over medium-high heat. Sprinkle chicken evenly with ¼ teaspoon salt and ⅛ teaspoon pepper. Coat pan with cooking spray. Place chicken in pan; cook 6 minutes on each side or until done.

2. Combine remaining ¼ teaspoon salt, remaining ⅛ teaspoon pepper, shallots, and next 6 ingredients (through sugar) in a bowl, stirring well with a whisk. Serve chicken over greens with sauce. **YIELD:** 4 servings (serving size: 1 chicken breast half, 1 cup greens, and about 2 tablespoons sauce).

CALORIES 231; **FAT** 7.6g (sat 1.6g, mono 4.1g, poly 1.2g); **PROTEIN** 35.4g; **CARB** 3.5g; **FIBER** 1.3g; **CHOL** 94mg; **IRON** 2mg; **SODIUM** 538mg; **CALC** 51mg

Pan-Seared Chicken with Italian Salsa Verde

The fresh flavors of parsley and mint carry the piquant capers, garlic, and vinegar in this simple chicken recipe. It's especially good atop fettuccine.

1 tablespoon all-purpose flour

¼ teaspoon salt

¼ teaspoon freshly ground black pepper

4 (6-ounce) skinless, boneless chicken breast halves

5 teaspoons olive oil, divided

¾ cup fresh flat-leaf parsley leaves

2 tablespoons water

2 tablespoons red wine vinegar

1 teaspoon bottled minced garlic

1 teaspoon capers, rinsed and drained

4 (2-inch) fresh mint sprigs

1 (2-ounce) slice peasant bread, crust removed

1. Combine first 4 ingredients in a large zip-top plastic bag; seal and shake well to coat. Heat 1 tablespoon oil in a large nonstick skillet over medium-high heat. Add chicken to pan; cook 6 minutes on each side or until done.

2. Place remaining 2 teaspoons oil, parsley, and next 5 ingredients (through mint) in a food processor; process 10 seconds or until finely chopped. Tear bread into pieces, add to processor, and process 4 seconds or until well blended. Thinly slice each chicken breast half, and serve topped with salsa verde. **YIELD:** 4 servings (serving size: 1 chicken breast half and 2 tablespoons salsa verde).

CALORIES 280; **FAT** 8.3g (sat 1.5g, mono 4.7g, poly 1.3g); **PROTEIN** 40.9g; **CARB** 8.1g; **FIBER** 1g; **CHOL** 99mg; **IRON** 2.7mg; **SODIUM** 345mg; **CALC** 51mg

EVEN *faster*

Institute a new house rule: The one who cooks is not the one who cleans up.

Chicken Scaloppine

Prepare chicken breasts scaloppine-style by pounding them into thin, quick-cooking servings, then dredge in lemon juice and breadcrumbs, and cook about 3 minutes on each side. The white wine sauce with capers complements the flavor of the lemon juice and makes a great topping for wild rice.

4 (6-ounce) skinless, boneless chicken breast halves

2 teaspoons fresh lemon juice

¼ teaspoon salt

¼ teaspoon black pepper

⅓ cup Italian-seasoned breadcrumbs

Cooking spray

½ cup fat-free, lower-sodium chicken broth

¼ cup dry white wine

4 teaspoons capers

1 tablespoon butter

1. Place each chicken breast half between 2 sheets of heavy-duty plastic wrap; pound to ¼-inch thickness using a meat mallet or small heavy skillet. Brush chicken with juice, and sprinkle with salt and pepper. Dredge chicken in breadcrumbs.

2. Heat a large nonstick skillet over medium-high heat. Coat pan with cooking spray. Add chicken to pan; cook 3 minutes on each side or until chicken is done. Remove from pan; keep warm.

3. Add broth and wine to pan, and cook 30 seconds, stirring constantly. Remove from heat. Stir in capers and butter. **YIELD:** 4 servings (serving size: 1 chicken breast half and 1 tablespoon sauce).

CALORIES 206; **FAT** 4.6g (sat 2.2g, mono 1.3g, poly 0.5g); **PROTEIN** 29.2g; **CARB** 7.7g; **FIBER** 0.6g; **CHOL** 76mg; **IRON** 1.6mg; **SODIUM** 657mg; **CALC** 27mg

EVEN *faster*

Buy 24 ounces chicken scaloppine, often in the meat case at your supermarket. Or try this dish with turkey scaloppine. Failing that, ask the butcher at your market to make scaloppine for you from a package of skinless, boneless chicken breast halves.

Chicken Taco Salad with Lime Vinaigrette

This Southwestern-influenced salad needs nothing on the side except some iced tea. Fresh lime gives it a citrusy punch.

Vinaigrette:

¼ cup chopped seeded tomato

¼ cup chopped fresh cilantro

2 tablespoons olive oil

1 tablespoon cider vinegar

1 teaspoon grated lime rind

1 tablespoon fresh lime juice

¼ teaspoon salt

¼ teaspoon ground cumin

¼ teaspoon chili powder

¼ teaspoon black pepper

1 garlic clove, peeled

Salad:

8 cups thinly sliced iceberg lettuce

1½ cups chopped roasted skinless, boneless chicken breast (about 2 breasts)

1 cup chopped tomato

1 cup chopped green bell pepper

1 cup finely diced red onion

½ cup (2 ounces) reduced-fat shredded sharp cheddar cheese

1 (15-ounce) can black beans, rinsed and drained

4 cups fat-free baked tortilla chips (about 4 ounces)

1. To prepare vinaigrette, combine first 11 ingredients in a blender or food processor; process until smooth.

2. To prepare salad, combine lettuce and next 6 ingredients (through black beans) in a large bowl. Add vinaigrette; toss well to coat. Serve with chips. **YIELD:** 4 servings (serving size: about 2 cups salad and 1 cup chips).

CALORIES 402; **FAT** 12.6g (sat 3.2g, mono 6.5g, poly 1.9g); **PROTEIN** 24.5g; **CARB** 51.6g; **FIBER** 8g; **CHOL** 35mg; **IRON** 3.6mg; **SODIUM** 861mg; **CALC** 236mg

QUICK TIP: Let the answering machine get that phone call! You're trying to get dinner on the table.

◀ Spicy Honey-Brushed Chicken Thighs

Because this simple entrée is sweet and spicy, serve it with sides or salads that are savory—or even lemony. Use regular potatoes, rather than sweet potatoes; leave the tomatoes out of the salad and go for cucumbers.

2 teaspoons garlic powder

2 teaspoons chili powder

1 teaspoon ground cumin

1 teaspoon paprika

¾ teaspoon salt

½ teaspoon ground red pepper

8 skinless, boneless chicken thighs

Cooking spray

6 tablespoons honey

2 teaspoons cider vinegar

1. Preheat broiler.

2. Combine first 6 ingredients in a large bowl. Add chicken to bowl; toss to coat. Place chicken on a broiler pan coated with cooking spray. Broil chicken 5 minutes on each side.

3. Combine honey and vinegar in a small bowl, stirring well. Remove chicken from oven; brush ¼ cup honey mixture over chicken. Broil 1 minute. Remove chicken from oven, and turn over. Brush chicken with remaining honey mixture. Broil 1 minute or until chicken is done. **YIELD:** 4 servings (serving size: 2 chicken thighs).

CALORIES 321; **FAT** 11g (sat 3g, mono 4.1g, poly 2.5g); **PROTEIN** 28g; **CARB** 27.9g; **FIBER** 0.6g; **CHOL** 99mg; **IRON** 2.1mg; **SODIUM** 528mg; **CALC** 21mg

> **QUICK TIP:** Always reach for a larger bowl than you think you need. Using a bowl that's too small can cause spills. Plus, you can't stir or whisk the ingredients as quickly.

Turkey Caesar Wraps

Although you could make these wraps with sliced deli turkey, the cutlets cooked at home will have less sodium per serving—and will still be warm when you roll them up, making these wraps irresistible.

12 ounces turkey cutlets (¼ inch thick)

½ teaspoon salt

¼ teaspoon freshly ground black pepper

Cooking spray

2 cups shredded romaine lettuce

1 cup halved cherry tomatoes

⅓ cup (1.3 ounces) grated fresh Parmesan cheese

⅓ cup shredded carrot

¼ cup light Caesar dressing

4 (8-inch) fat-free whole-wheat tortillas

1. Sprinkle cutlets with salt and pepper. Heat a large nonstick skillet over medium-high heat. Coat pan with cooking spray. Add cutlets to pan. Cook 2 minutes on each side or until done. Remove cutlets from pan, and cut into thin strips.

2. Combine turkey strips, lettuce, and next 4 ingredients (through Caesar dressing) in a medium bowl. Place 1 cup turkey mixture on each tortilla; roll up, and secure with wooden picks. **YIELD:** 4 servings (serving size: 1 wrap).

CALORIES 243; **FAT** 5.1g (sat 0.6g, mono 0.9g, poly 1.4g); **PROTEIN** 25.4g; **CARB** 24.1g; **FIBER** 2g; **CHOL** 39mg; **IRON** 2.1mg; **SODIUM** 721mg; **CALC** 63mg

EVEN *faster*

Substitute 2½ cups bagged coleslaw mix for the lettuce and carrots, if desired.

◀ Turkey and Oat Burgers

For these delicious burgers, remember the rule: If the package says "turkey meat," it includes only the meat. If it just says "turkey," it contains cartilage and other bits of the bird, all ground together. Or skip reading altogether, and hand the butcher a package of skinless turkey cutlets to grind for you.

1 cup old-fashioned rolled oats

1 cup finely chopped Vidalia or other sweet onion

1 tablespoon chili powder

¾ teaspoon salt

2 large egg whites, lightly beaten

1 (14.5-ounce) can no-salt-added tomatoes, drained and chopped

1½ pounds ground turkey

Cooking spray

6 (2-ounce) onion sandwich buns, toasted

6 curly leaf lettuce leaves

6 (¼-inch-thick) slices tomato

1. Combine first 7 ingredients. Divide mixture into 6 equal portions, shaping each into a ½-inch-thick patty.

2. Heat a grill pan over medium-high heat. Coat pan with cooking spray Add patties; cook 6 minutes on each side or until done. Place 1 patty on bottom half of each bun; top each with 1 lettuce leaf, 1 tomato slice, and top half of bun. **YIELD:** 6 servings (serving size: 1 burger).

CALORIES 285; **FAT** 4.3g (sat 1.2g, mono 0.8g, poly 0.9g); **PROTEIN** 33.1g; **CARB** 29.6g; **FIBER** 2.9g; **CHOL** 46mg; **IRON** 2.7mg; **SODIUM** 583mg; **CALC** 115mg

ON THE SIDE: Make Thanksgiving dinner on an average weeknight. Try these cutlets alongside baked sweet potatoes and a tossed green salad. You might even consider stirring up a saucepan of stuffing.

Turkey Cutlets with Spiced Cranberry Sauce

Purchased cranberry sauce can be reduced into a great sauce for these quick turkey cutlets. It's Thanksgiving any night of the week!

8 (2-ounce) turkey cutlets

½ teaspoon salt

½ teaspoon freshly ground black pepper

1 tablespoon unsalted butter

¼ cup fat-free, lower-sodium chicken broth

½ cup whole-berry cranberry sauce

¼ teaspoon ground cinnamon

⅛ teaspoon ground allspice

⅛ teaspoon ground cloves

1. Sprinkle cutlets with salt and pepper. Melt 1½ teaspoons butter in a large nonstick skillet over medium heat. Add 4 cutlets; cook 1½ minutes on each side or until done. Transfer to a plate; keep warm. Repeat procedure with remaining butter and cutlets.

2. Add broth to pan, scraping pan to loosen browned bits. Bring to a simmer; stir in cranberry sauce and next 3 ingredients (through cloves), returning to a simmer. Add turkey and any accumulated juices to the pan. Cook 1 minute. **YIELD:** 4 servings (serving size: 2 cutlets and 2 tablespoons sauce).

CALORIES 198; **FAT** 4g (sat 2.1g, mono 0.9g, poly 0.3g); **PROTEIN** 27.1g; **CARB** 13.4g; **FIBER** 0.7g; **CHOL** 82mg; **IRON** 1.5mg; **SODIUM** 374mg; **CALC** 15mg

EVEN*faster*

Want to save yourself a lot of cleanup afterward? Put bowls in the sink, and work there. Any spills and drips can be washed down the drain!

Yam Neua Yang

Yam Neua Yang (aka Spicy Beef Salad) calls out for jasmine or basmati rice—or even a Thai sticky rice, which is more labor intensive but also sweet and irresistible.

1 (1-pound) flank steak, trimmed

Cooking spray

⅓ cup sliced shallots

¼ cup chopped fresh cilantro

3 tablespoons fresh lime juice

1 tablespoon fish sauce

2 teaspoons sliced Thai red chiles or serrano chiles

2 medium tomatoes, cut into ¼-inch-thick wedges (about ¾ pound)

1. Prepare grill or broiler.

2. Place steak on grill rack or broiler pan coated with cooking spray; cook 6 minutes on each side or until desired degree of doneness.

3. Cut steak diagonally across grain into thin slices; cut each slice into 2-inch pieces.

4. Combine steak, shallots, and remaining ingredients, and toss gently. **YIELD:** 4 servings (serving size: 1 cup).

CALORIES 214; FAT 9.2g (sat 3.9g, mono 3.6g, poly 0.5g); PROTEIN 25g; CARB 7.6g; FIBER 1.1g; CHOL 59mg; IRON 2.8mg; SODIUM 407mg; CALC 17mg

savvy IN A SNAP

Fish sauce has been called "the soy sauce of Southeast Asia." It's pungent in the bottle but mellows gorgeously when heated.

Chinese Five-Spice Steak with Rice Noodles ▶

The delicate flavor and texture of these Asian noodles balances the highly seasoned beef. You can also serve the steak with basmati rice.

4 ounces uncooked wide rice sticks (rice-flour noodles)

¼ cup hoisin sauce

3 tablespoons lower-sodium soy sauce

1 teaspoon five-spice powder

1 (1-pound) flank steak, trimmed and cut into ¼-inch strips

2 teaspoons canola oil

2 tablespoons minced green onions

2 teaspoons bottled minced garlic

2 medium tomatoes, each cut into 6 wedges

2 green onions, cut into 2-inch pieces

1 tablespoon chopped fresh basil

1. Cook noodles according to package directions.

2. While noodles cook, combine hoisin sauce, soy sauce, five-spice powder, and steak in a large bowl. Heat oil in a large nonstick skillet over medium-high heat. Add minced green onions and garlic; sauté 30 seconds. Add beef mixture; cook 5 minutes, stirring frequently. Stir in tomato wedges, green onions, and basil; cook 2 minutes, stirring occasionally. Serve over cooked noodles. **YIELD:** 4 servings (serving size: 1½ cups beef mixture and 1 cup noodles).

CALORIES 374; FAT 12.1g (sat 4.3g, mono 4.3g, poly 2.1g); PROTEIN 28.2g; CARB 36.6g; FIBER 2.3g; CHOL 59mg; IRON 4.1mg; SODIUM 744mg; CALC 32mg

savvy IN A SNAP

Some **rice stick noodles** must be simmered on the stove like Italian pasta; others can be cooked by simply covering them with boiling water in a bowl and setting aside. Read the package directions carefully to know which kind you have.

1

Boil water faster
Put a lid on it—4 quarts of water comes to a boil 1 minute faster in a covered pot. (OK, just 1 minute. But if you're in a rush, every second counts—think what you can do with 60 minutes.)

2

Chop herbs *en masse*
To chop parsley or cilantro quickly, don't tediously pick leaves from the bunch; wash and dry the bunch while it's still bound together. Then make a diagonal cut (to avoid the thicker stems in the center) from the top of the bunch to chop off roughly the amount you'll need.

3

Peel blanched peaches
Place peaches in boiling water for about 30 seconds, remove with a slotted spoon, and plunge them into an ice bath for a few seconds more. The peels will slip off easily.

5

If it's flat, stack and slice several at once
This is perfect for items like shiitake mushroom caps, bacon, and bread.

4

Or just use nectarines
They're close enough to peaches for most recipes, and you won't have to bother with peeling at all.

Smash, don't peel garlic

Unless you need the garlic clove whole, just smash it with the flat side of your knife. The peel breaks apart so it's easy to remove. Mince away.

If you do need whole peeled cloves, try this

Drop whole cloves into a lidded bowl, cover, and shake vigorously. The peels often fall right off. (This only works about half of the time, but it's so cool when it does that we had to pass it on.)

Make a spice rub

While you have the spices out, make an extra batch to use on meat, shrimp, or poultry another night—it'll keep for months, so there's no rush to use it. Or try this tasty rub on chicken, pork, or steak: Combine 2 tablespoons brown sugar, 2 tablespoons paprika, 4 teaspoons ground cumin, 2 teaspoons kosher salt, and 1 teaspoon ground red pepper; store in a dry, airtight container. Yield: about 6 tablespoons (serving size: 1 teaspoon).

10

Make a pasta toss

If you're including vegetables like broccoli rabe or peas, throw them into your pot of boiling pasta for the last minute of cooking. Drain everything together, toss, and add the remaining ingredients—one less dirty pot. If your recipe calls for wilted greens such as spinach or arugula, just drain the pasta over the leaves, and they'll wilt on the spot.

Cook multiple toasted sandwiches or quesadillas

Use your broiler to cook several at once rather than using a skillet to cook batch after batch after (sigh) batch.

Quick Kofte

Kofte, Turkish meatballs often grilled on a stick, can be made from ground lamb, beef, or a combination. These are made with beef only, but you can try a 50/50 mix of ground lamb and beef, if you prefer.

½ cup prechopped onion

⅓ cup dry breadcrumbs

¼ cup chopped fresh mint

2 tablespoons tomato paste

1 teaspoon bottled minced garlic

½ teaspoon salt

½ teaspoon ground cumin

¼ teaspoon ground cinnamon

¼ teaspoon ground red pepper

⅛ teaspoon ground allspice

1 pound lean ground round

1 large egg white, lightly beaten

Cooking spray

8 (¼-inch-thick) slices plum tomato (about 2 tomatoes)

4 (6-inch) pitas, split

¼ cup plain low-fat yogurt

1. Preheat broiler.

2. Combine first 12 ingredients in a large bowl; stir just until combined. Divide mixture into 8 equal portions; shape each portion into a 2-inch patty. Place patties on a jelly-roll pan coated with cooking spray. Broil 4 minutes on each side or until desired degree of doneness. Place 1 tomato slice and 1 patty in each pita half; top each half with 1½ teaspoons yogurt. **YIELD:** 4 servings (serving size: 2 filled pita halves).

CALORIES 423; FAT 11.4g (sat 4.3g, mono 4.3g, poly 0.9g); PROTEIN 31.6g; CARB 46.7g; FIBER 3.2g; CHOL 75mg; IRON 4.3mg; SODIUM 766mg; CALC 114mg

QUICK TIP: Don't forget to check the refrigerator cases of your supermarket's produce section for chopped fresh onion, bell pepper, celery, carrots, and other vegetables.

Rosemary Pork Chops

Because there's no acid in this marinade, you can feel free to put the rub on the chops in the morning, set them on a plate, cover loosely with plastic wrap, and refrigerate all day. The flavor will be even more intense. Serve with Brussels sprouts.

1½ teaspoons chopped fresh rosemary

2 teaspoons bottled minced garlic

½ teaspoon salt

¼ teaspoon black pepper

4 (4-ounce) boneless center-cut loin pork chops (about ½ inch thick)

Cooking spray

1. Preheat broiler.

2. Combine first 4 ingredients. Rub mixture over both sides of pork chops. Place pork chops on a broiler pan coated with cooking spray; broil 3 minutes on each side or until desired degree of doneness. **YIELD:** 4 servings (serving size: 1 pork chop).

CALORIES 166; **FAT** 6.1g (sat 2.1g, mono 2.7g, poly 0.7g); **PROTEIN** 25g; **CARB** 1.4g; **FIBER** 0.5g; **CHOL** 62mg; **IRON** 1.1mg; **SODIUM** 342mg; **CALC** 32mg

ON THE SIDE: These would also be delicious—and fast—alongside the Grilled Salad (page 88).

Veal Scaloppine with Mustard Cream Sauce

What's the secret to a great cream sauce? Not too much cream. There should be just enough to coat the ingredients without weighing them down. What's even better, with less cream you spend less time at the stove boiling it down. A quick cook's dream!

8 (2-ounce) slices veal scaloppine

½ teaspoon freshly ground black pepper

⅛ teaspoon salt

1 tablespoon unsalted butter

½ cup fat-free, lower-sodium chicken broth

¼ cup whipping cream

1 tablespoon Dijon mustard

2 teaspoons minced fresh tarragon

1. Sprinkle veal with pepper and salt. Melt 1 teaspoon butter in a large nonstick skillet over medium heat. Cook one-third of veal 30 seconds on each side or until lightly browned. Transfer veal to a plate. Repeat procedure twice with remaining butter and veal.

2. Add broth to pan. Bring to a simmer, scraping pan to loosen browned bits. Add whipping cream, mustard, and tarragon. Cook, stirring constantly, 1 minute. Return veal and any accumulated juices to pan. Cook 30 seconds or until thoroughly heated, turning veal often. **YIELD:** 4 servings (serving size: 3 ounces veal and 3 tablespoons sauce).

CALORIES 203; FAT 9g (sat 5.4g, mono 2.8g, poly 0.5g); PROTEIN 24g; CARB 2.2g; FIBER 0.2g; CHOL 116mg; IRON 1mg; SODIUM 293mg; CALC 13mg

◀ Mole-Style Pork Chops

Unsweetened cocoa is the key ingredient to savory mole sauce; it adds a smooth, rich flavor without being overly sweet. Try it on pork or chicken for a delicious, Mexican-inspired dinner. Serve with rice and beans tossed with fresh cilantro.

1 tablespoon brown sugar

1 teaspoon smoked paprika

1 teaspoon ground cumin

1 teaspoon unsweetened cocoa

1 teaspoon ground chipotle chile pepper

½ teaspoon salt

4 (6-ounce) bone-in center-cut pork chops (about ½ inch thick)

Cooking spray

1. Heat a grill pan over medium heat.

2. Combine first 6 ingredients; rub evenly over both sides of pork. Lightly coat pork with cooking spray. Place pork on pan; cover and cook 3 minutes on each side or until done. Let stand 3 minutes. **YIELD:** 4 servings (serving size: 1 pork chop).

CALORIES 180; FAT 6.4g (sat 2.1g, mono 3g, poly 1.2g); PROTEIN 25.4g; CARB 4.4g; FIBER 0.8g; CHOL 70mg; IRON 0.5mg; SODIUM 376mg; CALC 11mg

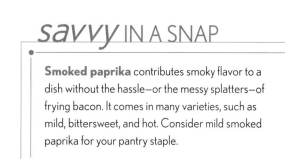

savvy IN A SNAP

Smoked paprika contributes smoky flavor to a dish without the hassle—or the messy splatters—of frying bacon. It comes in many varieties, such as mild, bittersweet, and hot. Consider mild smoked paprika for your pantry staple.

Lamb Chops with Herb Vinaigrette

Broiled lamb chops are a too-often-forgotten, quick recipe. Add garlic mashed potatoes and steamed broccoli florets for a complete meal. If you have bottled roasted red bell peppers in your refrigerator, you can substitute them for the pimiento.

½ teaspoon salt, divided

½ teaspoon black pepper

8 (4-ounce) lamb loin chops

2 tablespoons finely chopped shallots

1½ tablespoons water

1 tablespoon red wine vinegar

1½ teaspoons lemon juice

1½ teaspoons extra-virgin olive oil

1 teaspoon Dijon mustard

1½ tablespoons finely chopped fresh flat-leaf parsley

1½ tablespoons finely chopped fresh tarragon

1 tablespoon finely chopped fresh mint

1 tablespoon finely chopped pimiento

1. Preheat broiler.

2. Sprinkle ¼ teaspoon salt and black pepper over lamb. Place lamb on a broiler pan or roasting pan; place rack in pan. Broil 5 minutes on each side or until desired degree of doneness.

3. Combine shallots, 1½ tablespoons water, and vinegar in a small microwave-safe bowl; microwave at HIGH 30 seconds. Add remaining ¼ teaspoon salt, juice, oil, and mustard, stirring with a whisk. Add parsley and next 3 ingredients (through pimiento), stirring well. Serve vinaigrette over lamb. **YIELD:** 4 servings (serving size: 2 lamb chops and 1 tablespoon vinaigrette).

CALORIES 349; **FAT** 15.2g (sat 5.1g, mono 6.7g, poly 1.4g); **PROTEIN** 47.7g; **CARB** 1.9g; **FIBER** 0.2g; **CHOL** 150mg; **IRON** 4.6mg; **SODIUM** 482mg; **CALC** 37mg

savvy IN A SNAP

A **clean and amenable work space** encourages more efficient work—simply because you feel better. Mood, after all, has a direct effect on your speed.

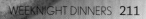

Chickpea-Vegetable Salad with Curried Yogurt Dressing

This is a great lunch or dinner in the summer when you're on the run. You can also make the dressing up to 2 days in advance; store it, covered, in the refrigerator.

Dressing:

⅓ cup chopped fresh cilantro

2 tablespoons olive oil

1 tablespoon lemon juice

1½ teaspoons curry powder

¾ teaspoon salt

½ teaspoon bottled minced garlic

¼ teaspoon freshly ground black pepper

1 (8-ounce) carton plain fat-free yogurt

Salad:

2 cups finely shredded carrot

1½ cups thinly sliced yellow or red bell pepper

1½ cups chopped plum tomato

½ cup golden raisins

¼ cup finely chopped red onion

2 (15½-ounce) cans chickpeas (garbanzo beans), drained

12 cups chopped romaine lettuce

1. To prepare dressing, combine first 8 ingredients in a small bowl; stir with a whisk.

2. To prepare salad, combine carrot and next 5 ingredients (through chickpeas) in a large bowl. Pour ½ cup dressing over carrot mixture, tossing gently to coat. Place 2 cups lettuce on each of 6 plates, and drizzle each serving with about 1 tablespoon dressing. Top each serving with 1⅓ cups carrot mixture. **YIELD:** 6 servings.

CALORIES 337; **FAT** 8g (sat 1.1g, mono 4.1g, poly 2g); **PROTEIN** 15.4g; **CARB** 55.4g; **FIBER** 8.9g; **CHOL** 1mg; **IRON** 5.7mg; **SODIUM** 573mg; **CALC** 201mg

QUICK TIP: Consider buying a large cutting board. You can chop or slice ingredients, and then simply slide them to different corners, rather than putting each chopped ingredient in its own little bowl to make space for others on a small board.

Bell Pepper and Fresh Mozzarella Couscous

Bottled roasted red bell peppers and superfast-cooking couscous make this a perfect recipe for your busiest day. It can be doubled to make two meals. Use any leftover artichoke hearts, bell peppers, and mozzarella for a vegetarian pizza.

½ cup water

⅓ cup uncooked couscous

⅛ teaspoon salt

¼ cup chopped bottled roasted red bell peppers

¼ cup canned artichoke hearts, rinsed, drained, and chopped

¼ cup (1 ounce) chopped fresh mozzarella cheese

1 tablespoon chopped fresh basil

1 tablespoon balsamic vinegar

1 teaspoon extra-virgin olive oil

⅛ teaspoon freshly ground black pepper

2 kalamata olives, pitted and sliced

1. Bring ½ cup water to a boil in a small saucepan; gradually stir in couscous and salt. Remove from heat; cover and let stand 5 minutes. Fluff with a fork.

2. Add bell peppers and remaining ingredients; toss gently to combine. Cover and chill.

YIELD: 1 serving (serving size: 2 cups).

CALORIES 390; **FAT** 13.6g (sat 4.9g, mono 5.2g, poly 0.8g); **PROTEIN** 13.1g; **CARB** 51.4g; **FIBER** 3.1g; **CHOL** 23mg; **IRON** 1.4mg; **SODIUM** 599mg; **CALC** 27mg

EVEN *faster*

5 WAYS TO PUT DINNER ON THE TABLE FASTER

1. MAKE SURE YOU HAVE EVERYTHING YOU NEED—prepped ingredients, equipment—ready to roll before you start cooking. Chefs call it *mise en place* (literally, "putting in place;" see page 14). Cooks who don't heed this rule can waste a lot of time backtracking in the middle of a recipe to prep ingredients they forgot.

2. DID WE MENTION THE IMPORTANCE OF *MISE EN PLACE?* Seriously: It bears repeating. Preparation is one of the big time-savers.

3. COOK SIMULTANEOUSLY ON AS MANY BURNERS AS YOU CAN. Professional cooks can work six or more; you can handle at least two or three.

4. KEEP A REFUSE BOWL ON THE COUNTERTOP. Avoiding extra trips to the garbage will save you time.

5. EMBRACE SANDWICH NIGHT. Just make your sandwich good, and use a few premium ingredients like bakery-fresh bread and quality condiments.

Prosciutto, Peach, and Sweet Lettuce Salad

Serve this light main-course salad with a hunk of crusty baguette and a glass of chilled riesling. Choose ripe, juicy peaches, and leave the peel on for more texture.

2 tablespoons fresh lemon juice

2 teaspoons honey

¼ teaspoon freshly ground black pepper

⅛ teaspoon salt

2 tablespoons extra-virgin olive oil

1 tablespoon finely chopped fresh mint

1 (6.5-ounce) package sweet butter lettuce mix

2 large ripe peaches, cut into wedges

3 ounces very thin slices prosciutto, cut into 1-inch pieces

3 ounces ricotta salata cheese, divided into 4 equal pieces

2 tablespoons dry-roasted sunflower seed kernels

Small mint leaves (optional)

1. Combine first 4 ingredients, stirring with a whisk. Gradually add olive oil, stirring constantly with a whisk. Stir in chopped mint.

2. Combine lettuce mix and peach wedges in a large bowl. Drizzle lettuce mixture with dressing; toss gently to coat. Arrange about 2 cups salad in each of 4 bowls; top each serving with ¾ ounce prosciutto, 1 piece ricotta salata, and about 2 teaspoons sunflower seed kernels. Garnish with mint leaves, if desired. **YIELD:** 4 servings (serving size: 1 salad).

CALORIES 209; **FAT** 13.5g (sat 3.2g, mono 5.9g, poly 2.2g); **PROTEIN** 10.4g; **CARB** 14.3g; **FIBER** 2.1g; **CHOL** 26mg; **IRON** 1.4mg; **SODIUM** 530mg; **CALC** 87mg

savvy IN A SNAP

Ricotta salata is a milky, mild, slightly salty cheese that's easy to crumble; you can substitute feta or goat cheese.

QUICK TIP: Crush the fennel seeds with a mortar and pestle, or use a heavy-duty zip-top plastic bag and a rolling pin.

◀ Fennel and Black Pepper–Crusted Lamb Chops

Lamb loin chops can hold up to the higher heat better than thinner rib chops. You can also substitute lamb T-bones.

Cooking spray

1½ teaspoons fennel seeds, lightly crushed

1 teaspoon ground coriander

¾ teaspoon cracked black pepper

½ teaspoon salt

¼ teaspoon garlic powder

4 (4-ounce) lamb loin chops, trimmed

1. Heat a grill pan over medium-high heat until hot. Coat pan with cooking spray. Combine fennel seeds, coriander, pepper, salt, and garlic powder. Press mixture onto both sides of lamb. Add lamb to pan, and cook 5 minutes on each side or until desired degree of doneness. **YIELD:** 2 servings (serving size: 2 lamb chops).

CALORIES 159; **FAT** 7.1g (sat 2.4g, mono 2.9g, poly 0.4g); **PROTEIN** 20.7g; **CARB** 2g; **FIBER** 1.3g; **CHOL** 64mg; **IRON** 2mg; **SODIUM** 645mg; **CALC** 42mg

Smoked Salmon, Goat Cheese, and Fresh Dill Frittata

Breakfast for dinner is always a great idea. Add some elegance by including goat cheese and smoked salmon in your frittata.

Cooking spray

2½ cups shredded peeled baking potato or refrigerated shredded hash brown potatoes

¼ teaspoon salt

¼ teaspoon pepper

½ cup (2 ounces) crumbled goat cheese

6 large egg whites

2 large eggs

3 ounces thinly sliced smoked salmon, cut into ¼-inch-wide strips

1 tablespoon chopped fresh dill

1. Preheat oven to 350°.

2. Heat a large ovenproof skillet over medium-high heat. Coat pan with cooking spray. Add potato; cook 5 minutes or until golden brown. Sprinkle with salt and pepper.

3. Combine goat cheese, egg whites, eggs, and smoked salmon in a medium bowl, and stir well with a whisk. Spread egg mixture evenly over potato in pan, and cook 2 minutes or until edges are set and bottom is lightly browned. Sprinkle with dill.

4. Bake at 350° for 5 minutes.

5. Increase oven temperature to broil (do not remove frittata from oven). Broil 3 minutes or until center is set. Carefully loosen frittata from pan with a spatula; gently slide frittata onto a platter. Cut into 4 wedges. **YIELD:** 4 servings (serving size: 1 wedge).

CALORIES 202; **FAT** 6.8g (sat 3.2g, mono 2.1g, poly 0.7g); **PROTEIN** 16.2g; **CARB** 18.5g; **FIBER** 1.6g; **CHOL** 128mg; **IRON** 1.5mg; **SODIUM** 589mg; **CALC** 100mg

ON THE SIDE: Try this quick dinner along with a Pesto Caesar Salad (page 92).

Greek Couscous with Shrimp

Wonderful Mediterranean ingredients Greek yogurt, kalamata olives, couscous, and grape tomatoes combine with quick seafood to produce a great weeknight meal.

1½ cups water

1⅓ cups uncooked couscous

⅜ teaspoon salt, divided

½ teaspoon freshly ground black pepper

3 tablespoons olive oil, divided

1½ pounds peeled and deveined medium shrimp

1 cup grape tomatoes, halved

½ cup thinly sliced green onions

⅓ cup pitted kalamata olives, halved

¼ cup plain 2% reduced-fat Greek-style yogurt

1. Bring 1½ cups water to a boil in a large saucepan over medium-high heat. Add couscous, ¼ teaspoon salt, and pepper to pan. Cover, remove from heat, and let stand 5 minutes. Fluff with a fork.

2. Heat a large skillet over medium-high heat. Add 1 tablespoon olive oil to pan; swirl to coat. Sprinkle shrimp with remaining ⅛ teaspoon salt. Add shrimp to pan, and sauté for 3 minutes or until done. Add shrimp to couscous mixture.

3. Combine remaining 2 tablespoons oil, tomatoes, onions, and olives in a large bowl; toss. Add tomato mixture to couscous mixture; toss to combine. Serve with yogurt.

YIELD: 4 servings (serving size: 2 cups couscous mixture and 1 tablespoon yogurt).

CALORIES 487; FAT 15.3g (sat 2.4g, mono 9.5g, poly 2.3g); PROTEIN 35.3g; CARB 49.8g; FIBER 3.8g; CHOL 195mg; IRON 4mg; SODIUM 564mg; CALC 114mg

Quick Paella ▶

Yes, it's possible to riff on the flavors of Spain's most famous dish and make a delicious paella. Boil-in-bag brown rice makes a fast, nutty, and nutritious foundation.

1 tablespoon olive oil

6 ounces Spanish chorizo, thinly sliced

2 (3.5-ounce) packages boil-in-bag brown rice

⅜ teaspoon salt

½ teaspoon hot smoked paprika

¼ teaspoon freshly ground black pepper

1½ cups water

1 (14.5-ounce) can no-salt-added diced tomatoes, undrained

1½ cups frozen shelled edamame

2 dozen mussels, scrubbed and debearded

1. Heat a Dutch oven over medium-high heat. Add oil to pan; swirl to coat. Add chorizo to pan; sauté 1 minute or until lightly browned, stirring occasionally. Remove rice from bags. Add rice to pan; sauté 1 minute, stirring frequently. Stir in salt, paprika, and pepper; sauté 30 seconds. Add 1½ cups water and tomatoes; bring to a boil. Cover, reduce heat to medium, and simmer 10 minutes or until rice is tender and liquid is almost absorbed.

2. Stir in edamame. Nestle mussels into rice mixture. Cover and cook 4 minutes or until mussels open and liquid is absorbed. Remove from heat. Discard any unopened mussels.

YIELD: 4 servings (serving size: 2 cups).

CALORIES 542; FAT 21g (sat 5.1g, mono 9g, poly 4.2g); PROTEIN 33.8g; CARB 55.6g; FIBER 8.1g; CHOL 27mg; IRON 4.9mg; SODIUM 562mg; CALC 42mg

Tex-Mex Confetti Pizza

Is there anything more prosaic than frozen corn? But when it's given a zing from paprika and combined with other toppings like cherry tomatoes and black beans, all laid onto supermarket pizza dough: voilà, a crowd-pleaser.

1 cup frozen whole-kernel corn, thawed and drained

1 tablespoon olive oil

1 teaspoon hot smoked paprika

⅛ teaspoon salt

1 pint grape tomatoes, halved

1 (15-ounce) can organic black beans, rinsed and drained

1 (16-ounce) package commercial pizza dough

¾ cup (3 ounces) crumbled queso fresco

1. Place a baking sheet in oven. Preheat oven to 450°.

2. Combine first 6 ingredients; toss. Roll dough out to a 13-inch circle; crimp edges to form a ½-inch border. Remove baking sheet from oven. Transfer dough onto preheated baking sheet. Spread bean mixture evenly over dough, leaving a ½-inch border, and top with queso fresco. Bake on bottom rack of oven at 450° for 20 minutes or until browned. Cut into 10 wedges. **YIELD:** 5 servings (serving size: 2 wedges).

CALORIES 353; **FAT** 9.7g (sat 2.3g, mono 4.4g, poly 0.8g); **PROTEIN** 12.3g; **CARB** 56.7g; **FIBER** 3.9g; **CHOL** 6mg; **IRON** 3.3mg; **SODIUM** 721mg; **CALC** 73mg

Quick Black Bean and Corn Soup

Cooking spray

1 cup frozen whole-kernel corn

3 (15-ounce) cans organic black beans, rinsed, drained, and divided

1½ cups fat-free, lower-sodium chicken broth

1 (14.5-ounce) can no-salt-added diced tomatoes, undrained

1 tablespoon chile paste with garlic (such as sambal oelek)

⅜ teaspoon salt

¼ cup plain 2% reduced-fat Greek-style yogurt

1. Heat a Dutch oven over medium-high heat. Coat pan with cooking spray. Add corn to pan, and sauté 4 minutes or until lightly browned, stirring occasionally.

2. Combine 2 cans of beans and broth in a blender; process until smooth. Add bean mixture, remaining can of beans, tomatoes, chile paste, and salt to corn, stirring to combine; bring to a boil. Cover, reduce heat to medium, and simmer 15 minutes, stirring occasionally. Serve with yogurt. **YIELD:** 4 servings (serving size: about 1¼ cups soup and 1 tablespoon yogurt).

CALORIES 295; FAT 1.6g (sat 0.3g, mono 0.4g, poly 0.6g); PROTEIN 17.8g; CARB 54.8g; FIBER 12.5g; CHOL 0.8mg; IRON 3.4mg; SODIUM 650mg; CALC 97mg

Quick Crisp Ravioli with Roasted Tomato Sauce

We are suckers for a bit of pan-fried crunchy goodness, and panko plus ravioli delivers. Use your favorite ravioli—we like cheese or spinach filling. Serve with garlicky broccoli rabe or wilted greens, such as chard or kale.

2 tablespoons water

1 large egg, lightly beaten

1 cup panko (Japanese breadcrumbs)

¼ cup (1 ounce) grated fresh Parmigiano-Reggiano cheese

1 (9-ounce) package fresh ravioli

3 tablespoons olive oil, divided

4 cups grape tomatoes, halved (about 2 pints)

½ teaspoon salt

¼ teaspoon freshly ground black pepper

3 garlic cloves, coarsely chopped

1. Combine 2 tablespoons water and egg in a shallow dish, stirring well. Combine panko and cheese in a shallow dish, stirring well with a fork. Dip each ravioli in egg mixture; dredge in panko mixture.

2. Heat a large skillet over medium-high heat. Add 1½ tablespoons oil to pan; swirl to coat. Add half of ravioli to pan in a single layer; sauté 1 minute on each side or until golden. Remove ravioli from pan using a slotted spoon; drain on paper towels. Keep warm. Repeat procedure with remaining 1½ tablespoons oil and ravioli. Wipe pan with paper towels.

3. Add tomatoes, salt, and pepper to pan; sauté 2 minutes, stirring frequently. Add garlic to pan; sauté 30 seconds, stirring constantly. Divide ravioli evenly among 4 plates; top each serving with ½ cup tomato sauce. **YIELD:** 4 servings.

CALORIES 399; **FAT** 19.2g (sat 6.1g, mono 9.9g, poly 1.6g); **PROTEIN** 14.6g; **CARB** 42.4g; **FIBER** 4.1g; **CHOL** 93mg; **IRON** 1.9mg; **SODIUM** 747mg; **CALC** 159mg

savvy IN A SNAP

Know what you're getting when you buy pregrated **Parmigiano-Reggiano cheese.** Some packages are the read deal; others are full of fillers and tasteless oils.

Fire Up That Wok

STIR-FRYING IS ONE OF THE FASTEST COOKING TECHNIQUES, mostly because it's done over high heat. It's also a lot of fun. You can do some intense, fairly easy cooking in no time—and sit down to a complex, flavorful dinner. Nothing beats the fresh taste of a stir-fry, partly because you can pack so many vegetables in the wok.

In some ways, stir-frying is the heart of our quick-cooking repertoire. We can begin with all those veggies, many of which can be found already chopped or minced in the produce section of our supermarkets. We can then go heavy on those very vegetables and light on the protein. And we can build the sauces, not with hours over the heat as in a braise or stew, but instead with a judicious use of bottled condiments, from chile sauce and oyster sauce to black vinegar and Worcestershire sauce.

It's true: Stir-fries require a well-stocked pantry. But that's still part of the good news. A little investment at the grocery store will pay off in many satisfying dinners, the various bottles and jars now squirreled away for when you're ready to use them. As a bonus, we've limited those special ingredients to things you'll find in a standard, large supermarket.

So fire up that wok, and let's get cooking. Dinner can be ready in minutes once you know a few secrets and tips.

THE FUNDAMENTALS of a good *stir-fry*

Simply toss and turn bite-sized pieces of food in a little hot oil in a wok over high heat, and in five minutes or less, the work is done. Vegetables emerge crisp and bright. Meats are flavorful, tender, and well seared.

Stir-frying fits hectic lifestyles and health-conscious tastes. It works wonders with fresh ingredients such as bell peppers, zucchini, and corn—and because foods cook in a flash, vegetables retain their color and texture. It's a versatile technique you can use every day.

Origins

Stir-frying was first developed in China as a cooking method that worked well on simple brick stoves. The typical stove top had a hole over the fire chamber. A round-bottomed wok fit over the lipped hole, capturing the heat efficiently. All it took was a small, hot fire to make the wok very hot. Oil and chopped food were stirred and tossed in the pan, cooking in minutes and making efficient use of precious fuel.

What stir-frying does

The high temperature required for stir-frying sears food quickly and preserves its natural juices. It takes only minutes (two to five, usually), so vegetables stay bright and crisp, meat browned and succulent. When the heat is high and the cooking quick, the Cantonese describe the result as *wok hay*—loosely translated as "the breath of a wok." It's a difficult quality to define, but you can experience it in the first few moments after food is removed from the wok. The food tastes vibrant and fresh, characterized by concentrated, harmonious flavors with a hint of smokiness. To appreciate *wok hay*, serve food immediately.

Best bets for stir-frying

Most vegetables cut into thin, bite-sized pieces are ideal, especially those with high moisture content, such as summer squash and bell peppers. Denser vegetables like broccoli work well, too, but may need to either be blanched first or allowed to steam briefly with a little liquid after the initial stir-frying to become tender. Leafy greens such as spinach cook in seconds once they hit the hot oil.

Tender cuts of meat—such as chicken breasts, flank steak, or pork tenderloin—stir-fry beautifully when cut into thin, bite-sized strips. Avoid large or tough chunks of meat from items such as pork shoulder or beef stew meat, which require long, slow cooking to become

tender. Shrimp, scallops, and firm-fleshed fish such as halibut work well, but delicate, flaky fish such as flounder or tilapia may fall apart.

Equipment

All you need for stir-frying is a wok and a broad, curved spatula. A wok, which is shaped like a big, wide bowl with high sloping sides, is designed for stir-frying. The curve of the pan makes it easy to scrape down the sides with a spatula and toss the food without accidentally turning it out of the pan.

The best choice for the typical home cooktop is a rolled carbon steel or enamel-clad cast-iron wok, 14 inches across, with a flat bottom. Carbon steel woks often cost less than $20 at retail stores or online sources, while enamel-clad cast-iron woks are pricier at about $160 or more. (Round-bottomed woks may work on gas burners but will not sit steadily on electric ranges.) Over time and with frequent use, carbon steel and cast-iron woks darken and develop a patina that effects a natural nonstick finish (see "Caring for your Wok" on page 233). Avoid pans that come with a nonstick finish as they can't be used over high heat and the finish deters browning.

In place of a wok, a 12-inch stainless-steel sauté pan with sloped sides can be used. Choose one that conducts heat well. Because these pans don't develop a nonstick patina, they often require more oil for cooking, and food may stick more readily. With the flatter shape and shallow sides of the pan, it's also a bit harder to move the food around.

You'll also need a wide spatula. Wok spatulas, shaped like wide shovels, are slightly curved so they can easily slide down the sides of the pan. A lid is helpful for briefly steaming dense vegetables at the end of cooking.

Size wise

When stir-frying, foods must be cut into thin, bite-sized pieces so they'll cook quickly. Generally, they should be of similar shape and size. If the sizes vary widely, foods will cook unevenly.

Mise en place

Stir-frying proceeds at a fast pace and requires attention. The total cooking time may only be five or so minutes, which doesn't allow time to prepare ingredients midstream. Read the recipe through; then cut, measure, and mix ingredients, and set them near the wok. Get out the serving dish. Then turn on the heat.

Fats

Choose an oil that can take high heat. An all-purpose, neutral-flavored oil such as canola oil works well. Avoid using butter, which burns easily at high temperatures.

Temperature

Preheat the wok over high heat until it is very hot, at least two minutes. It is hot enough to cook on when you see a little smoke rise from the wok, or if you flick a drop of water into the pan and it sizzles rapidly and instantly evaporates. Add oil, and rotate the wok so oil coats the surface. The oil will become hot immediately and ripple across the surface.

Make room

Limit vegetables to about 4 to 6 cups at a time (or 8 to 10 cups for leafy greens). If you use more than one kind of vegetable, add the thickest, densest pieces first, followed by smaller, thinner pieces, so everything is done cooking at the same time.

Keep moving

Once the food is in the pan, it needs to be constantly flipped to prevent burning. Use your spatula to efficiently scoop and turn the food.

BEST PANTRY STAPLES for *Asian cooking*

For quick cooking, you'll need some Asian staples in your pantry, ready for a stir-fry or Chinese-style braise. Here's what to stock:

Asian hot red chile sauce

A bottled condiment, the often fiery sambal oelek is a Southeast Asian favorite, a blend of chiles and vinegar. Sriracha is a Thai bottling, smooth like ketchup (but much hotter). Avoid versions that include sweeteners like corn syrup.

Peanut oil

Although refined peanut oil is great for frying, unrefined peanut oil has a more pronounced taste. Store either one in the fridge after opening. If it solidifies, run warm tap water over the neck of the sealed bottle to loosen up a tablespoon or two.

Fish sauce

The primary condiment of Southeast Asia is made from fermented fish, salt, and aromatics. It's quite stinky but mellows miraculously over the heat. If you've had Thai food, you've had fish sauce. Store opened bottles in the refrigerator.

Hoisin sauce

A thick condiment made from sweet potatoes, wheat, or rice with vinegar, sweeteners, and lots of aromatics. It's the sauce spread into the pancakes for Peking duck or moo shu pork. Although its name means "seafood sauce" in Cantonese, there's no seafood in the mix.

Oyster sauce

A molasses-like condiment, once made from oysters and salt, now made from a variety of seafood and aromatics. Cheaper bottles can be loaded with MSG.

Preserved black beans

Fermented, salted, dried black beans, common in many Chinese stir-fries. Store them in a sealed bag in the pantry.

Chinese black vinegar

A low-acid vinegar made from pressed, fermented glutinous rice and flavored with star anise and other aromatics. In a pinch, substitute equal parts Worcestershire sauce and balsamic vinegar.

Rice noodles

When dried, they're available in two forms: thin and thick. Keep both on hand for more options and variety.

Shaoxing wine

A rice wine common in Chinese cooking. Do not substitute "cooking wine," which is loaded with sodium. Instead, substitute dry sherry. For a nonalcoholic substitution, use lower-sodium vegetable broth with a splash of rice vinegar.

Rice wine vinegar

Available in two forms: seasoned (that is, with sugar and often salt) and unseasoned. Unless specified, all of these recipes call for the "unseasoned" bottle. Read the labels to be sure which one you have on hand.

Sesame oil

Sold in two varieties: dark (sometimes called toasted) and untoasted. The former has a more pronounced flavor, better in small quantities. Store it in the fridge once opened.

QUICK TIP: Omit the bell pepper, mushrooms, snow peas, and carrots; use 1 (16-ounce) bag frozen mixed vegetables (preferably a bag of Asian vegetables). There's no need to thaw them; just toss them into the wok after the green onions and onion wedges, and stir-fry 3 minutes.

Chicken-Cashew Stir-Fry

We can't resist this classic dish, a take-out favorite, especially because it combines both sweet and hot Asian flavors.

½ cup fat-free, lower-sodium chicken broth

1½ tablespoons cornstarch

3 tablespoons oyster sauce

1½ tablespoons honey

1 tablespoon lower-sodium soy sauce

2 teaspoons rice vinegar or white wine vinegar

½ teaspoon salt

2 tablespoons canola oil, divided

1 cup chopped green onions, divided

1 small onion, cut into 8 wedges

1 cup (3 x ¼-inch) julienne-cut red bell pepper

½ cup diagonally cut carrot

1 cup sliced mushrooms

1 cup whole snow peas

1 pound skinless, boneless chicken thighs, cut into bite-sized pieces

⅓ cup cashews

¼ cup cubed fresh pineapple

½ to 1 teaspoon crushed red pepper

6 cups hot cooked long-grain rice

1. Combine first 7 ingredients in a small bowl; set aside.

2. Heat 1 tablespoon oil in a wok or large nonstick skillet over medium-high heat. Add ½ cup green onions and onion wedges; stir-fry 1 minute. Add bell pepper and carrot; stir-fry 2 minutes. Add mushrooms and peas; stir-fry 2 minutes. Remove vegetable mixture from pan. Keep warm.

3. Heat remaining 1 tablespoon oil in pan over medium-high heat. Add chicken; stir-fry 5 minutes. Add broth mixture, vegetable mixture, cashews, pineapple, and crushed red pepper; bring to a boil, and cook 1 minute or until thick. Stir in remaining ½ cup green onions. Serve with rice. **YIELD:** 6 servings (serving size: 1⅓ cups stir-fry and 1 cup rice).

CALORIES 442; FAT 11.8g (sat 1.9g, mono 6.1g, poly 2.8g); PROTEIN 21.8g; CARB 60.8g; FIBER 2.9g; CHOL 63mg; IRON 3.8mg; SODIUM 553mg; CALC 57mg

caring FOR YOUR WOK

Treat a carbon steel or cast-iron wok much as you would a cast-iron skillet. Coat with oil, heat before the first use (this is called seasoning the pan), and keep dry to avoid rust. You'll need to follow the manufacturer's specific instructions. To remove any residual metallic taste before cooking in a new wok, stir-fry onions in the seasoned pan until the onions are charred. Discard the onions, wash the pan, and it's ready to use.

Clean carbon steel or cast-iron woks with soapy water and a gentle scrub, if needed. Don't scrub aggressively or you may remove the patina. If food is stuck, cool the wok, soak it in water until food is loose, and then gently scrub. Rinse well, and then heat the wok over high heat until completely dry. Lightly coat pan with oil before storing if it's used infrequently or is new.

Chicken, Asparagus, and Water Chestnut Stir-Fry

This simple, Cantonese-inspired main course is stocked with vegetables for lots of crunch in every spoonful. For even more, consider serving it over brown rice—or an exotic red rice. The extra nuttiness will serve to underscore all the aromatic fare.

1 pound skinless, boneless chicken breast, cut into 1-inch cubes

1 tablespoon cornstarch

2 tablespoons fat-free, lower-sodium chicken broth

2 tablespoons Chinese black vinegar (page 231)

2 tablespoons lower-sodium soy sauce

1½ teaspoons sugar

1½ tablespoons dark sesame oil

½ cup thinly sliced green onions (about 4 large onions)

1 tablespoon minced peeled fresh ginger

Cooking spray

2 cups (1-inch) sliced asparagus

1 cup coarsely chopped red bell pepper (about 1 small)

1 (8-ounce) can sliced water chestnuts, drained

1. Combine chicken and cornstarch in a medium bowl. Combine broth and next 3 ingredients (through sugar) in a small bowl.

2. Heat a wok over medium-high heat. Add oil; quickly tilt pan in all directions so oil covers pan with a thin film. Add onions and ginger to pan; stir-fry 30 seconds. Add chicken mixture. Coat chicken mixture with cooking spray; stir-fry 2 minutes. Increase heat to high. Add asparagus, bell pepper, and water chestnuts; stir-fry 2 minutes or just until vegetables are crisp-tender. Stir in broth mixture; cook, stirring constantly, 1 minute. Serve immediately. **YIELD:** 4 servings (serving size: 1¼ cups).

CALORIES 244; **FAT** 7.3g (sat 1.2g, mono 2.6g, poly 2.7g); **PROTEIN** 29.3g; **CARB** 16.1g; **FIBER** 4.6g; **CHOL** 66mg; **IRON** 3.1mg; **SODIUM** 372mg; **CALC** 54mg

savvy IN A SNAP

To quickly **core and seed a bell pepper,** hold the pepper by the stem. Slice down around the sides, taking off large strips of the pepper, leaving the core and seeds standing at the center.

Thai-Style Stir-Fried Chicken

Curry paste and coconut milk spice up a simple chicken and vegetable stir-fry. Once the ingredients are prepped, the cooking goes quickly, so have everything ready before you heat the pan.

¼ cup rice vinegar

2 tablespoons brown sugar

2 tablespoons fresh lime juice

2 teaspoons red curry paste

⅛ teaspoon crushed red pepper

1 pound skinless, boneless chicken breast, cut into bite-sized pieces

1½ tablespoons canola oil, divided

1 cup chopped onion

1 cup chopped carrot

1 (8-ounce) package presliced mushrooms

½ cup light coconut milk

1 tablespoon fish sauce

½ teaspoon salt

1 cup fresh bean sprouts

¼ cup chopped fresh cilantro

1. Combine vinegar, sugar, juice, curry paste, and crushed red pepper in a large zip-top plastic bag. Add chicken; seal and marinate in refrigerator 15 minutes, turning once.

2. Remove chicken from bag, reserving marinade. Heat 1 tablespoon oil in a wok or large nonstick skillet over medium-high heat. Add chicken; stir-fry 4 minutes. Remove chicken from pan; keep warm. Add remaining 1½ teaspoons oil to pan. Add onion and carrot; stir-fry 2 minutes. Add mushrooms; stir-fry 3 minutes. Add reserved marinade, scraping pan to loosen browned bits. Add coconut milk and fish sauce; bring to a boil. Reduce heat, and simmer 1 minute. Stir in chicken and salt; cook 1 minute. Top with sprouts and cilantro. **YIELD:** 4 servings (serving size: 1 cup chicken mixture, ¼ cup sprouts, and 1 tablespoon cilantro).

CALORIES 271; FAT 8.4g (sat 2.2g, mono 1.6g, poly 3.4g); PROTEIN 29.7g; CARB 19.6g; FIBER 2.9g; CHOL 66mg; IRON 2.2mg; SODIUM 767mg; CALC 43mg

savvy IN A SNAP

Preminced garlic and ginger are available in the produce section of almost all supermarkets. Look for glass bottles without any noticeable browning of the garlic or ginger inside. Also, avoid bottles with added sweeteners or sugars. Once opened, store these in your fridge for up to several months.

ON THE SIDE: Because Thai stir-fries and braises are often a sweet, sour, and spicy combo, they go great with sticky rice. Try this one over brown rice.

◄ Curried Chicken and Pineapple Stir-Fry

This Thai stir-fry, laced with coconut milk, is a balance of hot and sweet in each spoonful. One warning: The curry paste can be exceptionally hot. Read the label to make sure chiles are not the first ingredient—or use less until you get the hang of cooking with the stuff.

½ cup light coconut milk

1 tablespoon fresh lime juice

1 tablespoon fish sauce

2 teaspoons dark brown sugar

1 tablespoon peanut oil

1 red onion, cut into 1-inch pieces (about 1½ cups)

1 tablespoon minced garlic

1 tablespoon minced peeled fresh ginger

¾ pound skinless, boneless chicken breast, cut into 1-inch cubes

2 teaspoons green curry paste

2 cups cubed fresh pineapple

1½ cups whole snow peas

1. Combine first 4 ingredients in a small bowl.

2. Heat a wok or large nonstick skillet over medium-high heat. Add oil. Add onion, garlic, and ginger. Stir-fry 1 minute. Add chicken; stir-fry 2 minutes.

3. Stir in curry paste; add pineapple and snow peas. Stir-fry 2 minutes. Pour in coconut milk mixture; bring to a boil, and cook 1 minute or until mixture thickens, stirring gently.

YIELD: 4 servings (serving size: 1⅓ cups).

CALORIES 233; FAT 6.5g (sat 2.3g, mono 1.8g, poly 1.4g); PROTEIN 22g; CARB 21.6g; FIBER 2.5g; CHOL 49mg; IRON 1.6mg; SODIUM 460mg; CALC 44mg

EVEN *faster*

Look for cubed fresh pineapple in the refrigerator case of your super-market. The taste is much more vibrant than that of canned chunks.

Chicken and Broccoli in Black Bean Sauce

Preserved black beans give this stir-fry an earthy, sophisticated flavor, familiar in many Chinese dishes. For even more flavor, buy a bottle of unrefined peanut oil, which will offer more peanutty taste in every drop. And one final note: The piquant chiles are not to be eaten, but serve to impart their heat to the entire dish. Discard them from each bowl—or remove them from the mixture in the kitchen if you're offering this stir-fry to children.

¼ cup fat-free, lower-sodium chicken broth

3 tablespoons chopped preserved Chinese black beans

1 tablespoon minced garlic

1 tablespoon minced peeled fresh ginger

1 tablespoon dry sherry

1 tablespoon lower-sodium soy sauce

2 teaspoons sugar

1 tablespoon peanut oil, divided

1¾ cups thinly sliced green onions (about 5 medium)

6 small dried hot red chiles

¾ pound skinless, boneless chicken breast, cut into ½-inch-thick strips

1 (24-ounce) package frozen broccoli florets (about 6 cups), thawed

1. Combine first 7 ingredients in a bowl.

2. Heat a wok or large nonstick skillet over medium-high heat. Add 1½ teaspoons oil. Add onions and chiles. Stir-fry 1 minute or until fragrant. Add remaining 1½ teaspoons oil. Add chicken; stir-fry 2 minutes. Add broccoli florets; stir-fry 2 minutes. Add broth mixture; bring to a boil, stirring constantly. Cook 1 minute or until sauce coats vegetables.

YIELD: 4 servings (serving size: 1½ cups).

CALORIES 252; FAT 6.5g (sat 0.8g, mono 1.9g, poly 2.1g); PROTEIN 25g; CARB 16g; FIBER 4.8g; CHOL 49mg; IRON 2.1mg; SODIUM 313mg; CALC 91mg

Kung Pao Shrimp

A good kung pao stir-fry doesn't need to be deep-fried. In fact, stir-frying the protein rather than deep-frying it ensures that the essential flavors come through more prominently and yields a more satisfying dinner every time.

2 teaspoons cornstarch

1 tablespoon lower-sodium soy sauce, divided

1½ teaspoons dry sherry or Shaoxing wine, divided

1 pound peeled and deveined medium shrimp

1 tablespoon peanut oil

¼ cup chopped dry-roasted peanuts

1 tablespoon minced peeled fresh ginger

1 tablespoon minced fresh garlic

½ teaspoon crushed red pepper

1½ cups thinly sliced celery

1 cup chopped red bell pepper

¼ cup fat-free, lower-sodium chicken broth

1 teaspoon rice vinegar

¼ teaspoon salt

2 tablespoons green onion strips

1. Combine cornstarch, 1 teaspoon soy sauce, 1 teaspoon sherry, and shrimp.

2. Heat oil in a wok over high heat. Add peanuts and next 3 ingredients (through crushed red pepper); stir-fry 30 seconds. Stir in celery and bell pepper; stir-fry 2 minutes or until crisp-tender. Add shrimp mixture; stir-fry 2 minutes. Add remaining 2 teaspoons soy sauce, remaining ½ teaspoon sherry, and broth. Bring to a simmer; cook 1 minute or until slightly thickened. Remove from heat; stir in vinegar and salt. Top with onions. **YIELD:** 4 servings (serving size: 1¼ cups).

CALORIES 224; **FAT** 9.1g (sat 1.5g, mono 3.6g, poly 3.1g); **PROTEIN** 25.9g; **CARB** 9.1g; **FIBER** 2.3g; **CHOL** 172mg; **IRON** 3.4mg; **SODIUM** 574mg; **CALC** 91mg

savvy IN A SNAP

If you don't want to buy a whole head of **celery** for one meal, consider buying as many stalks as you need from the salad bar at your supermarket. Ounce for ounce, they may cost a little more—but actually may not. After all, if you throw out that whole head of celery after a couple of weeks, you'll have spent more for the celery than if you'd bought individual stalks. Or go even easier, and buy sliced celery from the salad bar. One medium stalk yields about ⅓ cup thinly sliced celery.

QUICK TIP: Use frozen corn kernels. Don't thaw them; just add them to the wok and stir-fry until thoroughly heated, about 2 minutes.

◄ Sizzling Shrimp with Corn Relish

Hot and sweet—there's just hardly a better combination. Although not a traditional accompaniment, you might consider serving this stir-fry with Grilled Salad (page 88) on the side. The vinegary mix against the sweet corn will make the meal all the more satisfying.

1½ tablespoons fresh lime juice

1 tablespoon fish sauce

½ teaspoon sugar

2 tablespoons canola oil

½ cup chopped shallots

1 tablespoon minced garlic

1 tablespoon minced jalapeño pepper (about 1 small)

1½ pounds peeled and deveined medium shrimp

1½ cups fresh corn kernels (about 3 ears)

⅓ cup chopped fresh cilantro

1. Combine first 3 ingredients in a small bowl.

2. Heat a 14-inch wok over high heat. Add oil, swirling to coat pan. Add shallots, garlic, and jalapeño; stir-fry 30 seconds or just until shallots begin to brown. Add shrimp; stir-fry 3 minutes or until shrimp are done. Add corn; stir-fry 1 minute or just until corn is thoroughly heated. Stir in juice mixture; sprinkle with cilantro. **YIELD:** 4 servings (serving size: 1 cup).

CALORIES 332; FAT 11.2g (sat 1.2g, mono 4.8g, poly 3.6g); PROTEIN 37.6g; CARB 19.9g; FIBER 2.1g; CHOL 259mg; IRON 4.8mg; SODIUM 612mg; CALC 101mg

Scallops and Bok Choy Stir-Fry

This scallop stir-fry is made with a traditional Cantonese "white sauce"—that is, "white" because it includes no soy sauce.

⅓ cup fat-free, lower-sodium chicken broth

2 tablespoons dry sherry

1 tablespoon minced peeled fresh ginger

1 teaspoon cornstarch

1 teaspoon minced garlic

½ teaspoon sugar

½ teaspoon salt

½ teaspoon ground black pepper

1½ pounds sea scallops (about 12 scallops), cut in half horizontally

1 tablespoon peanut oil

7 cups coarsely chopped bok choy (1 pound)

2 cups hot cooked basmati rice

1. Combine first 8 ingredients in a small bowl.

2. Pat scallop halves dry with paper towels. Heat a wok over high heat. Add scallop halves; cook 2 minutes on each side. Remove from pan, and keep warm. Reduce heat to medium-high; add oil to pan. Cook bok choy in hot oil 4 minutes or until crisp-tender, stirring frequently. Stir in broth mixture; cook 1 minute or until sauce thickens.

3. Spoon ½ cup rice onto each of 4 serving plates. Spoon bok choy mixture evenly over rice, and top evenly with scallops. **YIELD:** 4 servings (serving size: ¾ cup bok choy mixture, ½ cup rice, and about 6 scallop halves).

CALORIES 317; FAT 5.3g (sat 0.7g, mono 1.6g, poly 1.6g); PROTEIN 32.7g; CARB 32g; FIBER 1.6g; CHOL 56mg; IRON 2.4mg; SODIUM 780mg; CALC 161mg

MORE CHOICES: Use any variety of bok choy in this dish, even baby bok choy. However, all can be quite sandy. Pull the leaves off the stem, and wash them well. Blot them dry, and chop into bite-sized pieces. Baby bok choy leaves may not need any chopping at all!

Stir-Fried Shrimp with Spicy Orange Sauce

Although full-flavored oils are usually preferred in cooking, neutral-tasting canola oil works well here, allowing the flavors of orange juice, honey, ginger, and chiles to shine.

1½ pounds peeled and deveined large shrimp

1 tablespoon cornstarch

¼ cup fresh orange juice

2 tablespoons lower-sodium soy sauce

2 tablespoons honey

1 tablespoon rice wine vinegar

1 tablespoon chile paste with garlic (such as sambal oelek)

2 tablespoons canola oil

1 tablespoon minced peeled fresh ginger

3 garlic cloves, minced

⅓ cup chopped green onions

1. Place shrimp in a medium bowl. Sprinkle with cornstarch; toss well to coat. Set aside.

2. Combine juice, soy sauce, honey, vinegar, and chile paste, stirring with a whisk.

3. Heat oil in a wok or large nonstick skillet over medium-high heat. Add ginger and garlic to pan; stir-fry 15 seconds or until fragrant. Add shrimp mixture; stir-fry 3 minutes. Add juice mixture and onions; cook 2 minutes or until sauce thickens and shrimp are done, stirring frequently. Serve immediately. **YIELD:** 4 servings (serving size: ¾ cup).

CALORIES 301; **FAT** 10g (sat 1.1g, mono 4.6g, poly 3.2g); **PROTEIN** 35.3g; **CARB** 16.8g; **FIBER** 0.5g; **CHOL** 259mg; **IRON** 4.4mg; **SODIUM** 621mg; **CALC** 103mg

QUICK TIP: If your wok doesn't have a cover, consider using the lid from a large skillet, a large baking sheet (provided the wok's handles don't lift it ajar), or even a large piece of foil sealed tightly around the wok's edges.

MORE CHOICES: Although a classic like this is often served over rice, this stir-fry would be tasty over thick udon noodles—or even Chinese egg noodles.

Thai Coconut Mussels

This wok braise is more like a spicy and aromatic soup that's ready in minutes. It all adds up to bowls of comfort for chilly weather, especially with the heat of the green curry paste—which can admittedly be quite fiery, sometimes breathlessly so. You might want to cut down on how much you use until you get the feel for it. Serve with a piece of bread to soak up the delicious broth.

1 cup light coconut milk

1 cup fat-free, lower-sodium chicken broth

¼ cup fresh lime juice

1 tablespoon peanut oil

2 cups thin vertical slices onion
  (about 1 large)

1 cup chopped red bell pepper (1 medium)

1 tablespoon packed dark brown sugar

2 tablespoons minced peeled fresh ginger

2 teaspoons minced garlic

2 teaspoons green curry paste

60 mussels (about 2¼ pounds), scrubbed
  and debearded

1. Combine first 3 ingredients in a large bowl.

2. Heat a wok or large nonstick skillet over medium-high heat. Add oil. Add onion and bell pepper; stir-fry 2 minutes or until tender. Add sugar and next 3 ingredients (through curry paste); stir-fry 1 minute. Add coconut milk mixture; cook 1 minute.

3. Add mussels; cover and cook 6 minutes or until shells open. Remove from heat; discard any unopened shells. **YIELD:** 6 servings (serving size: 10 mussels and ⅔ cup broth).

CALORIES 216; **FAT** 6.8g (sat 1.5g, mono 1.9g, poly 1.8g); **PROTEIN** 21.6g; **CARB** 15.7g; **FIBER** 1.2g; **CHOL** 48mg; **IRON** 6.9mg; **SODIUM** 617mg; **CALC** 58mg

Shrimp Pad Thai

Celery is not traditional in this Thai favorite; however, it adds a lovely crunch as well as a delicate taste that works well with the hotter, more aromatic mélange in the wok. The rice stick noodles need time to soak in very hot water; use that time to prep the other ingredients so you're ready to cook when the noodles are.

8 ounces dried rice noodles

¼ cup fat-free, lower-sodium chicken broth

1 tablespoon dark brown sugar

3 tablespoons Chinese black vinegar (page 231)

1½ tablespoons fish sauce

1 teaspoon chili garlic sauce

1½ tablespoons peanut oil

⅔ cup sliced celery

½ cup thinly sliced green onions (3 onions)

2 teaspoons minced garlic

½ pound peeled and deveined medium shrimp

2 cups fresh bean sprouts

1 tablespoon chopped unsalted, dry-roasted peanuts

1. Place noodles in a large bowl; cover with hot tap water. Let stand 20 minutes. Drain well.

2. Combine broth and next 4 ingredients (through chili garlic sauce) in a small bowl.

3. Heat a wok or large nonstick skillet over medium-high heat. Add oil. Add celery, onions, and garlic; stir-fry 30 seconds. Add shrimp; stir-fry 3 minutes or until shrimp are done.

4. Add noodles to shrimp mixture. Add broth mixture; simmer 2 minutes, stirring often. Add bean sprouts and peanuts; cook 1 minute or until liquid is nearly absorbed, stirring frequently. **YIELD:** 4 servings (serving size: 2 cups).

CALORIES 369; **FAT** 7.6g (sat 1.2g, mono 3g, poly 2.4g); **PROTEIN** 15g; **CARB** 59.3g; **FIBER** 1.9g; **CHOL** 86mg; **IRON** 3.5mg; **SODIUM** 695mg; **CALC** 74mg

Spicy Sweet-and-Sour Pork

Here's an easy dinner loaded with fresh veggies, tender pork, and bold, Asian-inspired flavor.

¼ cup slivered almonds

1 pound pork tenderloin, cut into ¾-inch cubes

2 tablespoons cornstarch, divided

3 tablespoons lower-sodium soy sauce, divided

1 (8-ounce) can pineapple chunks in juice, undrained

¼ cup cider vinegar

¼ cup sugar

2 tablespoons ketchup

2 teaspoons Sriracha (hot chile sauce)

1 tablespoon canola oil

1 cup prechopped onion

1 teaspoon bottled minced ginger

½ teaspoon bottled minced garlic

1 cup chopped green bell pepper

¼ cup sliced green onions

1. Preheat oven to 400°.

2. Place almonds on a baking sheet; bake at 400° for 4 minutes or until toasted. Set aside.

3. Combine pork, 1 tablespoon cornstarch, and 1 tablespoon soy sauce; toss well to coat. Drain pineapple in a sieve over a bowl, reserving juice. Combine juice, remaining 1 tablespoon cornstarch, remaining 2 tablespoons soy sauce, vinegar, and next 3 ingredients (through Sriracha), stirring with a whisk.

4. Heat a wok or large nonstick skillet over medium-high heat. Add oil to pan; swirl to coat. Add pork to pan; cook 3 minutes, stirring frequently. Add onion, ginger, and garlic; sauté 1 minute. Stir in pineapple and bell pepper; cook 3 minutes, stirring frequently. Stir in vinegar mixture; bring to a boil. Cook 1 minute, stirring constantly. Sprinkle with almonds and green onions. **YIELD:** 4 servings (serving size: about 1½ cups).

CALORIES 335; FAT 9.4g (sat 1.4g, mono 6g, poly 2.3g); PROTEIN 27g; CARB 35.9g; FIBER 3g; CHOL 74mg; IRON 2.5mg; SODIUM 586mg; CALC 54mg

QUICK TIP: You don't need to cook rice to go along with a stir-fry. Stop at a Chinese restaurant on your way home, and buy a container or two, just as much as you need.

ON THE SIDE: Serve this aromatic favorite over coconut rice. Combine 1 cup uncooked basmati rice, 1¼ cups water, and ½ cup light coconut milk in a small saucepan; bring to a boil. Cover, reduce heat, and simmer 16 minutes or until liquid is absorbed.

CALORIES 184; **FAT** 3g (sat 2.7g); **SODIUM** 3.3mg

QUICK TIP: Look for bell pepper strips on the salad bar at your supermarket. Or look for bags of the strips in the freezer section. They may not be the "right" color, but they'll make your cooking a snap.

◄ Szechuan Pork

For the best taste, use natural-style, no-sugar-added peanut butter, a savory flavor against the fiery mix. If peanut allergies are a problem, use cashew butter or tahini.

6 ounces soba (buckwheat noodles), uncooked

2 teaspoons dark sesame oil

1 (1-pound) pork tenderloin, trimmed and cut into 2-inch strips

1 tablespoon chili garlic sauce

1 teaspoon bottled ground fresh ginger

¾ cup red bell pepper strips (about 1 small pepper)

¼ cup fat-free, lower-sodium chicken broth

1½ tablespoons lower-sodium soy sauce

1 tablespoon peanut butter

¾ cup (2-inch) diagonally cut green onions (about 4 green onions)

1. Cook noodles according to package directions, omitting salt and fat. Drain and rinse with cold water; drain.

2. Heat oil in a wok or large nonstick skillet over medium-high heat. Add pork, chili garlic sauce, and ginger to pan; stir-fry 2 minutes. Add bell pepper to pan; stir-fry 2 minutes. Add broth, soy sauce, and peanut butter to pan. Reduce heat to low; cook 1 minute or until sauce is slightly thick. Stir in onions. Serve over noodles. **YIELD:** 4 servings (serving size: 1 cup pork mixture and ½ cup noodles).

CALORIES 338; **FAT** 8.6g (sat 2.2g, mono 3.5g, poly 1.9g); **PROTEIN** 30.4g; **CARB** 36.8g; **FIBER** 1.7g; **CHOL** 63mg; **IRON** 2.9mg; **SODIUM** 693mg; **CALC** 40mg

Pork Chop Suey

This chop suey recipe is a quick and easy stir-fry that can be on the table in no time. You can substitute your favorite choice of meat for the pork or add different vegetables to make it your own.

1 (1-pound) pork tenderloin

1.1 ounces all-purpose flour (about ¼ cup)

2 tablespoons canola oil, divided

2 cups thinly sliced bok choy

1 cup sliced celery

1 cup red bell pepper strips

1 cup sliced mushrooms

1 (8-ounce) can sliced water chestnuts, drained

2 garlic cloves, minced

¼ cup fat-free, lower-sodium chicken broth

¼ cup lower-sodium soy sauce

1 tablespoon cornstarch

1 tablespoon dry sherry

½ teaspoon ground ginger

2 cups hot cooked long-grain rice

¼ cup sliced green onions

1. Trim fat from pork; cut pork into 1-inch pieces. Weigh or lightly spoon flour into a dry measuring cup; level with a knife. Combine flour and pork in a zip-top plastic bag; seal and shake well.

2. Heat 1 tablespoon oil in a wok or large nonstick skillet over medium-high heat. Add pork mixture; cook 3 minutes or until browned. Remove from pan; keep warm.

3. Add remaining 1 tablespoon oil to pan. Add bok choy and next 5 ingredients (through garlic); stir-fry 3 minutes. Combine broth, soy sauce, cornstarch, sherry, and ginger; stir well with a whisk. Add pork and broth mixture to pan; cook 1 minute or until thick. Serve over rice; sprinkle with onions. **YIELD:** 4 servings (serving size: 1½ cups chop suey, ½ cup rice, and 1 tablespoon onions).

CALORIES 382; **FAT** 10.1g (sat 1.4g, mono 5.4g, poly 2.6g); **PROTEIN** 29.5g; **CARB** 41g; **FIBER** 3.9g; **CHOL** 74mg; **IRON** 3.2mg; **SODIUM** 570mg; **CALC** 65mg

Sour Beans and Minced Pork

This spicy Szechuan dish is hot but also sweet and sour, thanks to the sweet green beans boiled in low-acid rice wine vinegar. The dish is best served over white rice, particularly a medium- or short-grain sticky rice. Make sure you use standard rice wine vinegar in the dish, not the sweetened variety, often called "seasoned rice vinegar." If you can find them, use Chinese long beans for more savory and authentic flair.

3 cups rice wine vinegar

1 pound green beans, cut into ¼-inch pieces

1½ tablespoons peanut oil

2 tablespoons minced peeled fresh ginger

1 tablespoon minced garlic

1½ teaspoons crushed red pepper

1 pound lean ground pork

¼ cup lower-sodium soy sauce

1. Bring vinegar to a boil in a large saucepan over high heat. Add beans; cook until crisp-tender, about 2 minutes. Drain, but do not rinse.

2. Heat a wok or large nonstick skillet over medium-high heat. Add oil and next 3 ingredients (through crushed red pepper). Stir-fry 30 seconds. Add pork, stirring to crumble; stir-fry until pork begins to brown, about 4 minutes. Add beans; stir-fry 1 minute. Add soy sauce; stir-fry until pork is browned, about 1 minute. **YIELD:** 4 servings (serving size: 1¼ cups).

CALORIES 279; **FAT** 15.7g (sat 4.9g, mono 6.8g, poly 3.2g); **PROTEIN** 24.6g; **CARB** 9.8g; **FIBER** 4.5g; **CHOL** 85mg; **IRON** 1mg; **SODIUM** 603mg; **CALC** 59mg

savvy IN A SNAP

Want cooked rice without any fuss? Consider buying a **rice cooker.** Dump in the rice, add water as indicated in the instructions, close the lid, and the machine does the rest. It may take a little longer to make rice in a rice cooker, but the results are often worth the extra minutes. The best rice cookers have "fuzzy logic," a computer chip that monitors humidity and other factors to make perfect rice every time.

Beef and Rice Noodle Stir-Fry

Don't cheat and skip soaking those rice noodles: They have to soften before they're added to the wok or skillet to make a successful stir-fry.

8 ounces uncooked thick rice noodles

½ cup fat-free, lower-sodium chicken broth

2 tablespoons oyster sauce

1 tablespoon hoisin sauce

½ teaspoon five-spice powder

1½ teaspoons dark sesame oil

1 tablespoon lower-sodium soy sauce

1 tablespoon seasoned rice vinegar

1 pound sirloin steak, cut into thin strips

1 tablespoon canola oil

6 green onions, cut into 1-inch pieces

1 tablespoon minced peeled fresh ginger

2 teaspoons minced garlic

1 cup thin green bell pepper strips (1 medium)

1. Soak rice noodles according to package directions; drain.

2. Combine broth and next 4 ingredients (through sesame oil) in a small bowl. Combine soy sauce and vinegar in a medium bowl. Add steak to soy sauce mixture; toss to coat.

3. Heat a wok or large nonstick skillet over medium-high heat. Add canola oil. Add beef mixture; stir-fry 2 minutes. Remove beef from pan. Add onions, ginger, and garlic; stir-fry 1 minute. Add bell pepper, and stir-fry 1 minute. Add noodles, broth mixture, and beef. Cook 2 minutes, tossing constantly. **YIELD:** 4 servings (serving size: 1¼ cups).

CALORIES 453; **FAT** 13.8g (sat 2.7g, mono 6.3g, poly 3.5g); **PROTEIN** 24g; **CARB** 56.8g; **FIBER** 1.6g; **CHOL** 42mg; **IRON** 3.4mg; **SODIUM** 646mg; **CALC** 56mg

Hunan Lamb

Although Hunan food can be an excuse for a hot-as-you-can-stand-it nightmare, the stir-fries from that region are actually quite aromatic and full-flavored, not just a mishmash of chile oils. You don't eat the dried chiles in this dish; they merely flavor it and should be discarded from each bowl—or before serving, if there are children at the table. Make sure you have some white rice on the side to cool things down.

¼ cup fat-free, lower-sodium chicken broth, divided

2 teaspoons cornstarch

¼ cup lower-sodium soy sauce

2 tablespoons rice vinegar

2 teaspoons sugar

2 teaspoons chile paste with garlic (such as sambal oelek)

1 tablespoon peanut oil

3 tablespoons minced peeled fresh ginger

6 dried Thai chiles

4 garlic cloves, slivered

1 pound boneless leg of lamb, cut into thin strips

2 cups sliced shiitake mushroom caps

2 cups thinly sliced red bell pepper (2 medium)

1. Combine 1 tablespoon chicken broth and cornstarch in a small bowl, stirring with a whisk. Combine remaining 3 tablespoons chicken broth, soy sauce, and next 3 ingredients (through chile paste) in another bowl.

2. Heat a wok or large nonstick skillet over medium-high heat. Add oil. Add ginger, chiles, and garlic. Stir-fry 30 seconds or until fragrant.

3. Add lamb; stir-fry 3 minutes. Add mushrooms and bell pepper; stir-fry 2 minutes or until crisp-tender. Stir in soy sauce mixture. Bring to a simmer; cook 1 minute. Stir cornstarch mixture with whisk; add to lamb mixture. Cook, stirring constantly, 30 seconds or until thick. **YIELD:** 4 servings (serving size: 1¼ cups).

CALORIES 257; FAT 8.9g (sat 2.4g, mono 3.6g, poly 1.7g); PROTEIN 28.3g; CARB 14.8g; FIBER 2.8g; CHOL 72mg; IRON 2.9mg; SODIUM 702mg; CALC 31mg

QUICK TIP: There's no need to slice the lamb yourself. Buy a piece of boneless leg meat or even a lamb loin, and ask the butcher at your supermarket to prep it for you. Or see if the meat case has any "lamb for stir-fry" prepackaged and ready to go. You can also do this with beef.

Sesame Beef and Asian Vegetable Stir-Fry

Black vinegar will give this traditional stir-fry a deeper, more complex taste; rice vinegar, a brighter, fresher flavor, is ideal for spring and summer.

¼ cup lower-sodium soy sauce, divided

¼ cup Chinese black vinegar (page 231) or rice vinegar, divided

4 teaspoons dark sesame oil

½ teaspoon five-spice powder

¾ pound top round, cut into ¼-inch strips

⅓ cup water

1 teaspoon cornstarch

2 teaspoons peanut oil, divided

3 tablespoons sesame seeds, toasted and divided

1 tablespoon minced peeled fresh ginger

2 garlic cloves, minced

2 cups red bell pepper strips

1½ cups frozen shelled edamame (green soybeans), thawed

1 cup sliced shiitake mushroom caps

1 (15-ounce) can whole baby corn, drained

½ cup diagonally cut green onions

3 cups cooked jasmine rice

1. Combine 2 tablespoons soy sauce, 2 tablespoons vinegar, sesame oil, and five-spice powder in a medium bowl, stirring with a whisk. Add beef; toss to coat. Let stand 10 minutes. Remove beef from bowl; discard marinade.

2. Combine remaining 2 tablespoons soy sauce, remaining 2 tablespoons vinegar, ⅓ cup water, and cornstarch, stirring with a whisk.

3. Heat 1 teaspoon peanut oil in a wok or large nonstick skillet over medium-high heat. Add beef; stir-fry 1 minute. Remove beef from pan. Add remaining 1 teaspoon peanut oil, 2 tablespoons sesame seeds, ginger, and garlic to pan; stir-fry 30 seconds. Add bell pepper, edamame, mushrooms, and corn; stir-fry 2 minutes. Add beef and cornstarch mixture; stir-fry 3 minutes or until sauce thickens. Remove from heat; stir in remaining 1 tablespoon sesame seeds and onions. Serve over rice. **YIELD:** 6 servings (serving size: 1 cup stir-fry and ½ cup rice).

CALORIES 434; **FAT** 14.4g (sat 3.3g, mono 4.8g, poly 3.5g); **PROTEIN** 21.7g; **CARB** 55.9g; **FIBER** 6.3g; **CHOL** 36mg; **IRON** 3.7mg; **SODIUM** 318mg; **CALC** 62mg

savvy IN A SNAP

Five-spice powder is a ground spice mix said to incorporate the five basic flavors of Chinese cooking (sour, sweet, bitter, savory, and salty). What's in any given bottle can vary widely, but look for cinnamon or cassia, star anise, and cloves on the label.

Spicy Beef and Bell Pepper Stir-Fry

This one's about as classic as it gets. The flavors are built through bottled condiments, so it's not much more trouble than dipping them out and tossing them in the wok. Try this dish over medium-grain brown rice, such as brown Arborio.

1 tablespoon canola oil

12 ounces flank steak, cut diagonally across grain into thin slices

1 red bell pepper, cut into thin strips

1 yellow bell pepper, cut into thin strips

3 tablespoons lower-sodium soy sauce

1½ tablespoons rice wine vinegar

1 tablespoon minced peeled fresh ginger

2 teaspoons chili garlic sauce

4 green onions, cut into 2-inch pieces

2 teaspoons toasted sesame seeds

1. Heat a wok or large nonstick skillet over medium-high heat. Add oil to pan; swirl to coat. Add steak to pan; cook 2 minutes, searing on 1 side. Add bell peppers; cook 2 minutes or until beef loses its pink color, stirring constantly. Remove beef mixture from pan.

2. Add soy sauce, vinegar, ginger, and chili garlic sauce to pan; bring to a boil. Cook 1 minute or until slightly thick. Add beef mixture and onions to pan; toss well to coat. Sprinkle with sesame seeds. **YIELD:** 4 servings (serving size: 1 cup).

CALORIES 216; **FAT** 11.5g (sat 3.1g, mono 5.4g, poly 1.8g); **PROTEIN** 20.8g; **CARB** 7.7g; **FIBER** 2.2g; **CHOL** 35mg; **IRON** 2.9mg; **SODIUM** 624mg; **CALC** 54mg

savvy IN A SNAP

Buy **toasted sesame seeds** in bulk, and store them in the freezer, where they'll stay fresh for up to 1 year.

Chicken-Peanut Chow Mein

Chow mein noodles are often labeled chucka soba. If you can't find them in the Asian section of the supermarket, substitute spaghetti or linguine. Chop and measure ingredients while you wait for the water to boil.

1 cup precut matchstick-cut carrots

1 cup snow peas, trimmed

2 (6-ounce) packages chow mein noodles

1 tablespoon dark sesame oil, divided

½ pound skinless, boneless chicken breast

3 tablespoons lower-sodium soy sauce, divided

¾ cup fat-free, lower-sodium chicken broth

2 tablespoons oyster sauce

1 teaspoon sugar

¼ teaspoon crushed red pepper

1 cup presliced mushrooms

2 teaspoons bottled ground fresh ginger

1 cup thinly sliced green onions

2 tablespoons dry-roasted peanuts, coarsely chopped

1. Cook carrots, snow peas, and noodles in boiling water 3 minutes; drain.

2. Heat 2 teaspoons oil in a wok or large nonstick skillet over medium-high heat. Cut chicken crosswise into thin strips. Add chicken and 1 tablespoon soy sauce to pan; stir-fry 3 minutes. Remove chicken from pan; keep warm.

3. Combine remaining 2 tablespoons soy sauce, broth, oyster sauce, sugar, and pepper, stirring well. Heat remaining 1 teaspoon oil over medium-high heat. Add mushrooms and ginger to pan; stir-fry 3 minutes. Add broth mixture, and cook 1 minute. Add noodle mixture and chicken to pan; cook 1 minute, tossing to combine. Sprinkle with onions and peanuts. **YIELD:** 4 servings (serving size: 1½ cups noodle mixture, ¼ cup onions, and 1½ teaspoons peanuts).

CALORIES 471; FAT 8.7g (sat 1.4g, mono 3g, poly 2.6g); PROTEIN 27.8g; CARB 72.6g; FIBER 2.7g; CHOL 33mg; IRON 2.2mg; SODIUM 807mg; CALC 43mg

Red Cooking Tofu

Here's a classic: a vegetarian braise from the wok that's both sophisticated and satisfying, particularly on a fall evening. The dish originally got its name because high-quality soy sauce takes on a reddish hue as it simmers a long time over the heat. However, because tofu cooks so quickly, you'll probably never see that color change—although you'll still enjoy all the traditional flavors of the dish!

1½ cups organic vegetable broth

¼ cup dry sherry

2 tablespoons lower-sodium soy sauce

1½ teaspoons sugar

2 teaspoons chile paste with garlic (such as sambal oelek)

1 tablespoon rice vinegar

2 teaspoons cornstarch

1 pound firm tofu, drained and cut into 1-inch cubes

1 (3.5-ounce) package shiitake mushrooms

1½ tablespoons peanut oil

¾ cup minced green onions (about 4 medium)

½ cup shredded carrot

1 tablespoon bottled minced garlic

1 tablespoon minced peeled fresh ginger

2 cups cooked brown rice

1. Combine first 5 ingredients in a 2-cup glass measure, stirring with a whisk. Combine vinegar and cornstarch in a small bowl, stirring with a whisk. Press tofu cubes gently between several layers of paper towels to remove excess moisture. Remove stems from mushrooms; slice mushroom caps to measure 2 cups.

2. Heat a wok over medium-high heat. Add oil. Add onions and next 3 ingredients (through ginger). Stir-fry 1 minute. Add broth mixture. Bring to a simmer; cover and reduce heat to medium. Cook 5 minutes. Add tofu and mushrooms; cover and simmer 5 minutes.

3. Increase heat to high. Stir cornstarch mixture with a whisk; stir into tofu mixture. Cook, gently stirring constantly, 1 minute or until mixture thickens. Serve over rice.

YIELD: 4 servings (serving size: 1 cup tofu mixture and ½ cup rice).

CALORIES 322; **FAT** 12.2g (sat 1.8g, mono 4.3g, poly 4.5g); **PROTEIN** 14.2g; **CARB** 37.1g; **FIBER** 3.4g; **CHOL** 0mg; **IRON** 2.5mg; **SODIUM** 737mg; **CALC** 244mg

ON THE SIDE: Although this quick braise seems to call out for rice, you could also serve it over a bed of steamed bok choy.

Singapore Mai Fun

Long popular on take-out menus, this curried noodle dish is a sure hit and ready in a snap. The leftovers are terrific cold—especially for breakfast!

1 (6-ounce) package thin rice noodles (py mai fun)

½ cup fat-free, lower-sodium chicken broth

3 tablespoons lower-sodium soy sauce

1 teaspoon sugar

½ teaspoon salt

Cooking spray

1 tablespoon peanut oil, divided

1 large egg, lightly beaten

½ cup red bell pepper strips

1 tablespoon grated peeled fresh ginger

¼ teaspoon crushed red pepper

3 garlic cloves, minced

8 ounces skinless, boneless chicken breast, thinly sliced

1 tablespoon curry powder

8 ounces medium shrimp, peeled and deveined

1 cup (1-inch) sliced green onions

1. Cook rice noodles according to package directions, omitting salt and fat. Drain.

2. Combine broth, soy sauce, sugar, and salt; stir until sugar dissolves.

3. Heat a wok or large nonstick skillet over medium-high heat; coat pan with cooking spray. Add 1 teaspoon oil. Add egg; stir-fry 30 seconds or until soft-scrambled, stirring constantly. Remove from pan.

4. Wipe pan clean with a paper towel. Heat remaining 2 teaspoons oil in pan over medium-high heat. Add bell pepper strips, ginger, crushed red pepper, and garlic; stir-fry 15 seconds. Add chicken, and stir-fry 2 minutes. Add curry powder and shrimp, and stir-fry 2 minutes. Stir in noodles, broth mixture, and egg; cook 1 minute or until thoroughly heated. Sprinkle with onions. **YIELD:** 6 servings (serving size: 1 cup).

CALORIES 237; **FAT** 4.6g (sat 1g, mono 1.7g, poly 1.3g); **PROTEIN** 19.7g; **CARB** 27.8g; **FIBER** 1.3g; **CHOL** 115mg; **IRON** 2.2mg; **SODIUM** 646mg; **CALC** 53mg

MORE CHOICES: You don't have to use both chicken and shrimp in this dish. Substitute 8 ounces broccoli florets or thinly sliced asparagus spears for either one.

Ants Climbing a Tree

A funny recipe title, for sure—but a very traditional dish. It's so named because the noodles look like the tangled limbs of a tree, and the ground pork bits like little ants all over them. The dish is supposed to be quite hot, an incendiary dish with the sweet noodles to knock the edge off some of the burn. If you want it even hotter, add a little more chile paste—or pass the jar at the table for those who want to take it way over the top.

6 ounces uncooked bean threads (cellophane noodles)

8 ounces lean ground pork

½ teaspoon dark sesame oil

1½ tablespoons lower-sodium soy sauce, divided

1½ tablespoons dry sherry, divided

1 cup fat-free, lower-sodium chicken broth

1 teaspoon chile paste with garlic (such as sambal oelek)

½ teaspoon sugar

1 tablespoon peanut oil

1 cup thinly sliced green onions (about 4 medium)

1 tablespoon minced peeled fresh ginger

2 teaspoons minced garlic

½ cup chopped fresh cilantro

4 lime wedges

1. Combine noodles and hot water to cover in a large bowl; let stand 10 minutes. Drain.

2. Combine ground pork, sesame oil, ½ teaspoon soy sauce, and ½ teaspoon sherry in another large bowl. Combine remaining 4 teaspoons soy sauce, remaining 4 teaspoons sherry, broth, chile paste, and sugar in a small bowl.

3. Heat a wok or large nonstick skillet over medium-high heat. Add peanut oil. Add onions, ginger, and garlic; stir-fry 30 seconds or until fragrant.

4. Add pork mixture; stir-fry 2 to 3 minutes or until pork is no longer pink. Stir in broth mixture; bring to a boil, stirring occasionally.

5. Add noodles. Toss 3 minutes or until liquid is absorbed. Top each serving with 2 tablespoons cilantro, and serve with lime wedges. **YIELD:** 4 servings (serving size: 1¼ cups noodle mixture, 2 tablespoons cilantro, and 1 lime wedge).

CALORIES 307; **FAT** 9.3g (sat 2.7g, mono 1.8g, poly 1.4g); **PROTEIN** 12.6g; **CARB** 42g; **FIBER** 1g; **CHOL** 43mg; **IRON** 1.8mg; **SODIUM** 475mg; **CALC** 31mg

MORE CHOICES: Substitute ground turkey or ground chicken for the ground pork, if desired.

Stir-Fried Tofu, Shiitake Mushrooms, and Chinese Peas

Here, fresh ginger is combined with salt; the mixture then sits for five minutes as the salt draws out some of the ginger juice, making the ginger drier—and better for stir-frying.

1 tablespoon julienne-cut peeled fresh
   ginger

½ teaspoon kosher or coarse sea salt

1 teaspoon cornstarch

1 tablespoon canola oil

2 cups thinly sliced shiitake mushroom caps

1 cup snow peas, trimmed

½ teaspoon minced bird chile or 1 teaspoon
   minced serrano chile

1 (12.3-ounce) package reduced-fat firm
   tofu, drained and cubed

½ cup (1-inch) sliced green onions

3 tablespoons lower-sodium soy sauce

1. Combine ginger and salt in a small bowl; let stand 5 minutes. Rinse ginger with cold water; pat dry. Combine ginger and cornstarch in bowl.

2. Heat oil in a wok or large nonstick skillet over medium-high heat. Add mushrooms, and stir-fry 2 minutes or until tender. Add ginger mixture, snow peas, and chile, and stir-fry 2 minutes. Add tofu; stir-fry 1 minute. Add onions and soy sauce; stir-fry 2 minutes. **YIELD:** 2 servings (serving size: 1¾ cups).

CALORIES 270; **FAT** 13.9g (sat 0.6g, mono 4.4g, poly 2.1g); **PROTEIN** 21g; **CARB** 16.5g; **FIBER** 3.6g; **CHOL** 0mg; **IRON** 3.9mg; **SODIUM** 728mg; **CALC** 105mg

Mao Pao Tofu

This classic is often ridiculously hot—a bowl of fire. We've cut down the heat a bit, but you can add it back by stirring in up to 8 dried, thin, long Asian chiles with the tofu. These are not to be eaten; they spice the dish as they soften over the heat but should be removed just before serving or at the table. For an even more authentic taste, add 1 teaspoon Szechuan peppercorns with the chile paste.

1 (3½-ounce) bag boil-in-bag rice

2 tablespoons lower-sodium soy sauce, divided

2 tablespoons dry sherry or Shaoxing wine, divided

½ pound lean ground pork

1 tablespoon peanut oil

1 (14-ounce) package extra-firm tofu, drained and cubed

3 tablespoons chopped green onions

1 tablespoon minced peeled fresh ginger

1 tablespoon chile paste with garlic (such as sambal oelek)

2 teaspoons minced garlic

¼ teaspoon salt

1 cup fat-free, lower-sodium chicken broth

2 teaspoons cornstarch

1 tablespoon water

1. Cook rice according to package directions.

2. Combine 1 tablespoon soy sauce, 1 tablespoon sherry, and pork; set aside.

3. Heat oil in a wok over high heat. Add tofu; stir-fry 3 minutes. Add pork mixture; stir-fry 3 minutes. Stir in onions and next 4 ingredients (through salt); stir-fry 30 seconds. Add remaining 1 tablespoon soy sauce, remaining 1 tablespoon sherry, and broth; cook 2 minutes. Combine cornstarch and water; stir with a whisk. Add to wok; cook 30 seconds or until slightly thick, stirring constantly. Serve over rice. **YIELD:** 4 servings (serving size: 1¼ cups tofu mixture and ½ cup rice).

CALORIES 342; FAT 14.3g (sat 3.8g, mono 2.7g, poly 4.6g); PROTEIN 23.3g; CARB 27.8g; FIBER 0.3g; CHOL 43mg; IRON 2.3mg; SODIUM 562mg; CALC 78mg

savvy IN A SNAP

Tofu is a bean curd made from soy milk. There's a bewildering array of tofu options available in supermarkets these days. In general, you'll find it three ways: firm, soft, and dried. Firm tofu, pressed into shape, holds its shape and can be eaten with chopsticks. Soft tofu is prized for its creamy texture and most often eaten with a spoon. Dried tofu has a cheesy, musky flavor. "Silken" tofu is less spongy, smoother, not grainy at all. It can be found in firm or extra-firm packages.

FAST & FANCY

Cooking for Company

DINNER PARTIES OFTEN GET LOST IN THE SHUFFLE of kids and soccer matches, long days at work, and late nights in front of the computer.

Too bad, because dinner parties are one of the times we get to be the most creative in the kitchen. And creativity is one of the prime ways to fight back against the day-in-day-out lives most of us lead.

What's more, stretching our cooking skills is a wonderful thing. People look forward to doing it at Thanksgiving. And everyone else sure looks forward to what's going to appear on the table! A dinner party's the same thing—but without the family angst.

But cooking for company doesn't mean the food has

to take all day to prepare. You can be a quick cook even when the fare is more formal and plated, when you plan to sit down in the dining room.

Because that's really the point, right? To share a meal with friends and family? Sure, you want the food to be spot-on, but nothing spoils the

ambience like an exhausted host or hostess. The meal is a time for everyone to sit back and relax. This means you, too.

So here are some elegant dishes that will still fit into your quick-cooking plan.

SUCCESSFUL *sautéing*

Use this quick and easy technique with tender produce to create speedy meals.

Sautéing is a basic cooking technique essential to many recipes. Soups and stews, for example, almost always begin with sautéed aromatics; sautéing browns the vegetables, which enhances the flavor of the soup. But it's also used to fully cook whole dishes—and do so quickly. Sautéed chicken breasts with a simple pan sauce, for example, may be ready in as few as 20 minutes, which is helpful on busy weeknights.

Because it cooks food fast, sautéing keeps the flavors vivid. This is especially welcome with ingredients such as tender asparagus. Just as hearty root vegetables benefit from long, slow braising, the delicate produce of spring prefers a light touch. With a few tips, this technique is easy to master.

Sautéing, defined

To sauté is to cook food quickly in a minimal amount of fat over relatively high heat. The word comes from the French verb *sauter*, which means "to jump," and describes not only how food reacts when placed in a hot pan but also the method of tossing the food in the pan. The term also refers to cooking tender cuts of meat (such as chicken breasts, scaloppine, or filet mignon) in a small amount of fat over moderately high heat without frequent stirring—just flipping it over when one side is browned.

What sautéing does

The browning achieved by sautéing lends richness to meats and produce. And because the food is cooked quickly, the integrity of the flavor and texture remains intact; asparagus, for example, retains its slightly grassy punch, as well as a pleasing crisp-tender bite.

Equipment

Use either a skillet (a wide pan with sloped sides) or sauté pan (a wide pan with straight sides) for this technique. Both have a large surface area so food is less likely to become overcrowded. Choose a pan with a dense bottom that evenly distributes heat. Nonstick, anodized aluminum, and stainless steel options all work well.

Best foods to sauté

Whether it's meat or vegetables, time in the pan is brief, so it's important that the food be naturally tender. Cuts such as beef tenderloin, fish fillets, and chicken breasts are good candidates; tougher cuts like brisket or pork shoulder are better for long cooking over low heat. The same principle holds for produce. Asparagus tips will be more successfully sautéed than beets. Many other tender vegetables, including baby artichokes, sugar snap peas, mushrooms, and bell peppers, lend themselves to this technique. That's not to say that denser, tougher vegetables can't be sautéed—they just may need to be blanched first (briefly cooked in boiling water) to get a head start on cooking.

Size matters

Cutting food to a uniform thickness and size ensures that it will cook evenly. Vegetables should be no larger than bite-sized, meat no larger than portion-sized. Meat that is too thick or vegetables that are too large run the risk of burning or forming a tough, overly browned outer crust in the time that it takes to completely cook them. Have the ingredients prepped before heating the pan.

Heat the pan

Be sure to warm the pan over medium-high heat for a few minutes. It needs to be quite hot in order to cook the food properly. If the heat is too low, the food will end up releasing liquid and steaming rather than sautéing.

Add fat

Fats such as butter, oil, or bacon drippings are used to coat the food to prevent it from sticking to the pan, aid in browning, and add flavor. Once the pan is hot, add the fat, and swirl to coat the bottom of the pan. (Heating the fat when you first heat the pan may cause food to stick.) Heat the fat for 10 to 30 seconds—until oil shimmers

or butter's foam subsides—and then add the food.

In general, use fats that have a high smoke point—peanut oil, regular olive oil, canola oil, or rendered pork fat. Once the fat begins to smoke, the flavor changes and can affect the food's taste. Butter adds great flavor, but it may burn, so you will either need to clarify it to remove the milk solids (which are prone to burning) or combine it with oil so there's less chance of burning. Oils that have low smoke points, like extra-virgin olive oil and many nut and infused oils, lose their characteristic taste when heated to high temperatures for sautéing. It's OK to sauté with these oils—just remember that their flavor will not be as pungent.

Don't overcrowd

It's crucial that only one layer of food cooks in the pan at a time. When sautéing cuts of meat, there should be at least a half-inch between each piece. Food releases steam as it cooks. If that steam doesn't have enough room to escape, it stays in the pan, and the food ends up steaming rather than sautéing and won't brown. If you've ever tried to

sauté a large amount of cubed beef for a stew, you may have experienced this problem. The solution is simply to sauté the food in smaller batches.

Toss and turn

When sautéing tender vegetables and bite-sized pieces of meat, stir frequently (but not constantly) to promote even browning and cooking. Dense vegetables such as cubed potatoes, though, should be stirred once every few minutes so that they don't fall apart as they grow tender. Portion-sized cuts of meat (chicken breasts, steaks, or pork medallions, for example) should be turned only once so they have enough time to form a nice crust, which will also keep the meat from sticking to the pan.

Stir-fry vs. sauté

Stir-frying and sautéing are techniques that share some similarities. Both methods cook food quickly in a small amount of fat. But stir-frying cooks food over intensely high heat, stirring constantly. Sautéing involves moderately high heat, and the food is not in continuous motion.

Grilled Halibut with Lemon-Caper Vinaigrette

Halibut is a light-textured white fish, a great foil to this simple vinaigrette, which masquerades as a sauce—and can be used on just about any grilled fish.

Vinaigrette:

1½ tablespoons fresh lemon juice

1 tablespoon extra-virgin olive oil

1½ teaspoons finely chopped shallots

1 teaspoon chopped capers

¼ teaspoon kosher salt

¼ teaspoon freshly ground black pepper

Fish:

Cooking spray

4 (6-ounce) halibut fillets

½ teaspoon kosher salt

2 tablespoons chopped fresh chives

Lemon wedge (optional)

1. To prepare vinaigrette, combine first 6 ingredients in a small bowl; stir with a whisk.

2. To prepare fish, heat a nonstick grill pan over medium-high heat. Coat pan with cooking spray. Sprinkle fish with ½ teaspoon salt. Add fish to pan; grill 4 minutes on each side or until desired degree of doneness. Spoon vinaigrette over fish. Sprinkle with chives. Garnish with lemon, if desired. **YIELD:** 4 servings (serving size: 1 fillet, about 2 teaspoons vinaigrette, and 1½ teaspoons chives).

CALORIES 221; **FAT** 7.4g (sat 1.1g, mono 4g, poly 1.6g); **PROTEIN** 35.6g; **CARB** 0.5g; **FIBER** 0.1g; **CHOL** 54mg; **IRON** 1.5mg; **SODIUM** 531mg; **CALC** 83mg

ON THE SIDE: Since the fish has a vinegary sauce, you'll want something creamy and slightly sweet on the side. Mashed potatoes to the rescue!

Tuna Steaks with Wasabi-Ginger Glaze

Chinese-style hot mustard has a sharp, spicy bite and can be used in place of wasabi paste in this easy glaze—which also pairs well with salmon, chicken thighs, or pork.

2 tablespoons lower-sodium soy sauce, divided

4 (6-ounce) tuna steaks (1 inch thick)

2 tablespoons ginger marmalade

2 teaspoons wasabi paste

Cooking spray

2 tablespoons chopped fresh cilantro

1. Spoon 1 tablespoon soy sauce over fish; let stand 5 minutes.

2. Combine remaining 1 tablespoon soy sauce, ginger marmalade, and 2 teaspoons wasabi paste in a small bowl, stirring with a whisk.

3. Heat a grill pan over medium-high heat. Coat pan with cooking spray. Add fish to pan; cook 2 minutes on each side. Spoon marmalade mixture over fish; cook 1 minute or until medium-rare or desired degree of doneness. Remove fish from pan; sprinkle with cilantro.

YIELD: 4 servings (serving size: 1 steak and 1½ teaspoons cilantro).

CALORIES 281; **FAT** 2.3g (sat 0.5g, mono 0.3g, poly 0.6g); **PROTEIN** 51.4g; **CARB** 7.7g; **FIBER** 0.1g; **CHOL** 98mg; **IRON** 1.8mg; **SODIUM** 397mg; **CALC** 37mg

ON THE SIDE:
Fluffy jasmine rice and steamed fresh asparagus will complete the meal.

Grilled Pastrami-Style Salmon ▶

The classic seasonings associated with beef pastrami taste fantastic on this grilled salmon. Purchase a whole center-cut salmon fillet so that it will cook more evenly than a cut that contains the thinner tail end. A quick sauté of zucchini shredded through the large holes of a box grater with some finely grated lemon zest and minced rosemary would make a fine side dish, or serve with coleslaw and a dinner roll.

1 tablespoon dark brown sugar

1 teaspoon kosher salt

1 teaspoon garlic powder

1 teaspoon ground ginger

1 teaspoon ground coriander

1 teaspoon coarsely ground black pepper

½ teaspoon ground allspice

1 (1½-pound) center-cut salmon fillet

½ teaspoon olive oil

Cooking spray

1. Preheat grill.

2. Combine first 7 ingredients. Place fish, skin side down, on a cutting board or work surface; brush evenly with oil. Sprinkle spice mixture evenly over fish; gently rub mixture into fish. Cover lightly with plastic wrap, and chill 15 minutes.

3. Place fish, skin side down, on grill rack coated with cooking spray; grill 10 minutes or until desired degree of doneness. **YIELD:** 4 servings (serving size: about 4½ ounces).

CALORIES 230; **FAT** 10.5g (sat 2.4g, mono 4.7g, poly 2.4g); **PROTEIN** 27.4g; **CARB** 4.9g; **FIBER** 0.6g; **CHOL** 65mg; **IRON** 0.8mg; **SODIUM** 532mg; **CALC** 26mg

Pan-Seared Trout with Walnut-Breadcrumb Topping

Nothing's more elegant than trout, a mild, fresh-tasting fish and a great dinner for two. If you're squeamish about removing the heads and tails, have your fishmonger do it for you. You can also double this recipe if you have a very large cast-iron skillet—or even triple it if you have more than one skillet. Look for fresh breadcrumbs at the bakery counter of most supermarkets. Or to make your own: Place bread slices in a food processor, and pulse until they reach your desired size.

2 teaspoons Dijon mustard

2 (6-ounce) trout fillets

¼ cup fresh breadcrumbs

3 tablespoons ground walnuts

½ teaspoon dried thyme

¼ teaspoon salt

¼ teaspoon freshly ground black pepper

1 tablespoon olive oil

1. Preheat oven to 500°.

2. Spread 1 teaspoon mustard over boned side of each fillet.

3. Combine breadcrumbs and next 4 ingredients (through black pepper) in a small bowl. Sprinkle over mustard, pressing to adhere.

4. Heat oil in a large cast-iron skillet over medium-high heat until smoking. Add fish, skin sides down.

5. Bake at 500° for 8 minutes or until desired degree of doneness. **YIELD:** 2 servings (serving size: 1 fillet).

CALORIES 405; **FAT** 21.8g (sat 4.4g, mono 8.4g, poly 7.9g); **PROTEIN** 39g; **CARB** 12.4g; **FIBER** 1.2g; **CHOL** 100mg; **IRON** 1.7mg; **SODIUM** 581mg; **CALC** 147mg

savvy IN A SNAP

Grind walnuts in a spice grinder. To remove any odors from the grinder, grind white rice to a powder, and then wipe it all out.

MORE CHOICES: You can also prepare the salmon on a jelly-roll pan 4 to 6 inches from a preheated broiler—or even in a grill pan over medium-high heat. Remember to coat the jelly-roll pan or grill pan with cooking spray.

Champagne and Orange-Steamed Lobster Tails en Papillote

Here's a quick, elegant, and simple entrée for company. Halve the ingredients if you want a special dinner for two.

8 orange slices

4 (5-ounce) lobster tails

2 tablespoons butter, cut into small pieces

¼ cup chopped fennel fronds

¾ cup dry Champagne or sparkling wine

¼ teaspoon kosher salt

1. Preheat oven to 425°.

2. Cut 4 (15 x 24–inch) pieces of parchment paper. Fold in half crosswise. Draw a large heart half on each piece, with fold of paper at center of heart. Cut out heart, and open. Layer 2 orange slices, 1 lobster tail, 1½ teaspoons butter, and 1 tablespoon fennel fronds near fold of each piece of parchment paper. Spoon 3 tablespoons Champagne over each serving. Starting at top of heart, fold edges of parchment paper, sealing edges with narrow folds. Twist end tip tightly to secure. Place packets on a baking sheet. Bake at 425° for 12 minutes. Remove from oven; let stand 5 minutes. Carefully open each packet. Remove meat from lobster tail; coarsely chop. Return meat to lobster tail shell; place on plate. Drizzle juices from 1 packet over lobster tail; repeat procedure with remaining 3 lobster tails and 3 packets. Sprinkle evenly with salt. **YIELD:** 4 servings (serving size: 1 lobster tail).

CALORIES 290; **FAT** 8.5g (sat 4g, mono 2g, poly 1.3g); **PROTEIN** 37.8g; **CARB** 8.8g; **FIBER** 0.8g; **CHOL** 143mg; **IRON** 2.1mg; **SODIUM** 480mg; **CALC** 105mg

savvy IN A SNAP

Look for **parchment paper** near the foil and wax paper at your grocery store.

Citrus-Glazed Scallops with Avocado Salsa

Although the sea scallops at the fish counter look fresh, they almost certainly arrived at the market frozen and have been thawed. Those scallops are much more economical when you buy them from the freezer case and thaw them overnight in a bowl in the fridge.

Scallops:

1½ pounds large sea scallops, cut in half horizontally

¼ teaspoon salt

¼ teaspoon freshly ground black pepper

Glaze:

¼ cup fresh lime juice

¼ cup fresh orange juice

2 tablespoons fresh lemon juice

1 tablespoon grated peeled fresh ginger

2 tablespoons honey

1 teaspoon olive oil

¼ teaspoon ground red pepper

1 garlic clove, crushed

½ cup chopped green onions

¼ cup finely chopped fresh cilantro

Salsa:

½ cup chopped seeded plum tomato

½ cup diced peeled avocado

¼ cup finely chopped red onion

1 tablespoon finely chopped fresh cilantro

1 tablespoon chopped jalapeño pepper

1 tablespoon fresh lime juice

½ teaspoon olive oil

⅛ teaspoon salt

⅛ teaspoon freshly ground black pepper

1 garlic clove, crushed

8 Bibb lettuce leaves (optional)

QUICK TIP: Always have a plan for cleanup. Run the dishwasher between courses—but don't ever wash dishes while guests are still at the table.

1. To prepare scallops, heat a large nonstick skillet over medium-high heat. Combine first 3 ingredients in a bowl; toss well. Add scallops to pan; cook 2 minutes on each side or until browned. Remove from pan; keep warm.

2. To prepare glaze, combine lime juice and next 7 ingredients (through garlic clove) in a small bowl; stir with a whisk. Add juice mixture to pan. Cook 7 minutes or until glaze becomes shiny and begins to thicken. Drizzle citrus glaze over scallops; add green onions and ¼ cup cilantro. Toss well.

3. To prepare salsa, combine tomato and next 9 ingredients (through garlic); toss well. Serve on lettuce leaves, if desired. **YIELD:** 4 servings (serving size: ⅔ cup scallops and ¼ cup salsa).

CALORIES 262; **FAT** 6.1g (sat 0.9g, mono 3.1g, poly 1g); **PROTEIN** 29.8g; **CARB** 22.5g; **FIBER** 2.2g; **CHOL** 56mg; **IRON** 1mg; **SODIUM** 503mg; **CALC** 56mg

Clams Casino Stew

This hearty stew was modeled on the 1950s classic: clams casino. For more flavor, ladle the stew over Parmigiano-Reggiano cheese melted under the broiler on baguette rounds.

2 bacon slices, chopped

1 cup chopped fennel bulb

1 cup thinly sliced leek (about 1 large)

1 tablespoon minced garlic

2 teaspoons minced fresh oregano

1 teaspoon paprika

¼ teaspoon crushed red pepper

2 (14.5-ounce) cans fat-free, lower-sodium chicken broth

2 tablespoons red wine vinegar

22 littleneck clams in shells (2 pounds), scrubbed

1. Cook bacon in a large saucepan over medium heat 5 to 6 minutes or until crisp, stirring occasionally. Remove bacon from pan with a slotted spoon, reserving drippings in pan.

2. Cook fennel, leek, and garlic in hot drippings 2 minutes or until leek is tender, stirring frequently. Stir in oregano, paprika, and crushed red pepper; cook 20 seconds.

3. Stir in broth and vinegar. Bring to a boil; add clams. Cover, reduce heat, and simmer 5 minutes or until shells open. Discard any unopened shells. Ladle into bowls; sprinkle with bacon. **YIELD:** 4 servings (serving size: 5 to 6 clams, about 1 cup sauce, and 1½ teaspoons bacon).

CALORIES 135; **FAT** 2.9g (sat 0.6g, mono 0.7g, poly 0.5g); **PROTEIN** 16g; **CARB** 8.9g; **FIBER** 1.3g; **CHOL** 38mg; **IRON** 15mg; **SODIUM** 598mg; **CALC** 77mg

savvy IN A SNAP

For this recipe you might consider 2 ounces **slab bacon,** diced into little cubes. It'll offer more chew—a good contrast to the clams.

Quick Cioppino

Although you might think this tomato and seafood stew comes from Italy, it's actually a San Francisco original, stocked with tons of flavor. It's perfect fare for a no-fuss dinner party.

2 tablespoons olive oil

1 cup chopped fennel bulb (about 5 ounces)

1 cup chopped onion

1 tablespoon minced garlic

2 teaspoons fresh thyme

2 teaspoons fresh rosemary, crushed

½ teaspoon salt

¼ teaspoon crushed red pepper

1 bay leaf

2 cups dry white wine

1½ cups bottled clam juice

1 (28-ounce) can no-salt-added crushed tomatoes

1 pound skinless halibut fillets, cut into 1½-inch cubes

1 pound medium shrimp, peeled and deveined

1. Heat oil in a Dutch oven over medium heat. Add fennel and next 7 ingredients (through bay leaf); cook, stirring often, 5 minutes or until onion is tender.

2. Add wine, clam juice, and tomatoes. Bring to a boil; cover, reduce heat, and simmer 15 minutes, stirring occasionally.

3. Add fish and shrimp; simmer, uncovered, 5 minutes or until shrimp are done and fish is desired degree of doneness. Discard bay leaf. **YIELD:** 6 servings (serving size: 1⅔ cups).

CALORIES 297; **FAT** 7.9g (sat 1.2g, mono 4.1g, poly 1.6g); **PROTEIN** 34g; **CARB** 12.2g; **FIBER** 3.2g; **CHOL** 141mg; **IRON** 4.7mg; **SODIUM** 483mg; **CALC** 145mg

ON THE SIDE: Serve this hearty stew over mashed potatoes, white rice, or instant polenta.

Balsamic Steak au Poivre

Crack the peppercorns with the back of a heavy skillet or in a mortar and pestle or spice grinder (don't grind too finely). Serve with a side of steamed haricots verts.

2 (8-ounce) New York strip steaks (about 1 inch thick), trimmed

¼ teaspoon kosher salt

2 tablespoons cracked mixed peppercorns

1 tablespoon olive oil

⅓ cup finely chopped shallots

½ cup fat-free, lower-sodium beef broth

2 tablespoons balsamic vinegar

1 tablespoon butter

1. Heat a large cast-iron skillet over high heat. Pat steaks dry with paper towels; sprinkle steaks evenly with salt. Press peppercorns onto both sides of steaks. Add oil to pan; swirl to coat. Add steaks to pan; cook 3 minutes on each side or until desired degree of doneness. Remove steaks from pan; let stand 5 minutes. Cut each steak in half.

2. While steaks rest, add shallots to pan; cook 1 minute or until almost tender. Stir in broth and vinegar, scraping pan to loosen browned bits. Bring to a boil; cook 2 minutes or until reduced by half. Remove from heat; stir in butter. **YIELD:** 4 servings (serving size: 3 ounces steak and 1½ tablespoons sauce).

CALORIES 236; **FAT** 12.7g (sat 4.8g, mono 5.9g, poly 0.7g); **PROTEIN** 25g; **CARB** 3.6g; **FIBER** 0.1g; **CHOL** 57mg; **IRON** 1.8mg; **SODIUM** 246mg; **CALC** 26mg

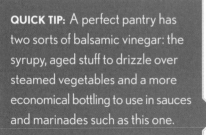

QUICK TIP: A perfect pantry has two sorts of balsamic vinegar: the syrupy, aged stuff to drizzle over steamed vegetables and a more economical bottling to use in sauces and marinades such as this one.

7 WAYS TO *demystify* WINE

Select and serve wines to their best advantage at your next dinner party.

Airplanes notwithstanding, there's a reason that wine generally doesn't come in single-serving containers. From the earliest times, wine has been a drink meant to be shared. Wine can make the food at a dinner party taste better in a way no other beverage can.

That said, serving wine raises numerous practical questions. Here are the answers to the most commonly asked questions.

1. How do you choose the right wine for the meal?

Pairing wine with food is about instinct and a good knowledge of how flavors work together. Let's say you have a menu of your own planned and aren't confident in your wine expertise. Take your menu with you to the best wine shop in town. Briefly describe the dishes to one of the salespeople, and ask him or her to recommend a wine and describe the flavors.

Remember: Pairing wine and food isn't a science, and there are no absolutely right or wrong answers.

2. How many wines should you offer your guests?

Sometimes serving a different wine with every course is in order, but it's also wonderful to serve just two—one matched to the appetizer and the other to the main dish. You can also sometimes pour two wines per course instead of just one. This encourages tasting, experimentation, comparison, and lively conversation as guests decide on their favorite.

3. How should the wines be served?

Assign one of your guests the role of "wine buddy." This person's job is to open wines and pour as needed, while you stay busy checking on the lamb and testing the vegetables. No matter whom you choose, your guests will love being the wine buddy. Try it—it works!

As to when to serve the wines, there are a few options. Serve an aperitif while guests are standing; empty glasses go to (or remain in) the kitchen. When you sit, the table is set with glasses for the wines to come. Pour the wines for the appetizer course and the main course at the same time. Though this is a little unconventional, guests can experiment with whichever wine they like; it also ensures a more relaxed atmosphere since you won't have to get up and down to remove or set glasses for each course.

4. How many bottles do you need?

A standard 750-milliliter bottle contains about five servings of wine. You can figure each guest will have a glass or two of wine with each course.

5. Which wineglasses are best?

Stick with large, inexpensive, stemmed wineglasses, and don't worry about having different ones for white and red wine; a single large glass works fine for both. It's nice to have enough glasses so that each guest can have a separate one for the aperitif wine, the appetizer course, and the main course.

If you're having a dinner party and are short on glasses, don't worry. Using the same glass for several wines is perfectly fine, and contrary to popular opinion, you don't need to (and in fact shouldn't) rinse the glasses with water between wines. A drop of the former wine won't hurt the next one.

6. Do you need to worry about letting the wine "breathe"?

Worry? No. But if you're serving a powerful young cabernet sauvignon or merlot, it will taste softer and more luscious if you pour it out into a carafe, pitcher, or decanter. This isn't decanting per se (you're not separating the wine from sediment), but you are aerating the wine by pouring it out of the bottle.

7. What about leftover wine?

Chill any opened bottles overnight to help preserve the wine. In the case of red wine, take the bottle out of the refrigerator an hour or so before enjoying a glass. And don't forget to drink a toast to remember your successful dinner party the night before!

Filet Mignon with Fresh Herb and Garlic Rub

A filet mignon comes from the small end of the tenderloin. It's a little-used muscle—and so very tender, almost buttery. There's not much more it needs except a great rub and a very hot skillet.

2 teaspoons bottled minced garlic

1½ teaspoons minced fresh basil

1½ teaspoons minced fresh thyme

1½ teaspoons minced fresh rosemary

½ teaspoon salt

¼ teaspoon black pepper

4 (4-ounce) beef tenderloin steaks, trimmed (1 inch thick)

Cooking spray

1. Combine first 6 ingredients in a small bowl; rub evenly over steaks.

2. Heat a large nonstick skillet over medium-high heat. Coat pan with cooking spray. Add steaks to pan, and cook 4 minutes on each side or until desired degree of doneness.

YIELD: 4 servings (serving size: 1 steak).

CALORIES 189; **FAT** 8.8g (sat 3.2g, mono 3.2g, poly 0.3g); **PROTEIN** 24.1g; **CARB** 0.8g; **FIBER** 0.2g; **CHOL** 71mg; **IRON** 3.1mg; **SODIUM** 349mg; **CALC** 9mg

ON THE SIDE: Serve these filets with steamed broccoli florets and roasted potato wedges. Place the florets in a microwave-safe bowl with a little water. Cover with wax paper, and microwave at HIGH 3 minutes or until crisp-tender.

Porcini-Dusted Chicken Scaloppine

This dish puts dried porcini mushroom powder to use as a flavorful coating for chicken cutlets. If fresh porcini or chanterelle mushrooms are available, use them for the sauce. Serve with steamed asparagus and garlic mashed potatoes.

½ cup dried porcini mushrooms (about ½ ounce)

4 (6-ounce) skinless, boneless chicken breast halves

½ teaspoon salt, divided

¼ teaspoon freshly ground black pepper, divided

1 tablespoon olive oil, divided

2 tablespoons minced shallot (about 1)

1 garlic clove, minced

3 cups sliced wild or cultivated mushrooms (about ½ pound)

½ cup dry white wine or dry vermouth

½ cup fat-free, lower-sodium chicken broth

3 tablespoons reduced-fat sour cream

1 tablespoon minced fresh flat-leaf parsley

1. Place porcini mushrooms in a spice or coffee grinder; process until finely ground. Slice chicken breast halves in half horizontally. Sprinkle chicken pieces with ¼ teaspoon salt and ⅛ teaspoon pepper. Sprinkle both sides of chicken with porcini powder, shaking off excess powder.

2. Heat 1 teaspoon oil in a large nonstick skillet over medium-high heat. Add 4 chicken pieces to pan; cook 1½ minutes on each side or until chicken is lightly browned and done. Remove chicken from pan; keep warm. Repeat procedure with 1 teaspoon oil and remaining 4 chicken pieces.

3. Heat remaining 1 teaspoon oil over medium heat. Add shallot and garlic to pan; cook 1 minute, stirring frequently. Add 3 cups mushrooms; cook 5 minutes or until liquid evaporates, stirring occasionally. Stir in wine, scraping pan to loosen browned bits. Increase heat to medium-high; cook 2 minutes or until liquid almost evaporates. Add broth to pan; simmer until liquid is reduced to ¼ cup (about 5 minutes). Stir in sour cream; cook 1 minute. Remove from heat; stir in remaining ¼ teaspoon salt, remaining ⅛ teaspoon pepper, and parsley. Serve sauce over chicken. **YIELD:** 4 servings (serving size: 2 chicken pieces and about 1½ tablespoons sauce).

CALORIES 269; **FAT** 7.3g (sat 2g, mono 3.1g, poly 1g); **PROTEIN** 43.2g; **CARB** 6.1g; **FIBER** 1.4g; **CHOL** 104mg; **IRON** 2.6mg; **SODIUM** 469mg; **CALC** 49mg

ON THE SIDE: Dry vermouth is a pantry staple and can stand in for white wine.

Chicken Française

We loved the subtle hint of lemon in the sauce for this classic French favorite. For a more pronounced lemon flavor, serve with lemon slices on each plate.

¼ cup all-purpose flour

¾ cup egg substitute

¼ cup (1 ounce) grated fresh Parmesan cheese

¼ cup chopped fresh parsley

¼ cup dry white wine

2 tablespoons fresh lemon juice

¼ teaspoon salt

⅛ teaspoon hot pepper sauce

3 garlic cloves, minced

8 (4-ounce) skinless, boneless chicken breast halves

1 tablespoon olive oil, divided

Cooking spray

2 tablespoons unsalted butter

¼ cup dry white wine

3 tablespoons fresh lemon juice

1. Place flour in a shallow dish. Combine egg substitute and next 7 ingredients (through garlic) in a second shallow dish.

2. Place each chicken breast half between 2 sheets of heavy-duty plastic wrap, and pound to ¼-inch thickness using a meat mallet or small heavy skillet. Dredge chicken in flour, and dip in egg substitute mixture.

3. Heat 1½ teaspoons oil in a large nonstick skillet coated with cooking spray over medium heat. Add 4 chicken breast halves; cook 4 minutes on each side or until done. Remove chicken from pan; keep warm. Wipe drippings from pan with a paper towel. Repeat procedure with remaining 1½ teaspoons oil and remaining chicken.

4. Melt butter in pan; add ¼ cup wine and 3 tablespoons juice. Bring to a boil; cook 10 seconds. Serve immediately over chicken. **YIELD:** 8 servings (serving size: 1 chicken breast half and 2 teaspoons sauce).

CALORIES 226; **FAT** 7.7g (sat 3.1g, mono 2.7g, poly 1.1g); **PROTEIN** 30.6g; **CARB** 5g; **FIBER** 0.2g; **CHOL** 76mg; **IRON** 1.7mg; **SODIUM** 231mg; **CALC** 60mg

Caramelized Onion Chicken Tenders

Chicken tenders? For fancy fare? Well, sure—especially when they have this gorgeous sauce to go on top. Sautéed green beans make a great side dish for this sweet, spicy chicken.

1 pound chicken breast tenders

½ teaspoon salt

¼ teaspoon freshly ground black pepper

1 teaspoon olive oil

½ cup sliced onion

½ cup seedless raspberry jam

1 tablespoon red wine vinegar

1 tablespoon lower-sodium soy sauce

1 teaspoon bottled ground fresh ginger

1 teaspoon fresh rosemary

1. Sprinkle chicken with salt and pepper. Heat oil in a large nonstick skillet over medium-high heat. Add onion, and sauté 2 minutes. Add chicken to pan; sauté 8 minutes or until chicken is done. Remove onion and chicken from pan.

2. Add jam and next 4 ingredients (through rosemary) to pan; cook 2 minutes, stirring constantly with a whisk. Return chicken mixture to pan; cook 4 minutes, stirring occasionally. **YIELD:** 4 servings (serving size: 3 ounces chicken and 1 tablespoon sauce).

CALORIES 246; **FAT** 2.6g (sat 0.5g, mono 1.2g, poly 0.4g); **PROTEIN** 26.6g; **CARB** 28.5g; **FIBER** 0.5g; **CHOL** 66mg; **IRON** 1.1mg; **SODIUM** 521mg; **CALC** 19mg

Chicken with Lemon-Leek Linguine

Add fresh flavors to a weeknight staple with this family-friendly menu. Go vegetarian by subbing vegetable broth and topping with goat cheese.

6 ounces uncooked linguine

4 (6-ounce) skinless, boneless chicken breast halves

½ teaspoon salt, divided

¼ teaspoon black pepper

¼ cup all-purpose flour

3 tablespoons butter, divided

3 garlic cloves, thinly sliced

1 leek, trimmed, cut in half lengthwise, and thinly sliced (1½ cups)

½ cup fat-free, lower-sodium chicken broth

2 tablespoons fresh lemon juice

2 tablespoons chopped fresh flat-leaf parsley

1. Cook pasta according to package directions, omitting salt and fat. Drain; keep warm.

2. Place chicken between 2 sheets of heavy-duty plastic wrap; pound to an even thickness using a meat mallet or small heavy skillet. Sprinkle chicken with ¼ teaspoon salt and pepper. Place flour in a shallow dish; dredge chicken in flour, shaking to remove excess.

3. Heat 1 tablespoon butter in a large nonstick skillet over medium-high heat. Add chicken, and cook 3 minutes on each side or until done. Remove chicken from pan; keep warm.

4. Melt 1 tablespoon butter in skillet over medium-high heat. Add garlic, leek, and remaining ¼ teaspoon salt; sauté 4 minutes. Add broth and juice; cook 2 minutes or until liquid is reduced by half. Remove from heat; stir in remaining 1 tablespoon butter. Add pasta to leek mixture; toss well to combine. Serve chicken over pasta mixture; sprinkle with parsley. **YIELD:** 4 servings (serving size: 1 chicken breast half and 1 cup pasta mixture).

CALORIES 474; **FAT** 11.5g (sat 6.2g, mono 2.7g, poly 0.9g); **PROTEIN** 46.8g; **CARB** 44g; **FIBER** 2.3g; **CHOL** 121mg; **IRON** 3.8mg; **SODIUM** 592mg; **CALC** 57mg

MORE CHOICES: For a more affordable alternative, use boneless loin pork chops cut into ¼-inch-thick slices instead of veal. To slice pork easily, place it in the freezer for 15 minutes before slicing.

Veal Scallops in Irish Whiskey Sauce

No doubt about it, this dish is a showstopper: sweet, salty, and irresistible. That said, the whiskey can flame over the heat. Don't worry—just follow some reasonable precautions. Turn off your overhead vent before you pour in the whiskey. And if the stuff does ignite, cover the skillet and move it off the heat for a minute or so until things calm down.

1 teaspoon Hungarian sweet paprika

½ teaspoon salt

½ teaspoon freshly ground black pepper

¼ teaspoon dried rubbed sage

¼ teaspoon ground ginger

1 pound (¼-inch-thick) veal scaloppine

2 teaspoons olive oil, divided

2 teaspoons butter, divided

2 tablespoons freshly chopped shallots

1 (8-ounce) package presliced mushrooms

¼ cup Irish whiskey

½ cup fat-free, lower-sodium chicken broth

2 tablespoons sherry

2 tablespoons chopped fresh parsley (optional)

1. Combine first 5 ingredients in a small bowl; sprinkle evenly over veal.

2. Heat 1 teaspoon oil and 1 teaspoon butter in a large nonstick skillet over medium-high heat. Add half of veal to pan. Cook 1 minute on each side or until lightly browned. Remove from pan, and keep warm. Repeat procedure with remaining oil, butter, and veal.

3. Reduce heat to medium. Add shallots and mushrooms to pan, and cook 1 minute. Add Irish whiskey, scraping pan to loosen browned bits. Add broth and sherry; simmer 5 minutes or just until sauce begins to thicken. Return veal to pan. Cover and simmer 1 minute or until thoroughly heated. Place veal on a serving platter, and top with mushrooms and sauce. Sprinkle with parsley, if desired. Serve immediately. **YIELD:** 4 servings (serving size: 2 veal slices and ¼ cup sauce).

CALORIES 208; **FAT** 10g (sat 3.4g, mono 4.5g, poly 0.9g); **PROTEIN** 23.5g; **CARB** 3.4g; **FIBER** 1.1g; **CHOL** 90mg; **IRON** 1.4mg; **SODIUM** 433mg; **CALC** 26mg

QUICK TIP: Although everyone likes to hang out in the kitchen, a crowd can slow down even the most experienced quick cook. Put nibbles and drinks in the living room, encouraging people to gather there.

Pork Medallions with Port Wine–Dried Cherry Pan Sauce

Here, pork tenderloin is cut into 16 medallions, an ideal shape and size for sautéing. Butter is whisked into the red wine mixture at the end, creating a rich, velvety sauce. Serve with plain or garlic-flavored couscous.

1 cup ruby port or other sweet red wine

⅓ cup dried sweet cherries

4 teaspoons seedless raspberry jam

1 teaspoon Dijon mustard

1 tablespoon olive oil

1½ pounds pork tenderloin, trimmed

½ teaspoon salt

¼ teaspoon freshly ground black pepper

1 tablespoon butter

Parsley sprigs (optional)

1. Combine first 4 ingredients.

2. Heat oil in a large skillet over low heat 2 minutes. Cut pork crosswise into 16 pieces. Sprinkle evenly with salt and pepper.

3. Place pork in pan; cook 4 minutes on each side or until golden brown. Remove pork from pan. Stir in wine mixture, scraping to loosen browned bits. Increase heat to high; bring to a boil. Cook until reduced to ½ cup (about 3 minutes). Remove from heat. Stir in butter with a whisk. Serve sauce over pork. Garnish with parsley, if desired. **YIELD:** 4 servings (serving size: 4 pork pieces and 2 tablespoons sauce).

CALORIES 366; **FAT** 12.4g (sat 4.3g, mono 5.6g, poly 1.6g); **PROTEIN** 35.6g; **CARB** 22.8g; **FIBER** 1.4g; **CHOL** 118mg; **IRON** 2mg; **SODIUM** 427mg; **CALC** 30mg

QUICK TIP: How much ground pepper from the mill is ¼ teaspoon? Do this experiment: Make a mark on your grinder, and turn the crank one full revolution from it. Measure what comes out. Now you know how many cranks it takes to get ¼ teaspoon, ½ teaspoon, and the rest.

Pan-Roasted Pork Chops with Brussels Sprouts and Tomatoes

Talk about easy elegance. This is a straightforward dish, delicate and light. The tomatoes break down a bit, mixing with the juices from the pork to create a terrific, simple sauce.

2 (6-ounce) bone-in center-cut pork chops (about ¾ inch thick)

¼ teaspoon salt

¼ teaspoon freshly ground black pepper

1 tablespoon canola oil

2 cups small Brussels sprouts (about 6 ounces), halved

1 cup grape tomatoes

1 tablespoon butter

1. Sprinkle pork chops evenly on both sides with salt and pepper. Heat a large nonstick skillet over medium-high heat. Add oil. Cook pork chops in hot oil 4 to 5 minutes on each side or until done. Remove from pan; keep warm.

2. Add Brussels sprouts and tomatoes to pan; sauté 6 minutes or until tomatoes begin to pop. Add butter; cook 1 minute or until butter melts, stirring constantly. Serve vegetables over pork chops. **YIELD:** 2 servings (serving size: 1 pork chop and 1⅓ cups vegetable mixture).

CALORIES 296; **FAT** 17.6g (sat 5.8g, mono 7.8g, poly 2.8g); **PROTEIN** 25g; **CARB** 10.8g; **FIBER** 4.3g; **CHOL** 70mg; **IRON** 2mg; **SODIUM** 374mg; **CALC** 74mg

QUICK TIP: Did you know that people actually slow down in dim light? A savvy quick cook has a bright, well-lit kitchen but a dining room with more ambient lighting, so guests relax and settle in.

QUICK TIP: Although dried herbs are certainly more convenient, fresh herbs hold up better to quick-cooking, high-heat methods like this one.

◀ Tuscan Pork Tenderloin

Roasting a small cut, such as pork tenderloin, at very high heat (here, 500°) creates a browned exterior and moist interior. (Cooking at lower temperatures will still produce fine results, but the pork won't develop a crust by the time it reaches the desired internal temperature.) The endive and shallots form a rack for the meat to rest on as it cooks—and a great side dish when it's done.

4 teaspoons olive oil, divided

2 teaspoons white balsamic vinegar

1 teaspoon kosher salt, divided

5 large shallots, halved

3 heads Belgian endive, quartered lengthwise (about 1 pound)

1½ teaspoons finely chopped fresh rosemary

1 teaspoon grated lemon rind

1 teaspoon fresh lemon juice

½ teaspoon fennel seeds, crushed

½ teaspoon freshly ground black pepper

2 garlic cloves, minced

1 (1-pound) pork tenderloin

1. Preheat oven to 500°.

2. Combine 1 tablespoon oil, vinegar, ½ teaspoon salt, shallots, and endive in a roasting pan; toss well to coat. Arrange vegetables evenly down center of pan.

3. Combine remaining 1 teaspoon oil, remaining ½ teaspoon salt, rosemary, and next 5 ingredients (through garlic) in a small bowl. Rub rosemary mixture onto pork. Arrange pork on top of vegetables. Bake at 500° for 17 minutes or until a thermometer registers 160°. Let vegetables and pork stand 10 minutes. Cut pork crosswise into 12 slices.

YIELD: 4 servings (serving size: 3 pork slices and about ¾ cup vegetables).

CALORIES 238; FAT 8.6g (sat 2g, mono 5.1g, poly 1g); PROTEIN 26.3g; CARB 14.4g; FIBER 4.2g; CHOL 74mg; IRON 2.4mg; SODIUM 537mg; CALC 55mg

Fennel and Rosemary-Crusted Roasted Rack of Lamb

A handful of well-chosen ingredients yields an impressive entrée. You can rub the lamb with the herb mixture in the morning, and refrigerate it until you're ready to pop it into the oven.

1 tablespoon fennel seeds, crushed

1 tablespoon chopped fresh rosemary

1 teaspoon freshly ground black pepper

¼ teaspoon salt

6 garlic cloves, minced

1 (12-ounce) French-cut rack of lamb (6 ribs), trimmed

Cooking spray

Rosemary sprigs (optional)

1. Preheat oven to 475°.

2. Combine first 5 ingredients in a small bowl. Rub lamb evenly with garlic mixture; place on a broiler pan coated with cooking spray. Bake at 475° for 15 minutes or until a thermometer registers 145° (medium-rare) to 160° (medium). Garnish with rosemary sprigs, if desired. **YIELD:** 3 servings (serving size: 2 ribs).

CALORIES 213; FAT 11.1g (sat 3.8g, mono 4.4g, poly 1g); PROTEIN 23g; CARB 3.6g; FIBER 1.2g; CHOL 75mg; IRON 2.6mg; SODIUM 279mg; CALC 54mg

MORE CHOICES: Rosemary definitely has a strong flavor. Substitute oregano or tarragon, if you prefer.

Farfalle with Creamy Wild Mushroom Sauce

This recipe received a high score for its rich flavor and ultracreamy texture. The exotic mushroom blend, a combination of shiitake, cremini, and oyster mushrooms, is sold in 8-ounce packages. If unavailable, use all cremini mushrooms.

1 pound uncooked farfalle (bow tie pasta)

1 tablespoon butter

12 ounces presliced exotic mushroom blend

½ cup chopped onion

⅓ cup finely chopped shallots

1 tablespoon minced garlic

1½ teaspoons salt, divided

¼ teaspoon freshly ground black pepper

¼ cup dry white wine or dry vermouth

⅔ cup whipping cream

½ cup (2 ounces) grated fresh Parmigiano-Reggiano cheese

2 tablespoons chopped fresh parsley

Minced fresh parsley (optional)

1. Cook pasta according to package directions, omitting salt and fat; drain.

2. Melt butter in a large nonstick skillet over medium-high heat. Add mushrooms, onion, shallots, garlic, 1 teaspoon salt, and pepper; cook 12 minutes or until liquid evaporates and mushrooms are tender, stirring occasionally. Add wine; cook 2 minutes or until liquid evaporates, stirring occasionally. Remove from heat.

3. Add pasta, cream, cheese, and 2 tablespoons parsley, tossing gently to coat. Stir in remaining ½ teaspoon salt. Garnish with minced fresh parsley, if desired. Serve immediately. **YIELD:** 8 servings (serving size: 1¼ cups).

CALORIES 336; **FAT** 11.4g (sat 6.9g, mono 3.1g, poly 0.4g); **PROTEIN** 12.1g; **CARB** 47.5g; **FIBER** 2.3g; **CHOL** 36mg; **IRON** 2.3mg; **SODIUM** 577mg; **CALC** 124mg

QUICK TIP: When you're chopping one shallot, chop a couple more. Store the extra in a small zip-top plastic bag in the freezer. No need to thaw them when you're ready to use them!

Pasta Primavera

Use fresh seasonal vegetables for a hearty meatless meal.

2 quarts water

1½ cups baby carrots, trimmed
   (about 6 ounces)

3 cups uncooked penne or cavatappi pasta
   (about 8 ounces)

1 teaspoon olive oil

2 cups pattypan squash, halved
   (about 8 ounces)

¾ cup shelled green peas

1 teaspoon salt

¼ teaspoon freshly ground black pepper

2 garlic cloves, minced

¼ cup dry white wine or dry vermouth

⅓ cup whipping cream

1 tablespoon fresh lemon juice

¼ cup (1 ounce) grated fresh Parmesan
   cheese

¼ cup thinly sliced fresh basil

¼ cup chopped fresh parsley

1. Bring 2 quarts water to a boil in a stockpot. Add carrots; cook 3 minutes. Remove with a slotted spoon. Add pasta to boiling water; cook according to package directions, omitting salt and fat. Drain.

2. Heat oil in a large nonstick skillet over medium-high heat. Add squash; sauté 3 minutes. Add carrots, peas, salt, pepper, and garlic; sauté 2 minutes. Stir in wine, scraping pan to loosen browned bits. Stir in cream and juice; cook 1 minute. Add pasta and cheese; stir well to coat. Remove from heat; stir in basil and parsley. **YIELD:** 4 servings (serving size: 2 cups).

CALORIES 373; **FAT** 11.8g (sat 6.1g, mono 3.6g, poly 1.1g); **PROTEIN** 13.9g; **CARB** 53.8g; **FIBER** 4.5g; **CHOL** 32mg; **IRON** 3.9mg; **SODIUM** 731mg; **CALC** 150mg

MORE CHOICES: For the meat lovers in the family, feel free to add chicken or shrimp to this pasta recipe.

SUPERFAST
SIDES

Big Flavors, Little Fuss

THE POOR SIDE DISH! WE QUICK COOKS TOO OFTEN FORGET ABOUT IT. We default to a little lettuce tossed with some bottled dressing or to a bag of green beans zapped in the microwave.

In fact, better sides don't take much time at all—and a little effort pays off big dividends as the more complex flavors play against the main course we've chosen for the meal. Some green beans fried in sesame oil, fried green tomatoes, a quick ratatouille—these offer big flavors without much fuss.

Many of these side dishes can become vegetarian suppers, particularly if you make two or three for the table: one with crunchy, fresh vegetables; one with luscious, stewed ones; and a whole grain to go alongside. Now that's a meal!

So let's work to get more fresh vegetables on the table, even when we're trying to cook quickly.

Good nutrition and good flavor should never be sacrificed for speed—and won't with these choices.

◀ Roasted Cauliflower, Chickpeas, and Olives

Cauliflower roasts into such mild sweetness that this Spanish-inspired side dish may win over even picky eaters. Enjoy it with sautéed, grilled, or roasted fish or chicken.

5½ cups cauliflower florets (about 1 pound)

10 green Spanish olives, halved and pitted

8 garlic cloves, coarsely chopped

1 (15-ounce) can chickpeas (garbanzo beans), rinsed and drained

3 tablespoons olive oil

½ teaspoon crushed red pepper

3 tablespoons fresh flat-leaf parsley leaves

1. Preheat oven to 450°.

2. Combine first 4 ingredients in a shallow roasting pan. Drizzle with oil; sprinkle with pepper. Toss well to coat. Bake at 450° for 22 minutes or until cauliflower is browned and crisp-tender, stirring after 10 minutes. Sprinkle with parsley. **YIELD:** 6 servings (serving size: about ⅔ cup).

CALORIES 147; **FAT** 8.4g (sat 1g, mono 5.5g, poly 1.3g); **PROTEIN** 4.4g; **CARB** 14.5g; **FIBER** 3.9g; **CHOL** 0mg; **IRON** 1mg; **SODIUM** 224mg; **CALC** 45mg

savvy IN A SNAP

To make cauliflower florets, cut the head in half through the stem. Working on the cut side, slice out the core on each end. Now begin slicing off the florets, working from the center outward.

Roasted Brussels Sprouts with Oregano

Roasting Brussels sprouts caramelizes some of the sugars and brings out a delicious flavor profile—one that may even appeal to fussy eaters.

1 pound small Brussels sprouts, trimmed and halved (4 cups)

1 tablespoon minced fresh oregano

1 garlic clove, minced

1 tablespoon olive oil

½ teaspoon freshly ground black pepper

¼ teaspoon salt

1. Preheat oven to 425°.

2. Place Brussels sprouts, oregano, and garlic in a large bowl. Drizzle sprouts with oil, and sprinkle with pepper and salt; toss to coat. Spread sprout mixture in a 13 x 9–inch metal baking pan.

3. Bake at 425° for 15 minutes, stirring after 8 minutes. **YIELD:** 4 servings (serving size: about ⅔ cup).

CALORIES 83; **FAT** 3.8g (sat 0.6g, mono 2.7g, poly 0.5g); **PROTEIN** 3.9g; **CARB** 10.7g; **FIBER** 4.4g; **CHOL** 0mg; **IRON** 1.7mg; **SODIUM** 176mg; **CALC** 55mg

savvy IN A SNAP

The smaller the **Brussels sprout,** the less bitter it can be. Plus, smaller Brussels sprouts cook more quickly. Trim off exterior leaves, and cut off any woody stems.

Buttery Lemon Broccolini

If you want to get a jump on this recipe, cook the Broccolini as directed, and plunge it into a bowl of ice water; drain, cover, and refrigerate for up to 2 days. You can also prepare the compound butter ahead of time and keep it in the fridge, too. Then, finish cooking the Broccolini in the skillet, and toss it with butter just before serving.

4 quarts water

1⅛ teaspoons salt, divided

2 (6-ounce) packages Broccolini

1 tablespoon butter, softened

½ teaspoon grated lemon rind

1½ teaspoons fresh lemon juice

⅛ teaspoon freshly ground black pepper

1. Bring 4 quarts water to a boil in a large saucepan; add 1 teaspoon salt. Place half of Broccolini in boiling water, and cook 5 minutes. Remove with a slotted spoon. Repeat procedure with remaining Broccolini. Drain; discard water.

2. Combine butter, rind, and juice, stirring with a fork until well blended.

3. Return Broccolini to pan over medium-high heat; stir in butter mixture, remaining ⅛ teaspoon salt, and pepper, tossing gently to coat. **YIELD:** 4 servings (serving size: 3 ounces Broccolini and about 1 teaspoon butter mixture).

CALORIES 61; **FAT** 2.8g (sat 1.8g, mono 0.7g, poly 0.1g); **PROTEIN** 3.1g; **CARB** 6.3g; **FIBER** 1.1g; **CHOL** 8mg; **IRON** 0.7mg; **SODIUM** 250mg; **CALC** 62mg

Broccoli with Crushed Red Pepper and Toasted Garlic

Here's an easy side dish, great next to anything roasted, steamed, or grilled. Don't use bottled minced garlic here—it can burn and turn bitter.

2 teaspoons olive oil

6 cups broccoli florets (about 1 bunch)

¼ teaspoon salt

¼ teaspoon crushed red pepper

3 garlic cloves, thinly sliced

¼ cup water

1. Heat oil in a large nonstick skillet over medium-high heat. Add broccoli, salt, pepper, and garlic. Cook 2 minutes. Add ¼ cup water. Cover, reduce heat to low, and cook 2 minutes or until broccoli is crisp-tender. **YIELD:** 4 servings (serving size: 1 cup).

CALORIES 53; **FAT** 2.7g (sat 0.4g, mono 1.7g, poly 0.4g); **PROTEIN** 3.3g; **CARB** 6.4g; **FIBER** 3.2g; **CHOL** 0mg; **IRON** 1mg; **SODIUM** 147mg; **CALC** 55mg

MORE CHOICES: Get more flavor by adding a few sprigs of thyme or oregano or even a large sprig of rosemary.

Sesame Green Beans

Here's a traditional Chinese take-out dish, morphed into a tasty side. The deep flavors really pay off in this simple dish.

1½ pounds green beans, trimmed (4 cups trimmed green beans)

2 teaspoons peanut or canola oil

2 teaspoons dark sesame oil

½ teaspoon crushed red pepper

1 tablespoon sesame seeds

2 teaspoons lower-sodium soy sauce

1. Bring a large saucepan of water to a boil. Add beans; cook 3 minutes. Drain and rinse with cold water until room temperature.

2. Heat a nonstick wok or nonstick skillet over medium heat. Add oils. Add green beans and pepper. Stir-fry 2 minutes. Add sesame seeds and soy sauce. Toss to coat.

YIELD: 4 servings (serving size: 1 cup).

CALORIES 106; **FAT** 5.7g (sat 0.9g, mono 2.3g, poly 2.2g); **PROTEIN** 3.7g; **CARB** 13.1g; **FIBER** 6.2g; **CHOL** 0mg; **IRON** 1.9mg; **SODIUM** 230mg; **CALC** 66mg

◄ Garlic-Roasted Kale

Roasting kale is an amazing process to watch—the leaves turn from a dusty dark green to dark emerald with brown-tinged curly edges that crunch. This vegetable side is delicious served hot from the oven; the leaves lose their crisp texture as the dish stands.

3½ teaspoons extra-virgin olive oil

¼ teaspoon kosher salt

10 ounces kale, stems removed and chopped

1 garlic clove, thinly sliced

1 teaspoon sherry vinegar

1. Preheat oven to 425°. Place a large jelly-roll pan in oven 5 minutes.

2. Combine first 4 ingredients in a large bowl; toss to coat. Place kale mixture on hot pan, spreading with a silicone spatula to separate leaves. Bake at 425° for 7 minutes. Stir kale. Bake an additional 5 minutes or until edges of leaves are crisp and kale is tender.

3. Place kale in a large bowl. Drizzle with vinegar; toss to combine. Serve immediately.

YIELD: 4 servings (serving size: about ⅔ cup).

CALORIES 72; **FAT** 4.7g (sat 0.7g, mono 3g, poly 0.8g); **PROTEIN** 2.3g; **CARB** 7.1g; **FIBER** 1.4g; **CHOL** 0mg; **IRON** 1.2mg; **SODIUM** 125mg; **CALC** 93mg

savvy IN A SNAP

Consider upgrading your salt choices. How about using **kosher salt or sea salt** in this easy side dish? The added minerals will offer new flavors and textures—and create a more enjoyable meal.

A *produce* GUIDE

Stay out of a cooking rut by trying new ingredients with our produce substitution guide.

One surefire way of contracting dinnertime cooking fatigue is to cook the same old thing over and over. Or perhaps you cook for kids or other adults who don't like to try new things? Challenge yourself or others in your house to try something new, and use this list of produce as a guide. You'll find some common substitutions that may make expanding your culinary repertoire a cinch.

If you like **onions,** try **shallots,** which are petite onions that look like large cloves of garlic. They have a lower water content than onions, so their flavor is more concentrated than that of onions. When you want full onion flavor without the bulk of a full-sized onion, shallots are ideal.

If you like **spinach,** try **arugula.** Although arugula is decidedly more intensely flavored than spinach (it has a peppery flavor), its texture is similar to that of spinach. If you'd like a change salads, sides, and mix-ins for soups, go bold and try arugula. It pai well with vinaigrettes and wilts quickly, much like spinach.

If you like **pineapple,** try **mango.** Mango's taste has been likened to a cross between a pineapple and a peach, and this tropical fruit can add sublime sweetness to salsas, relishes, smoothies, and salads.

If you like **basil,** try **mint.** Mint isn't just for garnishing dessert plates and adding to fruity cocktails. It's bursting with flavor and freshness and can impart delicious complexity to many dishes—both savory and sweet.

If you like **potatoes,** try **turnips** or **rutabaga,** which hold up to most popular potato-cooking methods. These root vegetables can be boiled and mashed or roasted and pureed.

If you like **cooked carrots,** try **parsnips.** The two look very similar, but parsnips have pale, cream-colored skin. Their tough, woody texture softens with cooking. Parsnips should be added to soups and stews in the last 30 minutes of cooking.

If you like **peaches,** try fresh **apricots,** ch are among the first fruits of summer. They have elicate flavor and creamy texture. They are great risps or tarts, much like peaches, but they're also good in savory dishes.

If you like **green onions,** try **leeks.** Leeks look like overgrown green onions, but they are actually milder and sweeter. Unlike green onions, they are best cooked because they're very fibrous when raw.

If you like **zucchini and squash,** try **baby squash** like **pattypan** and **scallopini squash,** which resemble flattened, scallop-shaped saucers. Baby squash boast mildly sweet, buttery flavor and tender flesh.

If you like **green beans,** try **okra.** We know. Okra might be a tough sell for many, but it has a mild flavor and, once cooked, a texture similar to that of the ever-popular green bean. Try it in Indian-Spiced Okra on page 307.

If you like **cabbage,** try **Brussels sprouts.** First, put aside any preconceived notions about Brussels sprouts. Then, buy the freshest sprouts available (look for small, firm sprouts with compact, bright-green heads), and cook them as quickly as possible to keep their flavors from getting too strong. And choose the right cooking method: They should be tender but still slightly crisp, and their color should remain intense; olive-drab sprouts have been overcooked.

Fried Green Tomatoes ▶

To lighten this classic, we added a fried crust to just one side of the tomato slices.

8 (½-inch-thick) slices green tomato (about 4 tomatoes)

⅜ teaspoon salt

¼ teaspoon freshly ground black pepper

½ cup yellow cornmeal

1 tablespoon canola oil

1. Sprinkle 1 side of each tomato slice evenly with salt and pepper. Dredge seasoned sides in cornmeal.

2. Heat oil in a large skillet over medium-high heat. Add tomato slices, coated sides down; cook 6 minutes, turning after 3 minutes. Serve immediately. **YIELD:** 4 servings (serving size: 2 slices).

CALORIES 147; **FAT** 3.9g (sat 0.3g, mono 2.3g, poly 1.1g); **PROTEIN** 3.5g; **CARB** 25.4g; **FIBER** 2.5g; **CHOL** 0mg; **IRON** 1.4mg; **SODIUM** 242mg; **CALC** 24mg

QUICK TIP: Use your old toothbrush to clean the kitchen sink stopper; it will get in all the little holes.

Spinach with Pine Nuts and Golden Raisins

This Spanish-inspired side dish is a sweet-savory combination of garlicky wilted spinach, buttery pine nuts, and golden raisins.

½ cup boiling water

⅓ cup golden raisins

2 tablespoons water

2 (9-ounce) packages fresh baby spinach

1 teaspoon olive oil

2 garlic cloves, minced

¼ teaspoon salt

¼ teaspoon freshly ground black pepper

4 teaspoons pine nuts, toasted

1. Combine ½ cup boiling water and raisins; let stand 15 minutes or until raisins are plump. Drain.

2. Combine 2 tablespoons water and spinach in a large Dutch oven over medium-high heat. Cook 3 minutes or until spinach wilts, stirring frequently. Remove from pan. Wipe pan with a paper towel.

3. Heat oil in pan over medium heat. Add garlic; cook 30 seconds, stirring frequently. Add spinach, raisins, salt, and pepper; cook 1 minute or until thoroughly heated. Stir in pine nuts. **YIELD:** 4 servings (serving size: ½ cup).

CALORIES 97; **FAT** 3.6g (sat 0.4g, mono 1.4g, poly 1.3g); **PROTEIN** 4.5g; **CARB** 15.2g; **FIBER** 3.5g; **CHOL** 0mg; **IRON** 3.9mg; **SODIUM** 250mg; **CALC** 136mg

savvy IN A SNAP

One serving of this dish packs in **114 milligrams of magnesium**—about 25 percent of your daily needs.

QUICK TIP: Use presliced or matchstick-cut packaged carrots, rather than diagonally slicing the carrots.

◄ Sautéed Carrots with Sage

You can easily double or triple this recipe to feed more, especially around a holiday table.

1 teaspoon butter

1 teaspoon olive oil

1½ cups diagonally cut carrot

2 tablespoons water

⅛ teaspoon salt

⅛ teaspoon freshly ground black pepper

2 teaspoons small fresh sage leaves

1. Melt butter in a large nonstick skillet over medium heat. Add oil to pan; swirl to coat. Add carrots and 2 tablespoons water. Partially cover pan, and cook 10 minutes or until carrots are almost tender. Add salt and pepper to pan; increase heat to medium-high. Cook 4 minutes or until carrots are tender and lightly browned, stirring frequently. Sprinkle with sage. **YIELD:** 2 servings (serving size: ½ cup).

CALORIES 75; FAT 4.4g (sat 1.5g, mono 2.2g, poly 0.4g); PROTEIN 0.9g; CARB 9g; FIBER 2.6g; CHOL 5mg; IRON 0.3mg; SODIUM 224mg; CALC 35mg

QUICK TIP: Use presliced mushrooms, rather than ones you've quartered yourself.

Braised Leeks and Mushrooms

Leeks are related to onions, but their flavor softens into a sweeter, more delicate one over the heat, a nice match to these earthy mushrooms and their buttery sauce.

6 leeks (about 3 pounds)

1 cup fat-free, lower-sodium beef broth

1 tablespoon tomato paste

¼ teaspoon salt

½ teaspoon fresh thyme

⅛ teaspoon black pepper

1½ teaspoons butter

2 cups quartered mushrooms (about 5 ounces)

1. Remove roots, outer leaves, and tops from leeks, leaving 6 inches of each leek. Cut each diagonally into thirds, then diagonally in half to form 6 triangular pieces. Rinse with cold water; drain well.

2. Combine beef broth, tomato paste, salt, thyme, and pepper in a bowl, and stir with a whisk.

3. Melt butter in a large nonstick skillet over medium-high heat. Add leeks and mushrooms, and sauté 6 minutes or until vegetables are lightly browned. Add broth mixture. Cover, reduce heat, and simmer 15 minutes or until leeks are tender. Uncover and simmer 7 minutes or until liquid almost evaporates, stirring occasionally. **YIELD:** 4 servings (serving size: ½ cup).

CALORIES 144; FAT 2.2g (sat 1g, mono 0.4g, poly 0.5g); PROTEIN 3.8g; CARB 29.3g; FIBER 2.9g; CHOL 4mg; IRON 4.6mg; SODIUM 204mg; CALC 115mg

Garlicky Lima Beans

Although it's more time-consuming, making this simple side dish with fresh lima beans yields tasty results. Look for them at farmers' markets and specialty grocery stores. If they have been shelled, inspect them carefully because they are quite perishable. Look for ones that have tender skins that are green or greenish-white in color and do not have any signs of browning. Boil them about 20 minutes, then drain, and continue with this recipe.

1 tablespoon olive oil

4 cups frozen lima beans, thawed

3 thyme sprigs

2 garlic cloves, crushed

1 bay leaf

½ teaspoon sea salt

¼ teaspoon freshly ground black pepper

1. Heat oil in a large nonstick skillet over medium-low heat. Add lima beans and next 3 ingredients (through bay leaf). Cook 5 minutes or until beans are warm, stirring frequently. Discard thyme sprigs and bay leaf. Stir in salt and pepper. **YIELD:** 8 servings (serving size: ½ cup).

CALORIES 105; **FAT** 2.4g (sat 0.4g, mono 1.3g, poly 0.5g); **PROTEIN** 5.4g; **CARB** 16.2g; **FIBER** 3.9g; **CHOL** 0mg; **IRON** 2.5mg; **SODIUM** 152mg; **CALC** 30mg

MORE CHOICES: This method is a delicious, basic way to cook any kind of fresh shell bean or pea. For another variation, drizzle the finished dish with olive oil and lemon juice. You can even sprinkle it with a few shavings of Parmigiano-Reggiano cheese.

Indian-Spiced Okra

Even folks who usually don't like okra enjoy the taste and texture of this highly seasoned dish. We've left the seeds in the chile for a moderate amount of heat.

¾ teaspoon brown mustard seeds

1 tablespoon canola oil

1 teaspoon ground coriander

1 teaspoon finely chopped serrano chile

½ teaspoon kosher salt

¼ teaspoon curry powder

1 pound small to medium okra pods, trimmed

1. Cook mustard seeds in a large heavy skillet over medium-high heat 30 seconds or until toasted and fragrant. Add canola oil and remaining ingredients; cook 1 minute, stirring occasionally. Cover, reduce heat to low, and cook 8 minutes, stirring occasionally. Uncover and increase heat to high; cook 2 minutes or until okra is lightly browned. **YIELD:** 6 servings (serving size: ⅔ cup).

CALORIES 47; **FAT** 2.6g (sat 0.2g, mono 1.4g, poly 0.7g); **PROTEIN** 1.7g; **CARB** 5.7g; **FIBER** 2.7g; **CHOL** 0mg; **IRON** 0.7mg; **SODIUM** 163mg; **CALC** 66mg

QUICK TIP: The heat in chiles is not water soluble; it's fat soluble. Pour a little oil onto your hands, rub them together, and wash them under warm water to help get rid of the burn.

Rapid Ratatouille

The more thinly you slice the vegetables, the more they'll melt into the classic consistency of this favorite side dish.

5 cups sliced zucchini

1½ cups vertically sliced onion

1 cup green bell pepper strips

1 teaspoon dried Italian seasoning

¼ teaspoon salt

1 (28-ounce) can no-salt-added whole tomatoes, drained and coarsely chopped

Grated Parmigiano-Reggiano cheese (optional)

1. Combine all ingredients except cheese in a shallow 2-quart glass or ceramic baking dish; cover and microwave at HIGH 14 minutes, stirring after 7 minutes. Sprinkle with cheese, if desired. **YIELD:** 6 cups (serving size: 1 cup).

CALORIES 45; FAT 0.3g (sat 0.1g, mono 0g, poly 0.1g); PROTEIN 2.3g; CARB 10.1g; FIBER 2.7g; CHOL 0mg; IRON 1.3mg; SODIUM 117mg; CALC 50mg

savvy IN A SNAP

To vertically slice an onion, slice off the root end and set the onion, cut side down, on the cutting board. Make thin slices down the onion, producing thin strips instead of rings.

Balsamic Succotash

High-quality, aged balsamic vinegar gives this old-time favorite an updated, sophisticated finish.

2 tablespoons unsalted butter

1 cup chopped onion

1 teaspoon bottled minced garlic

2 cups frozen whole-kernel corn

½ cup chopped red bell pepper

2 teaspoons fresh basil

1 (10-ounce) package frozen baby lima beans

½ cup fat-free, lower-sodium chicken broth

½ teaspoon sugar

⅛ teaspoon salt

⅛ teaspoon freshly ground black pepper

1 tablespoon balsamic vinegar

1. Melt butter in a large nonstick skillet over medium heat. Add onion and garlic; cook 3 minutes or until onion softens, stirring occasionally. Add corn, bell pepper, basil, and beans; cook 4 minutes, stirring occasionally. Add broth, sugar, salt, and black pepper; cook 7 minutes or until liquid almost evaporates. Remove from heat, and stir in vinegar. **YIELD:** 6 servings (serving size: ⅔ cup).

CALORIES 180; **FAT** 4.6g (sat 2.5g, mono 1.1g, poly 0.4g); **PROTEIN** 5.8g; **CARB** 28g; **FIBER** 4.9g; **CHOL** 10mg; **IRON** 1mg; **SODIUM** 222mg; **CALC** 44mg

QUICK TIP: For stove-top recipes, there's no need to thaw frozen corn kernels—just give them an extra minute over the heat.

Quick and Creamy Mashed Potatoes ▶

2 large Yukon gold potatoes (about 1½ pounds)

½ cup 1% low-fat milk

½ cup reduced-fat sour cream

1 teaspoon salt

½ teaspoon freshly ground black pepper

2 tablespoons minced fresh chives

1. Scrub potatoes; place in a single layer in a microwave-safe bowl (do not pierce potatoes with a fork). Cover bowl with plastic wrap (do not allow plastic wrap to touch food); vent. Microwave at HIGH 8 minutes or until tender. Let stand 2 minutes. Uncover; add milk and next 3 ingredients (through pepper), mashing with a potato masher until creamy. Stir in chives. **YIELD:** 7 servings (serving size: ½ cup).

CALORIES 101; **FAT** 2.3g (sat 1.5g, mono 0.7g, poly 0.1g); **PROTEIN** 4.1g; **CARB** 19g; **FIBER** 2.1g; **CHOL** 10mg; **IRON** 0.8mg; **SODIUM** 350mg; **CALC** 64mg

Cranberry-Glazed Sweet Potatoes

Here's the side dish for your next holiday gathering. Plus, it's made in the microwave, so it won't take up precious oven space! And, if not at a holiday table, it's a great side to that rotisserie chicken you brought home from the supermarket.

6 medium-sized sweet potatoes (about 3 pounds), peeled and cut into 1-inch pieces

½ cup firmly packed light brown sugar

2 tablespoons unsalted butter

2 tablespoons orange juice

½ teaspoon salt

1 cup whole-berry cranberry sauce

Orange rind strips (optional)

1. Place potatoes, covered, in a 2-quart microwave-safe casserole; microwave at HIGH 10 minutes or until tender. Combine sugar, butter, orange juice, and salt in a 2-cup glass measure. Microwave at HIGH 3 minutes, stirring every minute. Add sugar mixture and cranberry sauce to potatoes; toss gently. Microwave at HIGH 10 minutes or until thoroughly heated, basting with sauce twice during cooking. Garnish with orange rind, if desired. **YIELD:** 8 servings (serving size: ¾ cup).

CALORIES 249; **FAT** 3g (sat 1.8g, mono 0.8g, poly 0.2g); **PROTEIN** 2.7g; **CARB** 54g; **FIBER** 4.9g; **CHOL** 7mg; **IRON** 1mg; **SODIUM** 205mg; **CALC** 63mg

savvy IN A SNAP

Food splattered in a microwave can be hard to clean up. To do so, mix 1 cup water and ¼ cup white vinegar in a large, microwave-safe bowl; bring to a boil at HIGH in the microwave oven, probably about 3 minutes, depending on wattage. Leave untouched in the oven 5 minutes without further heating. The steam will loosen baked-on food and deodorize the oven for an easier cleanup job.

MORE CHOICES: Flavor the potatoes with any minced herb you desire. Or add a teaspoon or two of Dijon mustard for some real zing. You might also consider trying a little chutney, an elegant finish for this homey side dish.

Kidney Bean, Corn, and Pomegranate Salad

This unusual combination is one of our favorite salads. The leftovers are great for lunch: roll up in tortillas with sliced avocado.

1 (16-ounce) can no-salt-added dark
   red kidney beans, drained

1 (15.25-ounce) can no-salt-added
   whole-kernel corn, drained

½ cup pomegranate seeds (about 1
   pomegranate)

2 tablespoons chopped fresh cilantro

2 tablespoons chopped fresh parsley

⅓ cup bottled light olive oil vinaigrette

1. Arrange beans on 1 side of serving platter. Arrange corn on other side of platter. Sprinkle seeds, cilantro, and parsley over beans and corn. Drizzle olive oil vinaigrette over salad. **YIELD:** 4 servings (serving size: ¾ cup).

CALORIES 246; FAT 11.3g (sat 1.6g, mono 7.6g, poly 1.1g); PROTEIN 6.7g; CARB 31g; FIBER 6.5g; CHOL 0mg; IRON 0.8mg; SODIUM 109mg; CALC 31mg

QUICK TIP: To seed a pomegranate, slice it into quarters, and then dig into the chambers to get out the little seeds and their bright red flesh. It's a messy job. Work in the sink to make cleanup much easier.

Fresh herbs can take a dish from good to great.

What would pesto be without basil, or salsa sans cilantro? Whether used by the pinch or by the bunch, fresh herbs pull a recipe together by infusing the dish with unparalleled aromas and flavors. Sometimes, when the effect you seek is subtle, refined, and delicate, a hint of herbs is enough; other times, handfuls are required.

BASIL: Basil is one of the most important culinary herbs. Sweet basil, the most common type, is redolent of licorice and cloves. Basil is used in the south of France to make pistou; its Italian cousin, pesto, is made just over the border. Used in sauces, sandwiches, soups, and salads, basil is in top form when married to tomatoes.

CHIVES: Toss chives into a dish at the last minute because heat destroys their delicate onion flavor. Thinly slice them to maximize their taste, or use finely snipped chives as a garnish. Chives are great in dips and quesadillas, and on baked potatoes.

CILANTRO: Chances are you either love or hate this native herb of southern Europe and the Middle East. It has a pungent flavor, with a faint undertone of anise. The leaves are often mistaken for flat-leaf parsley, so read the tag. One of the most versatile herbs, cilantro adds distinctive flavor to salsas, soups, stews, curries, salads, vegetables, and fish and chicken dishes.

PARSLEY: Parsley can go in just about every dish you cook. It's mild, grassy flavor allows the flavors of other ingredients to come through. Curly parsley is less assertive than flat-leaf parsley (often called Italian parsley). Flat-leaf parsley is preferred for cooking because it stands up better to heat and has more flavor, while the more decorative curly parsley is used mostly for garnishing. Reach for either when a dish needs a little burst of color.

ROSEMARY: In Latin, rosemary means "dew of the sea"—appropriate since it is indigenous to the Mediterranean. Rosemary is one of the most aromatic and pungent of all the herbs. Its needlelike leaves have a pronounced lemon-pine flavor that pairs well with roasted lamb, garlic, and olive oil. Rosemary is also a nice addition to focaccia, tomato sauce, pizza, and pork, but because its flavor is strong, use a light hand.

SAGE: Sage is native to the northern Mediterranean coast, where it's used frequently in cooking. Sage's long, narrow leaves have a distinctively fuzzy texture and musty flavor redolent of eucalyptus, cedar, lemon, and mint. Italians love it with veal, while the French add it to stuffings, cured meats, sausages, and pork dishes. Americans, of course, associate it with turkey and dressing. Use it with discretion; it can overwhelm a dish.

DILL: Since ancient Roman times, dill has been a symbol of vitality. In the Middle Ages, it was thought to provide protection against witches and was used as an ingredient in many magic potions. In the kitchen, its feathery leaves lend a fresh, sharp flavor to many foods: gravlax, cottage cheese, cream cheese, goat cheese, omelets, seafood, cold yogurt soups, potato salads, and all kinds of cucumber dishes.

MINT: In the Mediterranean, mint is treasured as a companion to lamb and is often used in fruit and vegetable salads. Though there are many varieties, spearmint is preferred for cooking. You can add it to a bevy of dishes and drinks—lamb, peas, carrots, ice cream, tea, mint juleps, and mojitos. Spearmint's bright green leaves are fuzzy, very different from the darker stemmed, rounded leaves of peppermint.

OREGANO: Oregano grows wild in the mountains of Italy and Greece. The Greeks sprinkle it on salads, while the Italians shower it on pizza and slip it into tomato sauces. Add chopped oregano to vinaigrette, or use it in poultry, game, or seafood dishes. Oregano and marjoram are similar in looks and flavor and are often confused. Oregano has a more potent taste and aroma; marjoram is sweeter and more delicate.

TARRAGON: Tarragon is native to Siberia and western Asia and lends a sweet, delicate, licoricelike perfume and flavor to white wine vinegar. It pairs well with fish, omelets, and chicken cooked with mustard, and it is a crucial component of béarnaise sauce. Fresh tarragon isn't always easy to find, but you'll love its bittersweet, peppery taste. Heat diminishes its flavor, so add tarragon toward the end of cooking, or use it as a garnish. A little goes a long way.

THYME: Thyme comes in dozens of varieties; however, most cooks use French thyme. This congenial herb pairs well with many other herbs—especially rosemary, parsley, sage, savory, and oregano. Its earthiness is welcome with pork, lamb, duck, or goose, and it's much beloved in Cajun and Creole cooking. It's also the primary component of Caribbean jerk seasonings. Because the leaves are so small, they often don't require chopping.

KEEPING FRESH HERBS FRESH

• **Loosely wrap herbs** in a damp paper towel, and then seal in a zip-top plastic bag filled with air. Refrigerate for up to 5 days. Check herbs daily because some of them lose their flavor after a couple of days.

• **Store herbs bouquet-style** in the refrigerator when in bunches: Place, stems down, in a jar with water covering 1 inch of the stem ends, enclose in a large zip-top plastic bag, and change the water every other day. Most herbs will keep for up to 1 week this way.

• **To revive limp herbs,** trim ½ inch off the stems; place in ice water for a couple of hours.

• **In most cases, heat kills the flavor** of fresh herbs, so they're best added to a dish at the end of the cooking time.

◀ Herbed Couscous Pilaf

1 tablespoon olive oil

¼ cup finely chopped shallots

1 cup uncooked couscous

1 cup plus 2 tablespoons fat-free,
lower-sodium chicken broth

⅛ teaspoon salt

1 tablespoon chopped fresh flat-leaf
parsley

1 teaspoon chopped fresh thyme

1. Heat a small saucepan over medium-high heat. Add oil to pan, swirling to coat. Add shallots; sauté 2 minutes or until tender. Stir in couscous; sauté 1 minute. Add broth and salt; bring to a boil. Cover, remove from heat, and let stand 5 minutes. Fluff with a fork. Stir in parsley and thyme. **YIELD:** 4 servings (serving size: ¾ cup).

CALORIES 205; FAT 3.7g (sat 0.5g, mono 2.5g, poly 0.5g); PROTEIN 6.5g; CARB 35.6g; FIBER 2.6g; CHOL 0mg; IRON 0.8mg; SODIUM 189mg; CALC 20mg

MORE CHOICES: Swap out the olive oil with unsalted butter—or for a bolder flavor, a toasted nut oil.

Cabbage Slaw

4 cups shredded cabbage

1½ cups thinly sliced radishes

½ cup diagonally cut green onions

3 tablespoons olive oil

2 tablespoons fresh lemon juice

⅓ cup chopped fresh mint

½ teaspoon salt

¼ teaspoon ground red pepper

1. Combine first 5 ingredients; toss. Sprinkle with mint, salt, and pepper. **YIELD:** 6 servings (serving size: ½ cup).

CALORIES 81; FAT 6.9g (sat 1g, mono 4.9g, poly 0.8g); PROTEIN 1g; CARB 5g; FIBER 2g; CHOL 0mg; IRON 0.6mg; SODIUM 218mg; CALC 36mg

EVEN *faster*

You can make a simple side like this one in the small gaps during your day's schedule, saving the slaw back in the fridge until you're ready to eat. However, for all green vegetable sides, omit the salt until you're ready to serve the dish. It can leach moisture from the vegetables—here, turning the slaw watery during storage.

SWEET ENDINGS

Treat Yourself

QUICK COOKS *MAY* **OCCASIONALLY GIVE THE SIDE DISHES SHORT SHRIFT, BUT NOBODY EVER FORGETS ABOUT DESSERT!** That said, we've got some news you probably already know: There are almost no five-minute desserts. If you're really in a rush, your only option may be a bowl of berries topped with some sweetened low-fat yogurt.

But don't despair! There are still ways to streamline classic desserts so that making them is quicker, more efficient—and healthier, too.

Plus, many desserts can be made ahead sometime during the day. No, you're not saving time, but you're also not pressed to whip up a cake or cookies while you're trying to get dinner on the table.

Some desserts can even be made *way* ahead. Cookies can be kept in a sealed container on the counter for two or three days. And some desserts can be frozen. That's definitely a way to fit dessert into our "cook fewer times than you eat" scheme!

Still, how can you turn down a warm cake or some roasted plums just out of the oven? Once in a while, treat yourself to an easy, simple dessert *à la minute*. It's a great way to end a meal—and a nice way to thank yourself for having mastered the techniques and methods of cooking quickly.

Spicy Oatmeal Crisps

Ground pepper may sound like an odd ingredient in a cookie, but it complements the other spices well and makes a zesty, satisfying cookie.

3.4 ounces all-purpose flour (about ¾ cup)

1 teaspoon ground cinnamon

½ teaspoon baking soda

½ teaspoon ground allspice

½ teaspoon grated whole nutmeg

¼ teaspoon salt

¼ teaspoon ground cloves

¼ teaspoon freshly ground black pepper

1 cup packed brown sugar

5 tablespoons butter, softened

1 teaspoon vanilla extract

1 large egg

½ cup old-fashioned rolled oats

1. Preheat oven to 350°.

2. Weigh or lightly spoon flour into dry measuring cups; level with a knife. Combine flour and next 7 ingredients (through pepper) in a medium bowl. Place sugar, butter, and vanilla in a large bowl; beat with a mixer at medium speed until light and fluffy. Add egg; beat well. Stir in flour mixture and oats.

3. Drop by level tablespoons 2 inches apart onto baking sheets lined with parchment paper. Bake at 350° for 12 minutes or until crisp. Cool on pan 2 to 3 minutes or until firm. Remove cookies from pan; cool on wire racks. **YIELD:** 2 dozen (serving size: 1 cookie).

CALORIES 81; **FAT** 3.1g (sat 1.7g, mono 0.9g, poly 0.3g); **PROTEIN** 1.5g; **CARB** 12.2g; **FIBER** 0.7g; **CHOL** 15mg; **IRON** 0.6mg; **SODIUM** 71mg; **CALC** 12mg

QUICK TIP: Shave time whenever you can. While you can hardly overbeat the sugar, eggs, and butter, you need not spend long stirring the dry ingredients into them. Beat in the flour mixture at low speed just until there are no visible white streaks.

Coconut–Macadamia Nut Cookies

You can make these cookies a day or two ahead and store them in an airtight container. But be forewarned—these are so good, you should probably stash them somewhere out of sight so you don't eat them all yourself.

4.5 ounces all-purpose flour (about 1 cup)

1 cup old-fashioned rolled oats

1 cup packed light brown sugar

⅓ cup golden raisins

⅓ cup flaked sweetened coconut

¼ cup chopped macadamia nuts

½ teaspoon baking soda

¼ cup butter, melted

3 tablespoons water

2 tablespoons honey

Cooking spray

1. Preheat oven to 325°.

2. Weigh or lightly spoon flour into a dry measuring cup; level with a knife. Combine flour and next 6 ingredients (through baking soda) in a large bowl. Combine butter, 3 tablespoons water, and honey in a small bowl, stirring well to combine. Add butter mixture to flour mixture, stirring until well blended. Drop by level tablespoons 2 inches apart onto baking sheets coated with cooking spray. Bake at 325° for 10 minutes or until almost set. Cool on pan 2 to 3 minutes or until firm. Remove cookies from pan, and cool on wire racks. **YIELD:** 2½ dozen (serving size: 1 cookie).

CALORIES 90; **FAT** 3g (sat 1.5g, mono 1.2g, poly 0.2g); **PROTEIN** 1.1g; **CARB** 15.4g; **FIBER** 0.5g; **CHOL** 4mg; **IRON** 0.5mg; **SODIUM** 43mg; **CALC** 10mg

QUICK TIP: Pulsing nuts in a food processor until they are coarsely chopped is easier than chopping them on a cutting board.

Black Forest Cheesecake Parfaits ▶

In German restaurants and delis, this signature dessert is layered with chocolate, cherries, and whipped cream. Here, cream cheese replaces whipped cream for a zippier taste in these splurge-worthy parfaits.

4 cups frozen unsweetened cherries

½ cup black cherry preserves

½ cup sugar

2 tablespoons fresh lemon juice

¾ cup (6 ounces) ⅓-less-fat cream cheese

¾ cup chocolate wafer crumbs (about 15 cookies)

Grated lemon rind (optional)

1. Combine cherries and preserves in a medium saucepan; bring to a boil. Reduce heat to medium-low, and simmer 5 minutes. Remove from heat, and cool completely.

2. Combine sugar, juice, and cream cheese in a large bowl, and beat with a mixer at medium speed until smooth (about 2 minutes). Cover and chill.

3. Spoon 2 teaspoons crumbs into each of 8 (8-ounce) glasses; top each with 1½ table-spoons cream cheese mixture and 3 tablespoons cherry mixture. Repeat layers once, ending with cherry mixture. Garnish with rind, if desired. **YIELD:** 8 servings (serving size: 1 parfait).

CALORIES 236; **FAT** 6.8g (sat 3.7g, mono 2g, poly 0.7g); **PROTEIN** 3.5g; **CARB** 42.6g; **FIBER** 1.6g; **CHOL** 16mg; **IRON** 0.9mg; **SODIUM** 147mg; **CALC** 30mg

Mexican Chocolate Pudding

Mexican chocolate is a mélange of dark chocolate, sugar, cinnamon, and nuts. It's fairly grainy—but it makes a fine pudding! Grate the bars through the large holes of a box grater before you make this intense and flavorful dessert.

4 large egg yolks

1 teaspoon almond extract

6 tablespoons sugar

¼ cup cornstarch

2 tablespoons Dutch process cocoa

½ teaspoon salt

3 cups 1% low-fat milk

2 (3.1-ounce) blocks Mexican chocolate, grated

4 teaspoons unsalted butter

1. Combine egg yolks and almond extract in a medium bowl, stirring with a whisk until blended.

2. Combine sugar and next 3 ingredients (through salt) in a medium saucepan, stirring with a whisk until blended. Gradually add milk, stirring with whisk until smooth. Add chocolate; cook over medium heat until thick and bubbly (about 9 minutes), stirring constantly with whisk.

3. Gradually add half of hot milk mixture to egg yolk mixture, stirring constantly with whisk. Return milk mixture to pan. Cook over low heat 3 minutes or until thick, stirring constantly with whisk. Remove pan from heat.

4. Add butter, stirring with whisk until melted. Place pan in a large ice-filled bowl until pudding cools to room temperature (about 10 minutes), stirring often. **YIELD:** 8 servings (serving size: ½ cup).

CALORIES 217; **FAT** 9.1g (sat 4.5g, mono 3.1g, poly 0.7g); **PROTEIN** 5.4g; **CARB** 33g; **FIBER** 1g; **CHOL** 115mg; **IRON** 1mg; **SODIUM** 190mg; **CALC** 128mg

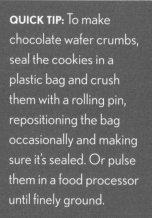

QUICK TIP: To make chocolate wafer crumbs, seal the cookies in a plastic bag and crush them with a rolling pin, repositioning the bag occasionally and making sure it's sealed. Or pulse them in a food processor until finely ground.

Chocolate-Frangelico Fondue

If the banana and strawberries are briefly chilled before serving, this creamy chocolate fondue will coat them better.

⅓ cup half-and-half

¼ cup fat-free milk

8 ounces semisweet chocolate, chopped

1¼ cups sifted powdered sugar

¼ cup water

2 tablespoons Frangelico (hazelnut-flavored liqueur)

2 tablespoons dark corn syrup

5 cups (1-inch) cubed purchased angel food cake (about 4 ounces)

2½ cups sliced banana

2½ cups quartered small strawberries

1. Combine first 3 ingredients in a medium saucepan; cook over medium-low heat 5 minutes or until smooth, stirring constantly. Stir in sugar, ¼ cup water, liqueur, and syrup. Cook 10 minutes or until mixture is smooth, stirring constantly. Pour into a fondue pot. Keep warm over a low flame. Serve with cake, banana, and strawberries. **YIELD:** 10 servings (serving size: ½ cup cake, ¼ cup banana, ¼ cup strawberries, and about ¼ cup fondue).

CALORIES 295; **FAT** 7.7g (sat 4.6g, mono 0g, poly 0.1g); **PROTEIN** 3.4g; **CARB** 56g; **FIBER** 3.1g; **CHOL** 3mg; **IRON** 0.3mg; **SODIUM** 98mg; **CALC** 41mg

MORE CHOICES: Substitute your favorite liqueur for the Frangelico.

Cuban Coconut Rice Pudding

This pudding uses starchy, medium-grain rice to achieve a creaminess reminiscent of risotto. Arborio, Valencia, or other medium-grain varieties of rice can be found at most supermarkets, sometimes in the specialty foods aisle or the Italian section.

3 cups water

1 cup Arborio or other medium-grain rice

4 whole cloves

1 (2-inch) piece vanilla bean, split lengthwise

1 (2-inch) cinnamon stick

1 (14-ounce) can fat-free sweetened condensed milk

½ cup evaporated fat-free milk

½ cup light coconut milk

½ cup golden raisins

1 tablespoon chopped crystallized ginger

1 teaspoon grated lemon rind

Dash of salt

½ teaspoon ground cinnamon (optional)

1. Place 3 cups water and rice in a large saucepan. Place cloves, vanilla bean, and cinnamon on a double layer of cheesecloth. Gather edges of cheesecloth together; tie securely. Add to rice mixture. Bring to a simmer over medium heat, stirring frequently. Reduce heat to low; cook 20 minutes or until rice is tender and liquid is almost absorbed.

2. Stir in milks and raisins; cook 10 minutes, stirring frequently. Stir in ginger, rind, and salt; cook 5 minutes, stirring frequently. Remove cheesecloth with spices. Pour rice mixture into a bowl or individual bowls; cover surface of pudding with plastic wrap. Chill. Sprinkle with cinnamon, if desired. **YIELD:** 8 servings (serving size: ½ cup).

CALORIES 286; **FAT** 1g (sat 0.7g, mono 0.1g, poly 0.1g); **PROTEIN** 7g; **CARB** 61.9g; **FIBER** 0.8g; **CHOL** 7mg; **IRON** 1.7mg; **SODIUM** 95mg; **CALC** 184mg

savvy IN A SNAP

So-called **"light" or "lite" coconut milk** is actually a second or further pressing of the coconut solids that make up regular coconut milk.

Rum Raisin Sauce on Frozen Yogurt

Here's a sweet, buttery sauce for your next frozen yogurt sundae. Save any leftovers, and stir a tablespoon or two into your morning hot cereal.

⅓ cup packed brown sugar

2 tablespoons water

1 tablespoon butter

1½ tablespoons all-purpose flour

1¼ cups 1% low-fat milk

⅓ cup raisins

1 tablespoon gold rum

3 cups vanilla low-fat frozen yogurt

1. Combine first 3 ingredients in a small saucepan over medium heat; cook 3 minutes or until butter melts, stirring occasionally. Combine flour and milk in a small bowl; stir with a whisk. Add milk mixture and raisins to pan, and stir well. Cook 5 minutes or until thick, stirring constantly. Remove from heat; stir in rum. Serve over frozen yogurt. **YIELD:** 6 servings (serving size: ½ cup frozen yogurt and ¼ cup sauce).

CALORIES 321; **FAT** 6.9g (sat 2.4g, mono 1.8g, poly 0.2g); **PROTEIN** 11.2g; **CARB** 53g; **FIBER** 0.3g; **CHOL** 73mg; **IRON** 0.4mg; **SODIUM** 95mg; **CALC** 326mg

QUICK TIP: The sauce can be made in advance and reheated in the microwave. Place it in a 2-cup glass measure; microwave at HIGH 1 minute or until heated, stirring every 30 seconds.

Ice Cream Treasures

Although not a quick dish because of how long the ice cream needs to set up, a dessert like this one is part of the quick cook's repertoire because it can be made so far in advance, during a little hole in your schedule over the course of a day.

1½ cups crushed chocolate-covered English toffee candy bars (6 ounces)

8 cups vanilla reduced-fat ice cream, softened

4 cups crispy rice cereal squares, crushed

2 cups multigrain toasted oat cereal

⅔ cup packed dark brown sugar

⅓ cup slivered almonds, toasted

⅓ cup flaked sweetened coconut, toasted

2 tablespoons butter, melted

1. Stir crushed candy into ice cream. Cover and freeze until ready to use.

2. Combine cereals, sugar, and next 3 ingredients (through butter) in a large bowl, stirring until well blended. Press half of cereal mixture into bottom of a 13 x 9–inch metal baking pan.

3. Let ice cream mixture stand at room temperature 20 minutes or until softened. Spread softened ice cream mixture over cereal mixture; top evenly with remaining cereal mixture. Cover and freeze 8 hours or overnight. **YIELD:** 16 servings (serving size: about ¾ cup).

CALORIES 265; **FAT** 8.4g (sat 4.1g, mono 2.7g, poly 0.7g); **PROTEIN** 5.2g; **CARB** 41.7g; **FIBER** 1g; **CHOL** 25mg; **IRON** 3.6mg; **SODIUM** 194mg; **CALC** 156mg

MORE CHOICES: Use any combination of cereals you like. This frozen dessert would also be delicious with chocolate ice cream and chopped walnuts instead of almonds.

Sherried Zabaglione with Berries

Serve this light custard sauce immediately to enjoy its frothy texture. A double boiler cooks the delicate custard gently and eliminates the chance of curdling. The water that heats the custard must simmer, not boil. Regulate the water before placing the custard on top. And be conservative: Once the top is in place, the water tends to heat up.

5 tablespoons sugar

3 tablespoons cream sherry

2 large eggs

3 tablespoons reduced-fat sour cream

2 cups blackberries

Mint sprigs (optional)

1. Combine first 3 ingredients in the top of a double boiler. Cook over simmering water until thick (about 4 minutes) and a thermometer registers 160°, stirring mixture constantly with a whisk. Remove top pan from heat; stir mixture with a whisk 2 minutes. Add sour cream, stirring gently with a whisk. Serve zabaglione immediately over berries. Garnish with mint sprigs, if desired. **YIELD:** 4 servings (serving size: ½ cup berries and about ¼ cup zabaglione).

CALORIES 157; **FAT** 4.2g (sat 1.7g, mono 1.4g, poly 0.6g); **PROTEIN** 4.2g; **CARB** 25.9g; **FIBER** 3.8g; **CHOL** 112mg; **IRON** 0.8mg; **SODIUM** 39mg; **CALC** 55mg

MORE CHOICES: Any berries will work with this tasty sauce. Or try Madeira wine instead of cream sherry.

Macerated Berries

Sugared and combined with alcohol, ripe berries give up their own juices until they swim in a delicious, sweet liquid. These are great on their own or over vanilla ice cream or plain yogurt.

2 cups sliced strawberries

2 cups fresh blueberries

1 cup fresh raspberries

1 tablespoon sugar

3 tablespoons fresh lemon juice

3 tablespoons Grand Marnier (orange-flavored liqueur)

Mint sprigs (optional)

1. Combine all ingredients except mint sprigs in a medium bowl, stirring gently. Cover and refrigerate at least 2 hours or overnight, stirring occasionally. Garnish with mint sprigs, if desired. **YIELD:** 4 servings (serving size: 1 cup).

CALORIES 133; **FAT** 0.8g (sat 0.1g, mono 0.1g, poly 0.4g); **PROTEIN** 1.3g; **CARB** 28.4g; **FIBER** 6g; **CHOL** 0mg; **IRON** 0.6mg; **SODIUM** 6mg; **CALC** 24mg

Vanilla-Roasted Strawberries

This delicious dessert needs a crunchy cookie or wafer on the side. The berries can bake and cool while you're eating dinner, a sweet little afterthought when the meal is done.

2 tablespoons unsalted butter

1 vanilla bean, split lengthwise

24 strawberries, tops removed

2 tablespoons light brown sugar

3 tablespoons dry red wine

1½ tablespoons balsamic vinegar

1 tablespoon chilled unsalted butter, cut into small pieces

1. Preheat oven to 400°.

2. Melt 2 tablespoons butter in a 9-inch square metal baking pan in oven. Remove pan from oven. Scrape seeds from vanilla bean into melted butter, reserving bean halves. Combine vanilla bean seeds and butter. Place strawberries, cut sides down, in pan; sprinkle with sugar. Tuck vanilla bean halves between berries in bottom of pan. Bake at 400° for 10 minutes or until berries are soft. Cool on pan 20 minutes.

3. Remove berries from pan with a slotted spoon, and transfer pan juices to a small skillet. Add wine and vinegar to pan; bring to a simmer over medium heat. Remove from heat; add chilled butter, stirring with a whisk. Drizzle sauce over berries. Serve immediately.

YIELD: 4 servings (serving size: 6 strawberries and 2 tablespoons sauce).

CALORIES 135; **FAT** 7.7g (sat 4.8g, mono 2.2g, poly 0.3g); **PROTEIN** 0.9g; **CARB** 16.7g; **FIBER** 3g; **CHOL** 21mg; **IRON** 0.8mg; **SODIUM** 5mg; **CALC** 25mg

MORE CHOICES: Substitute cranberry juice for the red wine, if you prefer.

Cinnamon Sugar Crisps

You've seen these familiar Chinese wrappers in pot stickers, but they're also great baked for crispy, crunchy snacks.

32 wonton wrappers

1½ tablespoons butter, melted

8 teaspoons cinnamon sugar

1. Preheat oven to 400°.

2. Arrange wrappers on baking sheets, and brush evenly with butter. Sprinkle each wrapper with ¼ teaspoon cinnamon sugar. Bake at 400° for 5 minutes or until crisp. Cool on wire racks. **YIELD:** 8 servings (serving size: 4 crisps).

CALORIES 123; **FAT** 2.6g (sat 0.5g, mono 1g, poly 0.9g); **PROTEIN** 3.2g; **CARB** 21.5g; **FIBER** 0.3g; **CHOL** 3mg; **IRON** 1.5mg; **SODIUM** 208mg; **CALC** 30mg

savvy IN A SNAP

Look for **wonton wrappers** in the refrigerator case of the produce section or in the dairy case—either way, they are almost always near the tofu.

Strawberry Soup

Strawberries in soup? Absolutely—they make for a unique, refreshing dessert.

3⅓ cups quartered strawberries

½ cup orange juice

½ cup riesling or other slightly sweet white wine

2½ tablespoons sugar

1⅓ cups plain fat-free yogurt

2 teaspoons finely chopped fresh mint

1. Place the first 4 ingredients in a blender; process until smooth. Pour strawberry puree into a bowl, and add yogurt, stirring with a whisk. Cover and chill. Spoon 1 cup soup into each of 5 bowls, and sprinkle with mint. **YIELD:** 5 servings.

CALORIES 116; **FAT** 0.5g (sat 0.1g, mono 0.1g, poly 0.2g); **PROTEIN** 4.3g; **CARB** 21.2g; **FIBER** 2.4g; **CHOL** 1mg; **IRON** 0.7mg; **SODIUM** 48mg; **CALC** 139mg

MORE CHOICES: Serve this soup with a few drops of aged, syrupy balsamic vinegar in each bowl. Offer crunchy biscotti on the side.

Chocolate-Granola Apple Wedges

If you can't find Braeburn apples, Gala or Fuji varieties also stand up to dipping and add a touch more sweetness.

2 ounces semisweet chocolate, finely chopped

⅓ cup low-fat granola without raisins

1 large Braeburn apple, cut into 16 wedges

1. Place chocolate in a medium microwave-safe bowl. Microwave at HIGH 1 minute, stirring every 15 seconds, or until chocolate melts.

2. Place granola in a shallow dish. Dip apple wedges, skin sides up, in chocolate; allow excess chocolate to drip back into bowl. Dredge wedges in granola. Place wedges, chocolate sides up, on a large plate. Refrigerate 5 minutes or until set. **YIELD:** 4 servings (serving size: 4 apple wedges).

CALORIES 132; **FAT** 4.8g (sat 2.6g, mono 1.4g, poly 0.1g); **PROTEIN** 1.5g; **CARB** 23.9g; **FIBER** 2.6g; **CHOL** 0mg; **IRON** 0.8mg; **SODIUM** 22mg; **CALC** 13mg

EVEN *faster*

Don't want to chop chocolate before melting it in the microwave? Use high-quality, semisweet chips.

Chocolate Bruschetta

Salt enhances the chocolate flavor. For best results, use good-quality chocolate and coarse sea salt. Garnish with fresh mint leaves instead of orange rind, if desired.

10 (1-ounce) slices diagonally cut French bread (about ¼ inch thick)

Cooking spray

5 ounces bittersweet chocolate (60 to 70% cocoa), finely chopped (about 1 cup)

¼ teaspoon coarse sea salt

Grated orange rind (optional)

1. Preheat broiler.

2. Lightly coat bread with cooking spray. Place bread on a baking sheet; broil 3 minutes on each side or until toasted. Remove bread from oven.

3. Reduce oven temperature to 350°.

4. Sprinkle each bread slice with about 1½ tablespoons chocolate. Bake 5 minutes or until chocolate melts. Sprinkle evenly with salt; garnish with orange rind, if desired. Serve warm. **YIELD:** 10 servings (serving size: 1 bruschetta).

CALORIES 150; **FAT** 4.3g (sat 2.4g, mono 0.7g, poly 0.1g); **PROTEIN** 3g; **CARB** 25.4g; **FIBER** 0.5g; **CHOL** 0mg; **IRON** 0.9mg; **SODIUM** 242mg; **CALC** 0mg

savvy IN A SNAP

Because the chocolate in this recipe is not melted stove top or in a microwave, but rather right on the bread, it needs to be chopped as finely as possible. **Use the large holes of a box grater,** and then sprinkle it on the bread as you would shredded cheese.

Spiced Figs in Red Wine

If you like, poach the figs and make the syrup up to two days ahead; cover and chill. If you want just a hint of flavor, take the rosemary sprig out of the wine mixture after 10 minutes. The longer it stays in the liquid, the stronger the rosemary flavor.

1 cup dry red wine

⅓ cup sugar

2 tablespoons fresh lemon juice

1 tablespoon honey

½ teaspoon vanilla extract

3 dried figs, halved

3 black peppercorns

1 (4-inch) rosemary sprig

1 (3-inch) thyme sprig

½ cup vanilla fat-free frozen yogurt

1. Combine first 9 ingredients in a small, heavy saucepan. Bring to a boil; cook 25 minutes or until reduced to ½ cup. Discard peppercorns, rosemary sprig, and thyme sprig. Remove figs with a slotted spoon; set aside.

2. Spoon ¼ cup sauce onto each of 2 dessert plates, and reserve remaining sauce for another use. Arrange figs and yogurt on top of sauce. **YIELD:** 2 servings (serving size: ¼ cup sauce, 3 fig halves, and ¼ cup yogurt).

CALORIES 201; **FAT** 0.3g (sat 0g, mono 0.1g, poly 0.2g); **PROTEIN** 2.5g; **CARB** 50.6g; **FIBER** 4.8g; **CHOL** 0mg; **IRON** 0.9mg; **SODIUM** 34mg; **CALC** 34mg

savvy IN A SNAP

If possible, buy **dried fruits** in bulk—or in clear packaging so you can see what you're getting. Choose dried fruits exactly as you would fresh: Look for juicy, plump, sweet-smelling fruits and berries without any mushy spots, mold, or visible decay.

Sugar-Roasted Plums with Balsamic and Rosemary Syrup

Small, sweet, dark-purple plums are ideal for this sophisticated dessert. Balsamic vinegar, water, and seasonings are reduced to an intense, syrupy glaze that contrasts with the sugar-coated plums. If you can't find small plums, use 6 medium ones, and halve them.

½ cup water

½ cup balsamic vinegar

6 tablespoons sugar, divided

10 black peppercorns

1 vanilla bean, split lengthwise

12 small unpeeled plums (about 3½ pounds)

2 rosemary sprigs

Rosemary sprigs (optional)

1. Preheat oven to 400°.

2. Combine ½ cup water, vinegar, 4 tablespoons sugar, and peppercorns, stirring with a whisk until sugar dissolves. Scrape seeds from vanilla bean; add seeds and bean to vinegar mixture. Place plums in an 11 x 7–inch glass or ceramic baking dish. Pour vinegar mixture over plums. Nestle 2 rosemary sprigs around plums in vinegar mixture. Sprinkle evenly with remaining 2 tablespoons sugar.

3. Bake at 400° for 20 minutes or until plums are tender (skin will begin to split on some plums).

4. Remove plums with a slotted spoon to a serving platter. Strain vinegar mixture into a small nonaluminum saucepan; discard solids. Bring vinegar mixture to a boil. Reduce heat to medium-high; cook until reduced to ¾ cup (about 5 minutes). Pour syrup evenly over plums; garnish with rosemary sprigs, if desired. **YIELD:** 6 servings (serving size: 2 plums and about 2 tablespoons syrup).

CALORIES 141; **FAT** 1g (sat 0g, mono 0g, poly 0.5g); **PROTEIN** 1.1g; **CARB** 34.6g; **FIBER** 2g; **CHOL** 0mg; **IRON** 0.2mg; **SODIUM** 5mg; **CALC** 6mg

MORE CHOICES: Pluots, plumcots, apriums, or even apricots would also work well in this recipe.

Hot Bushmills Sundaes

Not a dessert for the kids, but this is a great one for the grown-ups! The frozen yogurt acts as a cooling chaser to the whiskey-infused fruit.

1 (8-ounce) can unsweetened crushed pineapple

1 tablespoon cornstarch

1 tablespoon honey

¼ cup Bushmills Irish whiskey

3 cups vanilla fat-free frozen yogurt

1. Drain pineapple, reserving juice in a 2-cup glass measure. Add enough water to reserved liquid to measure ¾ cup. Add cornstarch and honey; stir with a whisk until smooth.

2. Microwave cornstarch mixture, uncovered, at HIGH 2½ to 3 minutes or until thick and bubbly, stirring after 1½ minutes. Stir in whiskey, and microwave at HIGH 30 seconds. Stir in pineapple, and microwave at HIGH 30 seconds.

3. Place ½ cup frozen yogurt in each of 6 bowls. Top each with ¼ cup sauce. **YIELD:** 6 servings.

CALORIES 124; **FAT** 0g (sat 0g, mono 0g, poly 0.1g); **PROTEIN** 3.8g; **CARB** 28.9g; **FIBER** 0.3g; **CHOL** 0mg; **IRON** 0.1mg; **SODIUM** 63mg; **CALC** 140mg

Chocolate-Amaretti Peaches

Look for amaretti cookies at specialty or gourmet markets; they have a distinctive almond-amaretto flavor and crunchy texture that make this easy peach dessert unforgettable.

½ cup amaretti cookie crumbs (about 8 cookies)

2 tablespoons brown sugar

4 large ripe peaches, halved and pitted

Cooking spray

8 teaspoons butter

1 ounce bittersweet chocolate, shaved

1. Preheat broiler.

2. Combine cookie crumbs and sugar in a small bowl.

3. Hollow out centers of peach halves using a melon baller. Fill each peach half with 1 rounded tablespoon cookie crumb mixture. Arrange peaches in an 11 x 7–inch glass or ceramic baking dish coated with cooking spray. Place 1 teaspoon butter on top of each filled half. Broil 2 minutes or until butter melts. Sprinkle evenly with chocolate. Cool 5 minutes before serving. **YIELD:** 8 servings (serving size: 1 filled peach half).

CALORIES 117; FAT 5.4g (sat 3.2g, mono 1.1g, poly 0.2g); PROTEIN 1.5g; CARB 17g; FIBER 1.6g; CHOL 10mg; IRON 0.3mg; SODIUM 42mg; CALC 9mg

Tropical Fruit Ambrosia with Rum

Travel to the islands with this dessert of chopped mango, kiwifruit, coconut, lime, and rum.

¼ cup sugar

¼ cup water

2 tablespoons white rum

2 tablespoons fresh lime juice

2 cups cubed peeled ripe mango (about 2 mangoes)

2 cups cubed peeled kiwifruit (about 6 kiwifruit)

2 tablespoons flaked sweetened coconut, toasted

1. Combine sugar and ¼ cup water in a small saucepan. Bring to a boil, and cook 1 minute or until sugar dissolves. Remove from heat; stir in rum and lime juice. Cool completely.

2. Combine mango and kiwifruit; add rum syrup, tossing gently. Sprinkle with coconut.

YIELD: 4 servings (serving size: 1 cup fruit and 1½ teaspoons coconut).

CALORIES 185; **FAT** 1.4g (sat 0.7g, mono 0.2g, poly 0.3g); **PROTEIN** 1.4g; **CARB** 41.3g; **FIBER** 4.6g; **CHOL** 0mg; **IRON** 0.6mg; **SODIUM** 14mg; **CALC** 33mg

MORE CHOICES: For a dessert without alcohol, substitute mango nectar or OJ for the rum.

QUICK TIP: Don't waste time waiting for the butter to soften for most cake and cookie recipes. Cool butter, just moments out of the fridge, will make more tender baked goods because the fat is still stiff enough to capture lots of air when it's beaten with the sugar.

◀ Monkey Bars

This moist snack cake just might remind you of that family favorite, banana bread.

½ cup raisins

1½ tablespoons dark rum or apple juice

4.5 ounces all-purpose flour (about 1 cup)

½ teaspoon baking powder

½ teaspoon baking soda

¼ teaspoon salt

¾ cup packed light brown sugar

¼ cup butter, softened

½ cup mashed ripe banana

3 tablespoons low-fat buttermilk

1 teaspoon vanilla extract

2 large egg whites

⅓ cup chopped walnuts

Cooking spray

1 tablespoon powdered sugar

1. Preheat oven to 350°.

2. Combine raisins and rum in a microwave-safe bowl. Microwave at HIGH 1 minute. Weigh or lightly spoon flour into a dry measuring cup; level with a knife. Combine flour and next 3 ingredients (through salt) in a bowl, stirring well with a whisk. Set aside.

3. Combine brown sugar and butter in a large bowl, and beat with a mixer at medium speed until well blended. Add banana and next 3 ingredients (through egg whites), beating well. Add flour mixture, beating just until combined. Stir in raisin mixture and walnuts.

4. Spread batter into an 8-inch square metal baking pan coated with cooking spray. Bake at 350° for 30 minutes or until golden. Cool completely in pan on a wire rack. Sprinkle with powdered sugar. **YIELD:** 16 servings (serving size: 1 bar).

CALORIES 135; FAT 4.7g (sat 2g, mono 1.1g, poly 1.3g); PROTEIN 2g; CARB 21.8g; FIBER 0.9g; CHOL 8mg; IRON 0.8mg; SODIUM 136mg; CALC 27mg

MORE CHOICES: Substitute your favorite whiskey, brandy, or Scotch.

Apricot-Oat Squares

Talk about easy! These bar cookies are made in a food processor, and then baked with preserves in the center. They'll keep for a couple of days in a sealed container on the counter—or for months in the freezer.

2.25 ounces all-purpose flour (about ½ cup)

2.37 ounces whole-wheat flour (about ½ cup)

1½ cups old-fashioned rolled oats

⅓ cup packed light brown sugar

6 tablespoons chilled butter

¼ teaspoon ground nutmeg

Cooking spray

¾ cup apricot preserves

1. Preheat oven to 350°.

2. Weigh or lightly spoon flours into dry measuring cups; level with a knife. Combine flours, oats, sugar, butter, and nutmeg in a food processor; pulse 5 times or until mixture resembles coarse meal.

3. Press two-thirds of oat mixture into bottom of an 8-inch square metal baking pan coated with cooking spray. Bake at 350° for 10 minutes. Spread preserves over warm crust. Sprinkle with remaining oat mixture, and press gently. Bake an additional 25 minutes or until lightly browned and bubbly. Cool completely in pan on a wire rack. **YIELD:** 16 servings (serving size: 1 square).

CALORIES 148; FAT 5g (sat 2.8g, mono 1.4g, poly 0.4g); PROTEIN 2.3g; CARB 24.9g; FIBER 1.5g; CHOL 12mg; IRON 0.8mg; SODIUM 52mg; CALC 14mg

Hello Dolly Bars ▶

These bar cookies are also known as seven-layer bars. They take less than 30 minutes to prepare and call for just 8 ingredients, making Hello Dolly Bars the perfect dessert for taking along to parties, the office, picnics—you name it.

1½ cups graham cracker crumbs (about 9 cookie sheets)

2 tablespoons butter, melted

1 tablespoon water

⅓ cup semisweet chocolate chips

⅓ cup butterscotch morsels

⅔ cup flaked sweetened coconut

¼ cup chopped pecans, toasted

1 (15-ounce) can fat-free sweetened condensed milk

1. Preheat oven to 350°.
2. Line bottom and sides of a 9-inch square metal baking pan with parchment paper; cut off excess parchment paper around top edge of pan.
3. Place crumbs in a medium bowl. Drizzle with butter and 1 tablespoon water; toss with a fork until moist. Gently pat mixture into an even layer in prepared pan (do not press firmly). Sprinkle chips and morsels over crumb mixture. Top evenly with coconut and pecans. Drizzle milk evenly over top. Bake at 350° for 25 minutes or until lightly browned and bubbly around edges. Cool completely in pan on a wire rack. **YIELD:** 24 servings (serving size: 1 bar).

CALORIES 123; FAT 4.4g (sat 2.3g, mono 1.3g, poly 0.6g); PROTEIN 2.1g; CARB 19.1g; FIBER 0.5g; CHOL 5mg; IRON 0.3mg; SODIUM 64mg; CALC 50mg

Scotch Bars

Dense and chewy, these bars are a classic combination of oats and butterscotch. You can make your own graham cracker crumbs—or buy them preground in the baking aisle.

2.25 ounces all-purpose flour (about ½ cup)

1 cup graham cracker crumbs (about 5 cookie sheets)

⅔ cup packed light brown sugar

⅓ cup quick-cooking oats

⅓ cup butterscotch morsels

1 teaspoon baking powder

1 tablespoon canola oil

1½ teaspoons vanilla extract

2 large egg whites

Cooking spray

1 tablespoon powdered sugar

1. Preheat oven to 350°.
2. Weigh or lightly spoon flour into a dry measuring cup; level with a knife. Combine flour and next 5 ingredients (through baking powder), stirring with a whisk.
3. Combine oil, vanilla, and egg whites, and add to flour mixture, stirring just until blended. Lightly coat hands with cooking spray.
4. Press batter evenly into an 8-inch square metal baking pan coated with cooking spray. Bake at 350° for 18 minutes or until a wooden pick inserted in center comes out clean. Cool in pan on a wire rack. Sift powdered sugar over top. **YIELD:** 16 servings (serving size: 1 bar).

CALORIES 118; FAT 2.9g (sat 1.3g, mono 0.7g, poly 0.5g); PROTEIN 1.5g; CARB 21g; FIBER 0.4g; CHOL 0mg; IRON 0.6mg; SODIUM 71mg; CALC 26mg

MORE CHOICES: Turn these into a chocolate dessert by substituting semisweet or dark chocolate chips for the butterscotch chips. Or try them with white chocolate.

MORE CHOICES: If you don't like pecans, try walnuts, skinned hazelnuts, unsalted peanuts, or even unsalted macadamia nuts. Chop them into small pieces for more flavor per bite.

QUICK TIP: Measure ingredients as close to the bowl as possible. Most spills happen while transporting. Bring the bag of sugar or flour to the bowl, rather than carrying a full measuring cup across the countertops.

◀ Pecan-Chocolate Chip Snack Cake

Even quick cooks need a slice of cake now and then! You can substitute chopped walnuts, almonds, or cashews for the pecans.

2.25 ounces all-purpose flour (about ½ cup)

¼ teaspoon baking soda

¼ teaspoon salt

¾ cup packed light brown sugar

1 teaspoon vanilla extract

2 large egg whites

⅓ cup chopped pecans

¼ cup semisweet chocolate chips

Cooking spray

2 teaspoons powdered sugar

1. Preheat oven to 350°.

2. Weigh or lightly spoon flour into a dry measuring cup; level with a knife. Combine flour, baking soda, and salt in a small bowl, stirring well with a whisk.

3. Combine brown sugar, vanilla, and egg whites in a large bowl; beat with a mixer at high speed 1 minute. Add flour mixture, beating just until combined. Stir in pecans and chocolate chips.

4. Spread batter into an 8-inch square metal baking pan coated with cooking spray. Bake at 350° for 18 minutes or until golden and crusty on top. Cool in pan 10 minutes on a wire rack. Sprinkle with powdered sugar. **YIELD:** 16 servings (serving size: 1 cake square).

CALORIES 87; **FAT** 2.6g (sat 0.6g, mono 1.3g, poly 0.6g); **PROTEIN** 1.2g; **CARB** 15.4g; **FIBER** 0.5g; **CHOL** 0mg; **IRON** 0.5mg; **SODIUM** 68mg; **CALC** 12mg

> **QUICK TIP:** Nothing speeds up your cooking like having fun. Savor the scents, sounds, and feel of a great recipe. If you enjoy what you're doing, you'll do it with more grace and ease.

Espresso-Walnut Cake

This cake was screaming for a streusel topping. We think it was well worth the extra little bit of effort.

Cooking spray

2 teaspoons all-purpose flour

¼ cup packed dark brown sugar

3 tablespoons finely chopped walnuts

1 teaspoon ground cinnamon

1 tablespoon instant espresso granules or 2 tablespoons instant coffee granules, divided

5 tablespoons butter

1 cup granulated sugar

2 large eggs

⅔ cup plain fat-free yogurt

2 teaspoons vanilla extract

½ teaspoon baking soda

¼ teaspoon salt

6 ounces all-purpose flour (about 1⅓ cups)

1. Preheat oven to 350°.

2. Coat an 8-inch square metal baking pan with cooking spray, and dust with 2 teaspoons flour.

3. Combine brown sugar, walnuts, cinnamon, and 1 teaspoon espresso granules in a small bowl.

4. Place butter in a large microwave-safe bowl. Cover and microwave at HIGH 1 minute or until butter melts. Add granulated sugar, stirring with a whisk. Add eggs; stir well. Stir in yogurt, vanilla, baking soda, and salt. Weigh or lightly spoon 6 ounces flour (1⅓ cups) into dry measuring cups; level with a knife. Add flour and remaining 2 teaspoons espresso granules, stirring just until blended (do not overstir).

5. Spread half of batter in prepared pan, and sprinkle with half of brown sugar mixture. Carefully spread remaining batter over brown sugar mixture, and sprinkle with remaining brown sugar mixture.

6. Bake at 350° for 25 minutes or until a wooden pick inserted in center comes out clean. Cool in pan 10 minutes on a wire rack. **YIELD:** 9 servings (serving size: 1 cake square).

CALORIES 284; **FAT** 9.4g (sat 4.5g, mono 2.6g, poly 1.7g); **PROTEIN** 5g; **CARB** 45.4g; **FIBER** 0.8g; **CHOL** 65mg; **IRON** 1.4mg; **SODIUM** 231mg; **CALC** 58mg

NUTRITIONAL ANALYSIS

How to Use It and Why

Glance at the end of any *Cooking Light* recipe, and you'll see how committed we are to helping you make the best of today's light cooking. With chefs, registered dietitians, home economists, and a computer system that analyzes every ingredient we use, *Cooking Light* gives you authoritative dietary detail like no other magazine. We go to such lengths so you can see how our recipes fit into your healthful eating plan. If you're trying to lose weight, the calorie and fat figures will probably help most. But if you're keeping a close eye on the sodium, cholesterol, and saturated fat in your diet, we provide those numbers, too. And

because many women don't get enough iron or calcium, we can help there, as well. Finally, there's a fiber analysis for those of us who don't get enough roughage.

Here's a helpful guide to put our nutritional analysis numbers into perspective. Remember, one size doesn't fit all, so take your lifestyle, age, and circumstances into consideration when determining your nutrition needs. For example, pregnant or breast-feeding women need more protein, calories, and calcium. And women older than 50 need 1,200mg of calcium daily, 200mg more than the amount recommended for younger women.

In Our Nutritional Analysis, We Use These Abbreviations

sat	saturated fat	**CARB**	carbohydrates	**g**	gram
mono	monounsaturated fat	**CHOL**	cholesterol	**mg**	milligram
poly	polyunsaturated fat	**CALC**	calcium		

Your Daily Nutrition Guide

	WOMEN ages 25 to 50	WOMEN over 50	MEN ages 25 to 50	MEN over 50
CALORIES	2,000	2,000 or less	2,700	2,500
PROTEIN	50g	50g or less	63g	60g
FAT	65g or less	65g or less	88g or less	83g*
SATURATED FAT	20g or less	20g or less	27g or less	25g*
CARBOHYDRATES	304g	304g	410g	375g
FIBER	25g to 35g	25g to 35g	25g to 35g	25g to 35g
CHOLESTEROL	300mg or less	300mg or less	300mg or less	300mg*
IRON	18mg	8mg	8mg	8mg
SODIUM	2,300mg or less	1,500mg or less	2,300mg or less	1,500mg*
CALCIUM	1,000mg	1,200mg	1,000mg	1,000mg

The nutritional values used in our calculations either come from The Food Processor, Version 8.9 (ESHA Research), or are provided by food manufacturers.

METRIC EQUIVALENTS

The information in the following charts is provided to help cooks outside the United States successfully use the recipes in this book. All equivalents are approximate.

Cooking/Oven Temperatures

	FAHRENHEIT	CELSIUS	GAS MARK
FREEZE WATER	32° F	0° C	
ROOM TEMPERATURE	68° F	20° C	
BOIL WATER	212° F	100° C	
BAKE	325° F	160° C	3
	350° F	180° C	4
	375° F	190° C	5
	400° F	200° C	6
	425° F	220° C	7
	450° F	230° C	8
BROIL			Grill

Liquid Ingredients by Volume

¼ tsp						=	1 ml	
½ tsp						=	2 ml	
1 tsp						=	5 ml	
3 tsp	=	1 tbl		=	½ fl oz	=	15 ml	
		2 tbls	=	⅛ cup	=	1 fl oz	=	30 ml
		4 tbls	=	¼ cup	=	2 fl oz	=	60 ml
		5⅓ tbls	=	⅓ cup	=	3 fl oz	=	80 ml
		8 tbls	=	½ cup	=	4 fl oz	=	120 ml
		10⅔ tbls	=	⅔ cup	=	5 fl oz	=	160 ml
		12 tbls	=	¾ cup	=	6 fl oz	=	180 ml
		16 tbls	=	1 cup	=	8 fl oz	=	240 ml
		1 pt	=	2 cups	=	16 fl oz	=	480 ml
		1 qt	=	4 cups	=	32 fl oz	=	960 ml
						33 fl oz	=	1000 ml = 1 l

Equivalents for Different Types of Ingredients

STANDARD CUP	FINE POWDER (ex. flour)	GRAIN (ex. rice)	GRANULAR (ex. sugar)	LIQUID SOLIDS (ex. butter)	LIQUID (ex. milk)
1	140 g	150 g	190 g	200 g	240 ml
¾	105 g	113 g	143 g	150 g	180 ml
⅔	93 g	100 g	125 g	133 g	160 ml
½	70 g	75 g	95 g	100 g	120 ml
⅓	47 g	50 g	63 g	67 g	80 ml
¼	35 g	38 g	48 g	50 g	60 ml
⅛	18 g	19 g	24 g	25 g	30 ml

Dry Ingredients by Weight

To convert ounces to grams,
multiply the number of ounces by 30.

1 oz	=	1⁄16 lb	=	30 g
4 oz	=	¼ lb	=	120 g
8 oz	=	½ lb	=	240 g
12 oz	=	¾ lb	=	360 g
16 oz	=	1 lb	=	480 g

Length

To convert inches to centimeters,
multiply the number of inches by 2.5.

1 in	=			2.5 cm
6 in	=	½ ft	=	15 cm
12 in	=	1 ft	=	30 cm
36 in	=	3 ft = 1 yd	=	90 cm
40 in	=			100 cm = 1 m

INDEX